D0425802

Colonization, Violence, and Narration in White South African Writing

Colonization, Violence, and Narration in White South African Writing: *André Brink, Breyten Breytenbach, and J. M. Coetzee*

Rosemary Jane Jolly

OHIO UNIVERSITY PRESS
ATHENS

WITWATERSRAND UNIVERSITY PRESS
JOHANNESBURG

Ohio University Press, Athens, Ohio 45701
© 1996 by Rosemary Jane Jolly
Printed in the United States of America
All rights reserved

Ohio University Press books
are printed on acid-free paper ∞™

01 00 99 98 97 96 5 4 3 2 1

Published 1996 in the Republic of South Africa by Witwatersrand
University Press, 1 Jan Smuts Avenue, Johannesburg, 2001, South Africa
ISBN 1 86814 297 3

Library of Congress Cataloging-in-Publication Data
Jolly, Rosemary Jane, 1963–
Colonization, violence, and narration in white South African Writing :
André Brink, Breyten Breytenbach, and J.M. Coetzee / Rosemary Jane Jolly
p. cm.
Includes bibliographical references and index.
ISBN 0-8214-1130-6 (cl). — ISBN 0-8214-1131-4 (pbk)
1. Afrikaans fiction—20th century—History and criticism. 2. South African
fiction (English)—20th century—History and criticism. 3. Brink, André
Philippus, 1935– —Criticism and interpretation. 4. Breytenbach,
Breyten—Criticism and interpretation. 5. Coetzee, J. M., 1940–
—Criticism and interpretation. 6. Violence in literature. I. Title.
PT6525.J65   1995
839.3′63509355—dc20   95-17570
                                                        CIP

Quotations from *Age of Iron* are reprinted by permission of Murray
Pollinger and Secker and Warburg Limited. The author thanks André
Brink, Breyten Breytenbach, J. M. Coetzee, and their publishers, Faber,
Persea, Penguin, Secker and Warburg Limited, Taurus, Viking and W. H.
Allen, for the use of quoted material from their works.

Cover Art: Garth Erasmus' "Emergency Series, I", courtesy of the artist and
Dangaroo Press

Cover and text designed and typeset by INARI INFORMATION SERVICES for Chris

Contents

ACKNOWLEDGMENTS

Many friends assisted me in the writing of this manuscript. Derek Attridge reviewed the manuscript in detail, offering invaluable suggestions and support. Thanks are also due to Linda Hutcheon, Ted Chamberlin, and especially Jim Howard for their guidance and friendship.

Other colleagues were also always ready to discuss the project with me: Garret Epp, Charmaine Eddy, Julian Patrick, and Christine Roulston.

I would like to thank the Canadian Research Consortium on Southern Africa and my colleagues in Southern African Studies at Queen's University—Alan Jeeves and Jonathan Crush—for their support.

I wish to acknowledge the support of my family, without whom the completion of this project would have been impossible. My father gave me my first copy of *Waiting for the Barbarians*; my mother offered tireless support and an attentive ear; my grandmothers, Doreen Jolly and Freda Lunn, have always been encouraging; and my in-laws adopted both my project and me without reserve. Finally, I thank Chris McMullen, whose patience and generosity enabled me to complete this book.

PREFACE

The soldier and the condemned man had
found some acquaintances in the teahouse,
who detained them. But they must have soon
shaken them off, for the explorer was only
halfway down the long flight of steps leading
to the boats when they came rushing after
him. Probably they wanted to force him at
the last minute to take them with him. While
he was bargaining below with a ferryman to
row him to the steamer, the two of them
came headlong down the steps, in silence, for
they did not dare to shout. But by the time
they reached the foot of the steps the
explorer was already in the boat, and the
ferryman was just casting off from the shore.
They could have jumped into the boat, but
the explorer lifted a heavy knotted rope from
the floor boards, threatened them with it and
so kept them from attempting the leap.

—Franz Kafka, "In the Penal Colony"

Kafka's "In the Penal Colony" has suffered from numerous readings characterized by facile allegorization; that is, attempts to redeem the events of the story
by placing them within a moral sphere whose very absence is one of the crucial
points—if not the crucial point—of Kafka's tale.[1] This phenomenon demonstrates one of the primary difficulties that writers of literary representations of
violence and critics of those representations confront: the desire to use the
rhetoric of such writings to establish the author, and sometimes her or his
readers, at a distance from the violations that constitute her or his subject.[2]
This is the function of the moralistic rhetoric of Kafka's less sophisticated
commentators; yet criticism of violence that posits the critic as "innocent," or
even as victim, in or by its representation of a scene of violence, is not always
so easy to spot. Perhaps Yeats was recognizing this difficulty when he wrote of

the liabilities of "passive suffering" in connection with his decision to leave the war poets out of his anthology of modern poetry.[3]

Writers on violence, be they authors of fiction or criticism, need to admit and to examine the territory that they occupy as spectators. The spectator of a scene of atrocity is in a position of privilege: she or he is not immediately involved in the scene that constitutes her or his subject. However, this position is, at the same time, rendered genuinely unenviable because of the spectator's tendency to repeat violations that stem from his or her response to the scene of violation. Kafka's explorer-as-spectator demonstrates both the effect of such contamination, and the violence that characterizes simplistic attempts to avoid it. He flees from the colony, only to reenact a scene of violence. His threatening of the colonists with the rope in order to preserve the boat as his refuge is a violent act of exclusion—an act that stems from an interpretation of what is acceptable and what is not that is as violent in its own right as that of the officer.

This act of exclusion contaminates Kafka's explorer at the very same time that he attempts, literally and figuratively, to put some distance between himself and the colony. I wish to consider it briefly in connection with the kind of reflections that critical discourses generated within the Western academy bring to bear on current, violent phenomena, of which developments in contemporary South Africa constitute a preeminent example. What role do such discourses play in a world whose problems appear to require a sense of increased internationalism, increased interdisciplinarianism and above all, keen urgency, for their articulation? What kind of critical function is the academy capable of in terms of our future? I ask these questions because, with the growth of postcolonial consciousness, we are becoming aware once again—if slowly!—that the Western academy has a history of operating in a position analogous to that of Kafka's explorer: it has often had the drive to explore but lacked the courage to assess its own implication in the knowledge it produces as a result of those explorations in moral terms.

An example of this failing—one that is of strategic relevance to this exploration—is produced by tracing Western authorities on the origin of violence. We need only glance at the traditions of philosophical, anthropological, and psychoanalytic thought to see that these disciplines reproduce variations of the master/slave, civilized/barbaric dichotomies not merely as the characteristics of history, but as the necessary origins of it, in discussions of violence that often amount less to explanation than they do to predetermination. The fact that fables of the origins of national, racial, and psychological violence are culturally specific and only selectively applicable—one history among many— is only beginning to dawn upon us (and is being wholeheartedly rejected by some: in this context, *The Closing of the American Mind* is a title whose ironic commentary on its own argument is surely lost on its author!). That these traditions—ones that form the basis of the kind of academic training both I on the one hand, and Brink, Breytenbach, and Coetzee on the other, received— inform my thoughts on violence is not something I have tried to deny; but I have attempted to demonstrate the limitations of such traditions in describing violations that they themselves are guilty of, the most obvious and pertinent of which, in terms of this study, are a number of imperialist assumptions of bewildering variety and complexity.

One of the problems of the genre of critical writing is its characteristic defensibility, the consequence of an expectation that it exhibit an armor so impenetrable, that it could never conceive of speaking to its own weakness. This problem becomes particularly acute when one develops the critical language with which to approach scenes of violence. The tendency always exists for the language that explicates violent situations to be perceived—by author, or reader, or both alike—as not merely explaining the crisis, but explaining it away. The mastery that is often posed as the apotheosis of the literary-critical genre tempts the critic to believe that she or he has somehow resolved the violence that the text reproduces by describing its parameters: surely a dangerous assumption.

Take, for example, two categories of literary identification that have traditionally been invoked to illuminate representations of violence in artistic work. The traditions of the sublime, and of gothic horror, may seem at first to offer tools for the analysis of the scenes of violence in South African prose that form the basis of this study. However, both the sublime as a philosophical term and the gothic as novelistic convention tend toward resolution: the one in terms of an aestheticization of emotional response, which again performs the function of distancing the moment of violence, and can offer pleasure as a consequence, (much as criticism that is eloquent enough to "explain away" its subject can);[4] the other in terms of the victory of social bonds over the subversive elements that are the catalysts of violence in the traditional gothic novel.[5] (The implicit credence given here to that old imperialist binary, civilized/atavistic, should not be overlooked as another reason why the category of the gothic is inadequate in the explication of the fiction of apartheid dissidence.)[6] To use the vocabulary of pain compensated for by pleasure, of victory over atrocity, in a discussion of violence in the context of contemporary South African prose, seems itself a violation of considerable proportions.

Our vocabulary tends to act like Kafka's explorer's rope, to distance us from the scene of violence in various ways. Occasionally it offers the phantom privilege of transcending the position of spectator through pornographic involvement in a scene of violence. This privilege is phantom precisely because pornographic response always contains the element of pleasure, and can be considered as yet another form of distancing for that reason; J. M. Coetzee's *Dusklands* is a novel at pains to point this out.

Even the postmodern preoccupation with the violence of representation can accomplish such a "resolution," a distancing, at the very same time that it purports to be based on principles calculated to avoid such pitfalls. After the Gulf crisis, the students of Victoria College at the University of Toronto organized a distinguished panel on the war between the Allies and Iraq.[7] The panel chose as the focus of the discussion the representation of Iraq in American and Canadian media, a move that resulted in an interesting discussion of the sophisticated orientalization of Iraq in film clips, news reports, and policy statements. This allowed us to identify the media's concentration on the accuracy of Allied weapons, rather than on the destruction they wreaked on their targets. Yet the discussion raised an awkward question in my mind: to what extent were we responsible for an analogous form of violation? Is it easier, and more comfortable, for us to use our analytical expertise to attack representations of the war, than to use them on a discussion of the incredibly complex, conflicting claims and suspect motivations that generated the tragedy itself? Surely it is necessary to forge ahead, our understandable apprehension notwithstanding?

Doubtless, postmodernism has forced us to distinguish once again between the subject and its representation. But to distinguish between violations and various conceptions of those violations articulated through representations, does not—and must not—mean that we should ignore the link between the two. How do our conceptions of what constitutes a violation either contribute to or hinder the occurrence of actual violence, be it domestic, political, or—and this is usually the case—inextricably both? This question is of paramount importance when it comes to the question of violation and the subject as subject to the exigencies of political and social power. Certainly, as postmodernism has indicated, defying the fixity of the dominant political ideology's construction can liberate the subject. But this postmodern defiance is a consequence of having had the opportunity to be defiant; the postmodern subject assumes a certain standard of material and political liberty to begin with. But what of the postcolonial subject, to whom the rhetoric of fractured subjectivity sounds like a description of her or his present, untenable position of oppression under colonialism, rather than a prescription for future liberation? Put simply, one can only entertain rejection of an image of one's identity as a personal, liberating choice if one has the basic political freedom to do so. This is the lesson of postcolonialism: to have an identity that is recognized is essential; the danger comes only when that identity is perceived by the powers that be as a fixed image to which the oppressed must either conform, or be punished. This fixed image constitutes my primary example of how a certain conception of subjectivity, in which "violation" is read as the failure to conform, results in the actual violence of interrogation and torture. To refuse to question the potential of our representations of violence to hinder or assist in generating a context in which active violence occurs—to encourage the realms of representation and actuality to be thought of in a relation of comfortable isolation from one another—is to encourage the split between theory and practice that is in danger of rendering the study of Humanities in the academy obsolete.

Our aversion to being trapped as spectators in a vision of horror—to be literally horrified—is understandable, to say the very least. Yet our tendency as critics of violence to fulfil our desire to run from the scene of horror by believing that we have "resolved" such scenes through our literary "treatment" of them, may unwittingly trap us in the scene of horror for longer than may otherwise have been the case. We need to develop ways of speaking about violence in literature which go beyond the safe, exclusive condemnation of certain representations of violence. Otherwise, we cannot identify how our present critical vocabulary contributes to a violent reality. My plea for a risk-taking vocabulary should not be mistaken for nostalgia for literary realism; my first chapter will demonstrate this. Rather, it is a request that we look at violence for longer than it takes either to denounce it and/or pronounce it inevitable. As Lucia Folena puts it,

> accusing a violence and simultaneously making it inevitable amounts to naturalizing and depoliticizing violence as a whole once more. What seems more important and profitable is identifying separate levels of violence, and showing that some of those levels are neither natural nor pre- or un-political. It is a matter of pluralizing violence, qualifying it, exploring the local and historical constitution of such levels (220).

This study is an attempt to meet Folena's challenge in the context of South African dissident writing. I have chosen André Brink, Breyten Breytenbach, and J. M. Coetzee, because their gender, race, and their primary linguistic heritage, place them in virtually untenable positions of powerful, privileged spectatorship—a factor that they have nevertheless chosen to recognize publicly, in terms of their dissident writing. That they have all been implicated in positions of domination three times over—as whites, as males, and as scions of Afrikaner families[8]—is a kind of safeguard against an all-too-easy glorification of dissidence and its counterpart, a facile vilification of all who entertain any position of power (a move that can be more popular than accurate or practical). I have also chosen them because they employ vastly different narrative forms in their depictions of violence. Brink is an Afrikaner whose writing, I will argue, participates in a development of the liberal tradition usually associated with earlier English-speaking writers, such as Alan Paton. He is also a writer whose work has had an enormously popular appeal in Europe and North America, and has done much to further the cause of antiapartheid sentiment internationally. Breytenbach's prison writings offer us the privilege of examining texts whose forms are generated by the experience of personal victimization, the experience that compelled him to write; they also prevent us from avoiding the difficult question of the relationship between actual experiences of violation and their literary re-presentations. J. M. Coetzee in turn offers us works that combine both theoretical clarity and stunning fictional vision in their approach to violence, and form the center of a controversy over what constitutes the most responsible form of fiction in a situation of such extreme political turmoil.

This is, ultimately, the crucial question: how do we construct the space between responsibility and violence in dissident rhetoric, whether it takes the form of fictional narratives—Brink's, Breytenbach's, Coetzee's—or critical prose, of which this project is an example? Coetzee's fifth novel, *Foe*, asks this very same question from the unique perspective of a South African writer who puts it into the mouth of a narrator who is "related" to him, in that she too wants to retell the history of the colonial encounter, and she too is at once both disadvantaged and privileged in various ways by her status as author. For this reason, I will begin this study with an introduction to *Foe*; and I will end it with a conclusion of that discussion, as a kind of measure of the progress that I hope to make toward explicating some of the questions *Foe* raises, both by reference to the other works of Coetzee, those of Brink and Breytenbach, and with respect to the heritage of critical discourses that I bring to bear upon the subject.

NOTES

1. The tendency to allegorize "In the Penal Colony," especially along religious lines, is discussed by Spann (114–6), who quotes from J. M. S. Pasley's commentary to illustrate his point. Pasley writes of the figure of the dead Commandant:

We are reminded of Jahvre as he is portrayed in the Book of Exodus, fighting for the Jews against the Egyptians, setting out a code of laws, and giving detailed specifications for the construction of the tabernacle, and even for the mixing of the holy unguent. The officer, with his brief-case containing the calligraphic commandments, calls up the figure of Moses hearing the tablets of the Law, which were engraved by the Lord's own hand (21).

This allegorization leads in turn to observations that carry an anti-Semitic implication:

Indeed the manner in which the officer handles the drawings, his dutiful hand-washing . . . and his concern lest they be touched by the uninitiated traveller, remind us *forcibly* of Jewish religious practice. Or again, the *"viele, viele Zieraten"* which surround and embellish the *"eigentliche Schrift"* may easily be related to the *massive overgrowth* of Jewish post-biblical exegesis, the *confusing decorations* of the Law (21; emphasis added).

2. This is the effect of Derrida's "Racism's Last Word," in which his condemnation of apartheid as "the ultimate racism in the world, the last of many" strikes me as a dangerous one, despite his defense that this piece was written as an appeal ("But, Beyond . . ." 157). It creates the impression, regardless of its author's intent, that all other societies have now been freed from racism.

3. Yeats writes in his introduction to the *Oxford Book of Modern Verse* that:

I have a distaste for certain poems written in the midst of the great war. . . . The writers of these poems . . . felt bound, in the words of the best known, to plead the suffering of their men. In poems that had for a time considerable fame, written in the first person, they made that suffering their own. I have rejected these poems for the same reason that made Arnold withdraw his *Empedocles on Etna* from circulation; passive suffering is not a theme for poetry (xxxiv).

4. For Burke, this distance is crucial for the effect of the sublime:

When danger or pain press too nearly, they are incapable of giving any delight, and are simply terrible; but at certain distances, and with certain modifications, they may be, and they are delightful. . . . (40).

5. Rosemary Jackson points out that in Gothic fiction

many fantasies play upon a *natural* fear of formlessness, absence, "death", to rein-force an *apparently "natural"* order of life—but that order is in effect an arbitrary one which identifies the "norm" as a middle-class, monogamous and male-domi-nated culture. In the name of defeating the "inhuman", such fantasies attempt to dismiss forces inimical to a bourgeois ideology (122).

6. The gothic novel has, of course, been deeply implicated in the processes of colonialism through its representation of the racial other as "inhuman." Patrick Brant-linger gives an excellent discussion of what he calls the tradition of "Imperial Gothic" in his book, *Rule of Darkness*. He examines such authors as Rudyard Kipling, Robert Ballantyne, Rider Haggard, and Joseph Conrad in this context.

7. Held on February 25, 1991 at Alumni Hall, Victoria College.

8. When asked by David Attwell to what extent his struggles against Afrikanerdom have been analogous to those of Breyten Breytenbach, Coetzee was careful to explain

that his family did not participate in the kind of Afrikaner nationalism to which Breytenbach responds with such (self) disgust; Coetzee pointed out that, unlike
Breytenbach, English has been Coetzee's primary means of expression since childhood.
However, he concludes his remarks with a caveat about the moral danger involved in
detaching himself completely from his Afrikaner heritage:

> The whites of South Africa participated, in various degrees, actively or passively, in
> an audacious and well-planned crime against Africa. Afrikaners as a self-defining
> group distinguished themselves in the commission of that crime. Thereby they lent
> their name to it. It will be a long time before they have the moral authority to
> withdraw that brandmark. . . . Is it in my power to withdraw from the gang? I
> think not. Breytenbach may have the power, but only because he first paid a price.
> More important, is it my heart's desire to be counted apart? Not really. Further-
> more—and this is an afterthought—I would regard it as morally questionable to
> write something like the second part of *Dusklands*—a *fiction*, note—from a posi-
> tion that is not historically complicit (*Doubling* 342–3).

INTRODUCTION

> The violence of representation
> is the suppression of difference.
>
> — Armstrong and Tennenhouse,
> *Violence and Representation*

SUSAN BARTON'S DILEMMA

It may seem strange to introduce this exploration of violence and literature in the South African context without a description of that context in historical or sociopolitical terms, or a conventional introduction to the life and times of the author on whose fiction this introduction is based, namely J. M. Coetzee. The motivation behind this is twofold. I have no desire to spectacularize, and thus to exoticize, the violence of South Africa which motivated the founding questions of this study. The making of South Africa into an international spectacle that allows for the operation of a specious voyeurism under the guise of a dubiously "justified" moral condemnation is an approach that, since it replicates the twin violations of pornographic involvement and the myth of objectivity I described in the preface, I wish most strenuously to avoid. Secondly, I do not want to jeopardize my project—that of illustrating the practical connections between issues of representation and issues of violence—by simplifying the context of those connections. For this reason I choose not to "domesticate" either Coetzee or the novel examined in this introduction, *Foe*, by defining them exclusively, and thus sensationally, with reference to the specifics of their country of origin. Such specifics will be included as they are required by the argument, but not as objects of self-evidence. For the moment, I would like to use Coetzee's *Foe*, often referred to as the most "theoretical" of his fictions, to speak to the risks taken by a writer who makes it her or his practice to represent a number of different ways in which violence is exercised against the subject.

Foe, Coetzee's fifth novel, which was published in 1986, is very much a novel that reflects the time and place of its genesis. Obviously, in light of my opening remarks, I do not mean to suggest that the novel should be made to reflect, through the deployment of a simplistic allegorical reading, apartheid South Africa in 1986, or simply the history of that particular location.[1] Rather, I want to point out that in *Foe*, Coetzee examines the conflict between a number of contemporary interests—those of postmodernism, feminism, and postcolonialism—from a specific context, that of the South African academy, in which the examination of such discursive claims is a task of particular historic moment. I intend to look at *Foe* as an allegory of narrative strategies employed by these discourses, since Coetzee's allegory is calculated to draw attention to the fact that acts of narration are always also, necessarily, acts of violation at the figurative level. The consequences of such figurative violence, *Foe* suggests, must be evaluated in terms of its implications for the actual, discursive context in which the narrative operates.

As Dovey proposes, *Foe* can be read as an exploration of the relationships among postmodern, postcolonial, and feminist discourses (*Novels* 330; "Intersection" 119).[2] Undoubtedly, the characters in *Foe* lend themselves to the kind of analysis that Dovey has undertaken. They do so, that is, to the extent that they can be read as representations of the various critical approaches that Dovey has named. Cruso can certainly be read as a representation of the colonizer, Susan Barton as a representation of the feminist novelist, Friday as a representation of the colonized subject, and Foe as a postmodern representation of the eighteenth-century master-writer. Yet to the degree that these characters exceed their respective qualities as representatives of these discourses, and instead become characterized by their interactions with one another as bodies that are simultaneously racially and sexually differentiated, they sabotage any simplistic interpretation of themselves as representative of distinct critical approaches, and insist instead upon their status as belonging to a novelistic, rather than critical, discourse. In this capacity they act not merely as representatives of various kinds of critical discourses, but rather as a critique of those discourses. They do so by embodying the violations that established categories of thought can enact upon (in this case) a fictional body, here specifically that of Coetzee's text itself. By means of analogy, the figures in *Foe* also demonstrate the pitfalls into which the conventions of fictional critiques of racial, sexual, and colonial violence frequently leap.

The act of placing, or rather, re-creating events in narrative, which is the preoccupation of storymaking, is always cast in an ambiguous light by Coetzee in his own fictional narratives. Many of his narrators occupy the shaky ground on which Coetzee himself, Brink and Breytenbach stand: these figures are all, as Stephen Watson has pointed out, faced with the dilemma of being "reluctant colonizers" (377–78); or, following Attwell, who uses Simon During's construct of "postcolonizing," they are all "postcolonizers" (*J. M. Coetzee* 22). Magda, the magistrate, the doctor of *Michael K.*, and the ailing female narrator of *Age of Iron* all criticize various acts of colonization; but they do so from positions of privilege under the system of colonization, positions that (and they are aware of this) place their criticisms in the light of an inexorable irony that threatens to make them "lose their voice." Their acts of narration are attempts to control and influence situations that are out of the narrators' hands; their criticisms of those situations come, as it were, out of their mouths perforce.[3]

The production of any narrative, fictional or critical, depends upon the creation of a certain textual logic—the creation of an essentially fictional discourse—which performs the task of privileging certain subjects over others. *Foe*'s narrative strategy points out that the translation of events "out of hand" into their situation within a master(ing) narrative involves a violence analogous to that of colonization. As *Foe* documents the struggles over what stories get told, how they get told, and to whom they "belong," the novel seems to illustrate that, as Nancy Armstrong and Leonard Tennenhouse put it, "the violence of representation is the suppression of difference" (8). This violation becomes evident, ironically, when the narrative fails to master its subjects: when it "loses its voice."

The first of *Foe*'s narrative strategies is never to claim that it is free from bias in presenting Susan Barton's history; indeed, as the novel progresses, its narrative suggests that such a task would be impossible. The first section of the novel records the events that Susan Barton, in subsequent sections of the novel, attempts to turn into her story. Although these events are presented as "the truth" by Susan Barton herself, the narrative of the novel marks them as being part of her narrative: they are recorded as constituting her narration, a first-person narration that remains for the most part within inverted commas.[4] Thus the novel distinguishes between Susan Barton's narrative and its own narrative framework, and in doing so, questions the claims her narrative makes.

For at least the first half of the novel, the single justification of a narrative for Susan Barton is its ability to convey "the truth." This monolithic goal of Susan Barton's writing enterprise turns out to be at odds with her desire to present her experience on the island in a "factual" account. The first few pages of *Foe* may well lead us to suspect the implication of this contradiction, namely, that Susan Barton's narrative is interrupted—and will ultimately be halted—when it is confronted by the notion that a number of "truths" may be operating simultaneously. Susan Barton recounts in chronological order the events of her being shipwrecked, her arrival on the island, her meeting with Friday, and her introduction of herself to Cruso. Her first "failure" to tell us her story comes when she is unable to account for, and therefore is unable to recount, Cruso's history. This is because his accounts of his past are numerous and contradictory. Susan Barton resorts to blaming this gap on the failure of his memory. However, even this rhetorical gesture cannot disguise the interruption in her narrative. The lapse is precipitated by a breakdown in the operation of her logic of "the truth":

> 'With these words I presented myself to Robinson Cruso, in the days when he still ruled over his island, and became his second subject, the first being his manservant Friday.
>
> 'I would gladly now recount to you the history of this singular Cruso, as I heard it from his own lips. But the stories he told me were so various, and so hard to reconcile one with another, that I was more and more driven to conclude age and isolation had taken their toll on his memory, and he no longer knew for sure what was the truth, what fancy. . . . So in the end I did not know what was truth, what was lies, and what was mere rambling.
>
> 'But let me return to my relation, (11–12).

Susan Barton's history is, finally, a history of her inability to tell the story she wants to tell; it is not at all the story she originally desires. From the beginning, Susan Barton as narrator seems to be aware of threats to her control of the narrative. Part One closes with the disclosure that she has been addressing a "Mr Foe," and her simultaneous claim that the story of the island "belongs" to her. She wants Foe to recognize her not merely as character, but as owner-author of the tale:

> 'Do you think of me, Mr Foe, as Mrs Cruso or as a bold adventuress? Think what you may, it was I who shared Cruso's bed and closed Cruso's eyes, as it is I who have disposal of all that Cruso leaves behind, which is the story of his island' (45).

In spite of her exclusive claim to the story of the island, Susan Barton decides she needs help from Foe in telling the story. Susan Barton enlists Foe's assistance because she comes to feel that her version of the story is not "the truth" of her story; yet she nevertheless comes to resent Foe's "edition" of the story for the very same reason. She sets down the facts of her story for Foe, and decides that this history "'is a sorry, limping affair'" (47). She wants the telling of the story to retrieve or redeem her experiences on the island. Yet she discovers that in the process of writing down this history she has not resurrected herself as castaway and author. Instead, she has violated herself by defacing herself in her own narrative:

> 'When I reflect on my story I seem to exist only as the one who came, the one who witnessed, the one who longed to be gone: a being without substance, a ghost beside the true body of Cruso. Is that the fate of all storytellers? Yet I was as much a body as Cruso. . . . Return to me the substance I have lost, Mr Foe: that is my entreaty. For though my story gives the truth, it does not give the substance of the truth . . .' (51).

So Susan Barton turns to Foe for help, choosing him because she has been told that he is an author who has heard a number of confessions and is held to be "'a very secret man'" (48). Susan Barton may have done well to be suspicious of Foe's reputed "secrecy." The nature of his "interest" (48) is com-mercial, and his project of telling Susan Barton's story for her is calculated to this end. Susan Barton herself has the notion of commercial success in mind: she wants to produce the first female castaway narrative so that she will be recognized both as author and castaway, and will consequently gain financial independence. It is ironic, then, that she relinquishes her sole right over the story to Foe in the hope that he will fulfill her twin goal of telling "the truth" and making the story popular, all in order to "bring her back to life." Having remarked that her memoir took her three days to write, she comments to Foe:

> 'More is at stake in the history you write, I will admit, for it must not only tell the truth about us but please its readers too. Will you not bear it in mind, however, that my life is drearily suspended till your writing is done?' (63)

Foe, and following him, Susan Barton, attempt to transform her nar-rative into a popular travel adventure, because this is the form that has been used for stories such as hers, and is therefore the only one capable of producing the recognition, commercial and other, which Susan Barton believes this enter-prise will afford her. Susan Barton comes to her storytelling task with a belief that the literary stereotypes upon which the form of the travel narrative rests bear "the truth" about the figures they employ. She desires and expects Cruso to be Defoe's Robinson Crusoe. She laments the fact that he brought only a knife from the shipwreck and bemoans his failure to keep a journal (16–17).

Later, Susan Barton develops the same response to Foe's invocation of such stereotypes as Cruso had demonstrated earlier in response to her demand that he "be" Robinson Crusoe. Foe believes that Barton's history cannot be-come story without the addition of the exotic paraphernalia of the eighteenth-century travel narrative: gun powder and muskets saved from a legendary shipwreck, cannibals, and so on. Just as Cruso had pointed out to Susan Barton the difficulties of keeping a journal and the impracticability of the advantages supposedly gained by doing so, Susan Barton now queries Foe about the validity of such stereotypes:

> 'Now I ask: Who can keep powder dry in the belly of a wave? Furthermore: Why should a man endeavour to save a musket when he barely hopes to save his own life? As for cannibals, I am not persuaded, despite Cruso's fears, that there are cannibals in those oceans' (54).

When Susan Barton becomes impatient with what she perceives to be Foe's recalcitrance, she literally takes over his place. In his absence, she tries to write her story at his bureau, using his paper, pen, and ink. Yet, as in the case of the fictional daughter she believes Foe is trying to foist on her, she is never able to escape the ghost of (De)Foe or the stereotypes he attempts to employ in telling her story. This is so despite the fact that these "ghost" stereotypes of eighteenth-century fiction—the author who relates "true confessions," the cannibal, the castaway, and so on—disturb her attempt to produce "the truth" in story. The exotica required by the form of the travel tale violate Susan Barton's notion of the truth; however, she is nevertheless driven to consider employing them in order to achieve the recognition she desires.[5]

The "validity" that these fictions offer Susan Barton is the "validity" of closure, the one feature that her account, judged by her own standards, "lacks." Realizing that her narrative may seem too dull to her readers, and that they may reject it for its frequent inability to account for the circumstances it describes, she asks herself how long it will be before she is "'driven to invent new and stranger circumstances.'" She then proceeds to list examples of events that did not occur while she was on the island, but that could "make up" the story. One of these events, for example, provides Cruso's odd occupation of terrace-building with a rationale: "'at last, the coming of a golden-haired stranger with a sack of corn, and the planting of the terraces.'" Yet Susan Barton mourns the violation that such additions/editions inflict upon her sense of true narrative: "'Alas,'" she asks, "'will the day ever arrive when we can make a story without strange circumstances?'" (67)

Susan Barton's attitude toward what she calls "strange circumstances" is paradoxical. Although she considers "make-up" stories to be a violation of the truth of narrative, she nevertheless considers the incidents in her narrative which she is unable to explain—its truly "strange circumstances"—to be a violation of that narrative as well. Her approach, which assumes (at least until

Part Three of the novel) that narrative not only should, but is also capable of, telling "the truth," is one that desires closure and expects all mysteries to be re-solved in the course of narrative. In this scheme of things, puzzles or mysteries become "symptoms" that it is the duty of narrative to "treat." It is no wonder then that Susan Barton, as long as she clings to this view of narrative, is daunted by the task that she believes lies before her. This task consists of resolving the numerous puzzles or mysteries that belong to the story that she believes Cruso has bequeathed to her; the task of restoring her inheritance.

Susan Barton approaches this task by what she perceives to be the necessary means, that is, by rescuing or saving the "facts" of the story both for posterity and prosperity. The metaphor of salvation resonates throughout the tale of Susan Barton's endeavors. This metaphor describes what Susan Barton believes narrative can do for her and her ghostly companions, "shipwrecked" by Coetzee in a narrative that imposes the problem of its own dis-closure on its own fictional narrator. Susan Barton has the desire of any castaway to be saved. However, in Coetzee's novel this desire is given metafictional expression in the linking of Susan Barton's desire to be saved literally—that is, from the island— to her desire to be saved literarily, in and by her own narrative.[6] Susan Barton's original desire is to be saved from the island. Once this desire has been fulfilled, however, it is replaced by her desire to save the island, or her experience of it, in narrative, by completing that narrative.

In the context of this notion of narrative, closure and salvation amount to one and the same thing. Susan Barton conceives of narrative as essentially teleological in both its form and function. Narrative is seen to heal or "fix" events, eliminating all elements of controversy or doubt surrounding them. Such a narrative relieves author and reader alike of any responsibility to enquire further about those events. This essentially recuperative notion of narrative demands not only that Susan Barton "fix" the holes in her story; it also dictates that she cannot be sure of who she is, or of her own author-ity— that she cannot be sure of her own salvation—until the story is written down. In this context it is not surprising that she feels that her life is suspended until her story is written down. Her inability to bridge the faults in the narrative threatens her goal of salvation for herself and the figures that accompany her on her quest. Her attempts to restore the holes in the fabric of the narrative provide us with a record of failure that suggests what she herself begins to suspect. This history of "failed" narrative proposes that closure is impossible without violation. What kind of salvation, if any, is possible, the text ultimately asks, without invoking the violation of closure?

Cruso's terraces form only the first of numerous puzzles or mysteries that frustrate Susan Barton's attempt to "save the island" and close her story.

The terraces, and Cruso himself, introduce the puzzles that follow them. They pose a threat to Susan Barton's project because they refuse to be translated into narrative, refuse to be "saved." The mysteries that present themselves most immediately to Susan Barton, those that she names to Friday, are those that center around the figures of Cruso and Friday: the terraces, Friday's tongue, Friday's apparent submission to Cruso, Friday's and Cruso's lack of desire for Susan Barton, and Friday's "scattered petals" ritual (83–87). We might expect Friday and Cruso to present such problems to Susan Barton's potentially recuperative narrative, since they are both figures who were reluctant to be saved in the first place: both characters are forced into being saved by Susan Barton (39–41). Their actions suggest that neither Cruso nor Friday wished to leave the island; and neither survives his "salvation," as it were. Cruso physically does not survive the colonizer's version of a (reversed) "middle passage" back to England, and Friday does not survive the translation into English; English is incapable of describing—of circumscribing—him.

The rejection of salvation through narrative, signalled by the refusal or rejection of the figures of Friday and Cruso to be translated into narrative, suggests a violation demonstrated in and inflicted by Susan Barton's narrative throughout the fiction. This violation has its basis in the inability of narrative, especially a narrative that attempts to de-scribe characters as figures of "the truth," to deal with bodies as bodies, rather than as figures of speech. The "treatment" of the body as a figure of speech violates the body by translating it into a term in a representative scheme. This denies the substantiality of the body and effectively effaces the body from the text. The metaphor used to convey this violation of the body by narrative in *Foe* is that of cannibalism. The only cannibals in *Foe* are its narrator-characters, and the only cannibalism is that which they inflict upon their subjects in the process of turning them into stories. Foe, in the process of trying to turn Susan Barton into a story, is depicted actually biting her, then sucking the wound and murmuring, "'This is my manner of preying on the living'" (139). This eating up of the body by narrative turns characters into "ghosts" (Susan Barton's word for it); and ultimately even the narrator-characters, Foe and Barton, are so afflicted. If the characters of *Foe* turn out to be not so much characters as they are "ghosts" or figures, then it is because the fiction as a whole—its metanarrative—recognizes that narrative does to characters precisely what Foe says loss of their preferred diet does to cannibals: "'They lose their vivacity when deprived of human flesh,'" he remarks (127).

Cruso and Friday are the first "bodies" to suggest that the translation of themselves into narrative is a violation. Cruso's physical resistance to the sailors that transport him from the island to the ship indicates his constant resistance to being translated into narrative and to being given a history that will become famous abroad. Despite the fact the he himself can be (and has been)[7] read as a colonizer, Cruso refuses to submit to Susan Barton's colonization of him in writing and by writing. His refusal to keep an account of himself, which in Susan Barton's mind is tantamount to a refusal to account for himself, indicates his rejection of the written word. His death indicates that he is never saved in the manner that Susan Barton thinks he should be. In this sense he dies out of Susan Barton's narrative; he never becomes one of the "ghosts" of the after-story.[8] However, his death does serve to alert Susan Barton to the violation that her narrative has enacted upon him, despite the fact that she will not recognize this violation as it pertains to other figures, particularly that of Friday, for quite some time to come:

> 'On the island I believe Cruso might yet have shaken off the fever, as he had done so often before. . . . But now he was dying of woe, the extremest woe. With every passing day he was conveyed farther from the kingdom he pined for, to which he would never find his way again. He was a prisoner, and I, despite myself, his gaoler' (43).

Susan Barton's other "prisoner" is of course Friday. Friday cannot speak.[9] By virtue of this he is resistant to Susan Barton's colonizing narrative. Although he cannot speak out against his "savior," his demeanor is not that of the saved but of the enslaved:

> 'But when he was brought aboard Friday would not meet my eye. With sunken shoulders and bowed head he awaited whatever was to befall him' (40–41).

Friday is the first figure to become a ghost of his former self, the first body to be cannibalized by Susan Barton's post-island narrative project. Once he is in England he loses his vivacity, "'grows old before his time'" (55). In England Susan Barton begins the long and difficult project of "restoring" Friday, a project doomed to failure. Susan Barton shows him one of Foe's novels, and tries to persuade him of the immortal quality of words. "'Is writing not a fine thing, Friday?'" she asks him. "'Are you not filled with joy to know that you will live forever, after a manner?'" (58). She attempts to teach Friday the English names of the various utensils he uses to fulfill the tasks she sets for him. She tries to convince herself that she is doing so to restore him to his original self, to give him back his tongue. She assumes that as long as language—her language—is restored to him, his (lost) history will be restored to him. She appears to believe that this history will somehow replace his colonization by Cruso and/or others. She describes this time-honored colonialist strategy of giving voice to the mute(d) other in order to save him for "civilization:"[10]

> 'I seek the first sign that he comprehends what I am attempting . . . [which is] to build a bridge of words, over which, when one day it has grown sturdy enough, he may cross to the time before Cruso, the time before he lost his tongue, when he lived immersed in the prattle of words as unthinking as a fish in water; from where he may by steps return, as far as he is able, to the world of words in which you, Mr Foe, and I, and other people live' (60).

Once again, however, Susan Barton comes to doubt the motive behind her liberal-humanist project. She asks herself whether the blunt, silent, and obvious domination of Friday by Cruso may not be preferable to a superficially well-intentioned liberalism that is, ultimately, insidious in terms of its ability to camouflage its own intent:

> 'I tell myself I talk to Friday to educate him out of darkness and silence. But is that the truth? There are times when benevolence deserts me and I use words only as the shortest way to subject him to my will. At such times I understand why Cruso preferred not to disturb his muteness. I understand, that is to say, why a man will choose to be a slaveowner' (60–61).

Despite this realization, Susan Barton continues to try to communicate with Friday using figures that are familiar to her, but which Friday cannot recognize. She tries to extract the truth of his past from him, using drawings. She shows him a picture of a Cruso-like figure cutting out a black man's tongue, and then one of a black slave-trader, cutting out a black boy's tongue. However, she doubts her own strategy when he does not respond, reflecting that these pictures may not look anything like the scene of Friday's mutilation. Or, she remarks, what she sees as an act of extreme violation—the dismemberment or dysfunction of Friday's tongue—may not be a violation from another perspective, but rather a cultural norm.[11]

Having torn up the pictures, Susan Barton tries to communicate with Friday next through music, but this too fails. She tries to play the flute with him, but their combined playing is "'jangled and jarred'" (98). She plays her flute as Friday dances, at first believing that she is offering him a form of companionship in the process. However, when she ceases playing she is angered to find that Friday continues to dance, as if she had never existed; as if, she says, his soul were "'more in Africa than in Newington'" (98).[12] She acknowledges for the first time that it is possible that Friday has not communicated with her, not because he has been unable to do so, but because he has no desire to do so.

As the history of Susan Barton's attempts to "free" Friday unfolds, it becomes clear that Susan Barton is not trying to liberate Friday at all, but to control him by gaining access to him through communication on her terms. In this respect, she has saddled herself with an impossible task. However, she does not realize that this task is self-imposed. As a consequence, she blames Friday for her sense of being overburdened. To Susan Barton, Friday is a version of the white, in this case, woman's, burden. It is no wonder that she tells Friday, referring to her task of storytelling, that "'Sometimes I believe it is I who have become the slave'" (87), or that she later complains to Foe that Friday is a tyrant riding on her shoulders, from whom she cannot free herself (148).[13]

Susan Barton's next attempt to "liberate" Friday, or rather, to free herself from him, is to grant him his freedom legally. She inscribes his bill of freedom from Cruso (not, tellingly, from herself) and puts it in a bag around his neck. The fact that his declaration of "freedom" needs to be worn like a chain around his neck signifies that this method of dispensing with Friday will also fail.[14] Susan Barton's notion of taking Friday to Bristol and literally shipping him back to Africa (no doubt a deliberate play on the "put them back on the boat" attitude) represents a kind of "apartheid" approach to what is perceived to be the problem of the heterogeneity brought about by the colonial encounter. It is another simplistic attempt at recuperation, one which tries to restore both Friday and Susan Barton herself to an impossible original innocence. "Africa" here becomes a territorial metaphor for a kind of heathen prelapsarian Eden capable of containing Friday and thus releasing Susan Barton from her "burden." Once again Susan Barton's strategy aims, like her bridge of words, to "restore" Friday by writing the enslavement of Friday's body out of history.

If Susan Barton's bemoaning her fate—her enunciation of Friday, the figure of the colonial encounter, as burden—sounds like the statements of a number of South African writers concerning the burden of being expected to write about, and in this way somehow resolve, the violations of apartheid, perhaps we should not disregard this coincidence altogether. (The story of *Foe* is not only the story of the white South African dissident author. My return to a reading of *Foe* at the conclusion of this book is intended to demonstrate, among other points, my unwillingness to reduce it to such a parable.) Susan Barton's failed attempts to heal the breaches of her narrative, which represent unresolved violations of various kinds, can function as a useful reminder of the limitations of narrative, including critical narrative, in terms of its ability to "treat" the symptoms of violence. Forms of narrative that assume—or rather, presume—that narrative can "redeem" us in the face of such atrocities invoke a kind of closure that is irredeemably specious. Such closure participates not only in the rhetorical violence of a premature literary closure, but also thereby implicates itself in the broader discursive violence of promoting the myth that absolute unity, based on a notion of monolithic community, is both desirable and attainable.

The realization of the limitations of narrative in "dealing with" atrocity has perhaps been late in coming to the white South African literary tradition. It has proven difficult for authors to depict the horror of South Africa, precisely because they tend to enact a superficial "treatment" of the situation in their fiction. The failure of South African fiction to recognize the dangers of this "therapeutic" approach can be described in terms of South African literary history as the failure of white liberalism. I am thinking here of novels such as Alan Paton's *Cry, the Beloved Country*, in which the pastoral convention is used to make the hierarchies of racism palatable, if not ultimately invisible. The relationship between aesthetic merit and political practice assumed in such narratives is regarded with suspicion by later novelists who have inherited the liberal tradition, such as Nadine Gordimer, whose *Burger's Daughter* rejects the propositions of liberal humanism in terms of its content, if not its form.

The question of the relationship between narrative convention and subject matter brings us to a number of related questions that provide a starting point for the concerns of this book. How does the form of a narrative interact with its subject—in this case, the multiple violences of sexism, racism, and colonialism—to create a "treatment" of such violence? What kinds of narratives avoid this pitfall, and to what other violations are such alternative narratives vulnerable? What approaches do they offer in place of the superficially "therapeutic"? I will tackle the first of these questions by beginning with a discussion of the liberalism of André Brink's fiction, a liberalism that has been less scrutinized by critics of the liberal tradition in white South African writing in English.[15] I will then consider the latter questions by discussing the prison writings of Breyten Breytenbach and, finally, other novels of J. M. Coetzee.

NOTES

1. Many reviewers and critics reduce Coetzee's fiction to allegories of the contemporary South African situation (a consequence of the investment of the press in the construct of the "committed South African writer," a label that Coetzee rejects). Teresa

Dovey and Lois Parkinson Zamora have offered much more satisfying allegorical readings of Coetzee's work: Dovey focuses on his fictions as Lacanian allegories in her book *The Novels of J. M. Coetzee* and Zamora looks at his politically informed use of Hegelian allegories. David Attwell's book, *J. M. Coetzee: South Africa and the Politics of Writing*, is valuable for its careful delineation of how Coetzee's fictions resist or exceed philosophical allegories, rather than conforming to them.

2. The text supports this approach in numerous instances. Susan Barton's replacement of Foe as narrator within the novel, and the implication that she therefore also re-places the father-narrator, Daniel Defoe, suggests the feminist interest of *Foe*'s narrative. This is further demonstrated by Sue Barton's rejection of the "daughter" Foe has created for her, the second "Susan Barton." Susan Barton's rejection of this "daughter" can be read as a rejection of the "sinful" history of the female character of Defoe's *Roxana*; a "history" that culminates in Roxana's refusal to recognize her daughter, Susan. The figure of Friday has a long history of representing the colonized subject. This history extends from *Robinson Crusoe* itself through Mannonian readings that identify Friday and Caliban, to his figuring in *Foe* as colonized and therefore disabled, at least in relation to the power of narrative, since his tongue is rendered (as) dysfunctional. Finally, the novel is obviously metafictional. Susan Barton's repetition of the novel's opening lines in the version of the shipwreck story she tells to Cruso alert us to the metafictional aspect of *Foe* early on. The use of metafiction in *Foe* to review the history of narratives of colonization has encouraged a number of critics to approach the novel as a postmodern work of historiographical metafiction (Hutcheon, *A Poetics of Postmodernism* 107–8, 114, 198–99, and *A Politics of Postmodernism* 76; Gräbe; and Marais, "The Deployment of Metafiction in an Aesthetic of Engagement").

3. As Watson notes in his essay, this inability of "the colonizer who refuses" to effect any radical change in her or his position—not even through the expression of her or his refusal—is described by Memmi in his book, *The Colonizer and the Colonized*:

> He [the colonizer who refuses] may openly protest, or sign a petition, or join a group which is not automatically hostile toward the colonized. This already suffices for him to recognize that he has simply changed difficulties and discomfort. It is not easy to escape mentally from a concrete situation, to refuse its ideology while continuing to live with its actual relationships. From now on, he lives his life under the sign of a contradiction that looms at every step, depriving him of all coherence and all tranquillity (20).

4. The narrative of the third part is not given in inverted commas, but the dialogue between Susan Barton and Foe that she relates there marks the narrative as her own.

5. In an article entitled "Oppressive Silence: J. M. Coetzee's *Foe* and the Politics of the Canon," Derek Attridge discusses this conundrum in relation to Coetzee's fiction. He explores the difficulty of writing about the marginal in a form that draws attention to the subject of the dispossessed by engaging, and thus participating in, the Western literary canon.

6. Dovey points this out: "the desire to save oneself or another functions as a metaphor for the desire to translate the self or the other into writing" (*The Novels of J. M. Coetzee* 347).

7. Dovey identifies Cruso as a neocolonizer (*The Novels of J. M. Coetzee* 346); Robert M. Post, in an extremely reductionist reading of *Foe*, identifies him as representing "the Afrikaner government of South Africa" ("The Noise of Freedom" 145).

8. Indeed, it is precisely because of his death that Susan Barton later believes that he may have had some key to the telling of the tale that she does not. Through the unequivocal nature of death he has paradoxically remained a source of the substantial to Susan Barton, an effect that she reflects upon as she begins to doubt her own integrity:

> 'Had I known, on the island, that it would one day fall to me to be our storyteller, I would have been more zealous to interrogate Cruso. . . . when he lay dying on the *Hobart* I might have said: "Cruso, you are leaving us behind, you are going where we cannot follow you. Is there no last word you wish to speak, from the vantage of one departing?"' (89).

9. Here I do not mean merely that Friday cannot physically speak, but more significantly, that he is not given speech by the author; that he cannot therefore "speak" in the language of the novel.

10. Brian Macaskill and Jeanne Colleran, who for the most part give a sufficiently complex reading of *Foe*, offer a description of Friday which appears to suggest that Coetzee's project employs this strategy of giving a voice to the other:

> Coetzee produces here a distinctively postmodern emblem of the gothic by opening Friday's mouth, by revealing fully *the extent to which* Foe *must be, indeed, always has been, Friday's narrative* although others (both inside and outside the text) have tried to appropriate it or to dictate to it, or to allegorize it along the way (453; emphasis added).

Once again, this reading of Friday appears to want to resolve, rather than to describe, his violation.

11. This possibility is overlooked by the majority of critics, including David Attwell, Teresa Dovey, and Brian Macaskill and Jeanne Colleran.

12. Perhaps the only point at which Susan Barton can be said to be beginning to recognize Friday as a bodily presence, rather than as a figure of her own speech, is when she, in despair and not knowing what else to do, follows Friday's example and dances in the barn. She discovers that the movement comforts and warms her: "'I danced till the very straw seemed to warm under my feet. I have discovered why Friday dances in England, I thought, smiling to myself'" (103).

13. This is of course an ironic reversal of the opening scene of the novel, in which Friday carries Susan Barton to the interior of the island, because her feet cannot withstand its thorny vegetation, to which Friday is accustomed: "'So part-way skipping on

one leg, part-way riding on his back . . . I ascended the hillside, my fear of him abating in this strange backwards embrace'" (6).

14. The marks left by this "chain" reappear in the "unnamed" narrative that concludes the novel. This could well be interpreted as a self-referential gesture on Coetzee's part, an ironic commentary by the author on *Foe*'s efficacy as a bill of freedom. (David Attwell remarks upon the fact that in the final section, Friday has "a scar on his neck, 'like a necklace, left by a rope or chain' (155), *unobserved before in the novel*" [*J. M. Coetzee* 116; emphasis added]. It seems to me that the connection between the bill of freedom and the scar is a relatively strong one.)

15. One exception to the rule is Vernon February, who proposes that Brink's novels are more problematic than condemnation or praise based on their antiracist stance would suggest (124–27).

Violence, Afrikaner Liberalism, and the Fiction of André Brink

> The novel-form Conrad inherited is the novel-form in which most writers, black and white, write today. For comedy of manners is the basis of protest fiction, fiction of good guys and bad guys, racist guys and liberal guys. Comedy of manners is the basis of realism that mirrors society to identify refinements of behaviour that are social or anti-social, heroic or anti-heroic. . . .
>
> The novel-form Conrad inherited—if I may re-state my theme in a more complex way—was conditioned by a homogenous cultural logic to promote a governing principle that would sustain all parties, all characterizations, in endeavouring to identify natural justice, natural conscience behind the activity of a culture.
>
> —Wilson Harris, "The Frontier on which *Heart of Darkness* Stands"

1. Introduction

Due to the international popularization of the antiapartheid cause over the past few decades, André Brink, like all contemporary South African dissident writers who have achieved international recognition, is asked with tedious regularity about the role of the South African writer. Unlike J. M. Coetzee, whose (consistent) response to such queries is to reject the very notion of such a role, Brink appears to be content for his writing to be discussed with this much-invoked construct—that of the South African dissident author as champion of the antiapartheid cause—in mind.[1] Brink's two collections of essays, entitled *Mapmakers: Writing in a State of Siege* (1983) and *Literatuur in die Strydperk* [Literature in the Stage of Struggle] (1985), demonstrate his interest in the sociopolitical context of works by dissident authors of various nationalities, and his desire to describe in particular the political and imaginative challenges that South Africa poses for the dissident writer. Brink's comments on his novels reflect this concern with the conjunction of the political and the aesthetic; his response to being invoked as the representative "South African author" in the domestic and international media is to accept responsibility for that role, using the authority it grants him as an opportunity to educate his readers. André Brink's critical and fictional work, precisely because of the exemplary conscience it exhibits with respect to the ethics of what Brink himself refers to as "writing in a state of siege," provides a good introduction to the privileges and constraints under which the white South African dissident Afrikaner works, as well as an outline of Brink's particular response to those conditions.[2]

While acknowledging the "closeness" of his work "to the realities of South Africa today," Brink claims that it is his "stated conviction" that "literature should never descend to the level of politics; it is rather a matter of elevating and refining politics so as to be worthy of literature" (Ross interview 55). Brink's novels challenge South African political authority and encourage his readers, both in and outside South Africa, to do the same. Brink has developed an aesthetics "*in response* to [the] outrages of the state" (J. M. Coetzee, "Brink and Censor" 63), using his essays and speeches to discuss his political intentions directly, in markedly public forums. He has indicated, for example, that the interracial love affair between Joseph Malan and Jessica Thomson, and the details of its description, were calculated to cause the offense that resulted in the highly publicized banning of *Looking on Darkness*, his first novel to be rewritten in English (published in 1974).[3]

The subject matter of Brink's following novels develop the alliance between his political and literary prerogatives. *An Instant in the Wind* (1976), a historical novel set in the nineteenth century, describes a similarly doomed interracial love affair between a black slave, Adam, and an inhabitant of the Cape who is of European origin, Elizabeth Larsson. *Rumours of Rain* (1978) deals with the inability of the novel's narrator and protagonist, an Afrikaner entrepreneur named Martin Mynhardt, to come to terms with the changes wrought in his life by the increasing demand for black rights—a demand made by his own workers and supported by his son, Louis, and his mistress, Bea, and defended in court by his erstwhile best friend, Bernard.

Brink's subsequent novels have continued to exhibit an interest in the subject of racial relations: *A Chain of Voices* (1982), another historical novel, describes a slave rebellion and *The Wall of the Plague* (1984) details the decision of a "coloured" woman living in exile in France to return to South Africa in order to participate in the antiapartheid movement from within the country. In *States of Emergency* (1988), Brink explores the relationship between the actual state of emergency imposed on the country by President P. W. Botha at the time of Brink's writing of the novel, and his attempt to deal with the implications of this political condition within a fictional construct. *Act of Terror* (1991) describes an attempt to assassinate the South African president, concentrating on the involvement of an Afrikaner, Thomas Landman, in the plot. *On the Contrary* (1993), his third historical novel, is based on the figure of Estienne Barbier, who rebelled against Dutch authorities at the Cape and was executed for his dissidence. *The First Life of Adamastor* (1993) retells the Adamastor myth from the perspective of a leader of the Khoi, who inhabited the Cape at the time of "first contact."

That Brink appears to believe that his role as a South African dissident requires him to express a particular kind of political commitment in his fiction is indicated more generally in the speech he gave on accepting the Martin Luther King Memorial Prize for *A Dry White Season* (1979). This novel describes the investigation of an Afrikaner into the circumstances surrounding the deaths of a black child and his father while in police custody. "In *A Dry White Season*," he stated, "I have tried to accept that responsibility one owes to one's society and one's time" (*Mapmakers* 204).

Brink's subject matter is deliberately provocative. The recurring descriptions of sexual intercourse, and particularly of interracial sexual relationships, and his portrayals of interracial violence, especially that involving police brutality, have received condemnation by a significant number of readers within South Africa.[4] Brink's unfailing insistence on treating topics that were proscribed under the terms of South Africa's extensive censorship legislation ensured that his works drew their fair share of attention from the Publications Control Board.

In an essay entitled "Literature and Offence" in *Mapmakers* Brink proposes that the notion of offense is critical, not incidental, to the aesthetic project embodied in his novels. He begins by distinguishing between language that is in general use, the "language of society" or pragmatic discourse, and that of the creative writer, or literary discourse. Brink states that the language used by society at large is conditioned by and rooted in convention, since such language is, of necessity, "generalize[d] and systematize[d] . . . within a structure of common denominators." The creative writer's language usage, Brink argues, runs counter to that of society:

> the writer must hone blunted words anew, rekindle the fire of "original inspira-
> tion" in them, rediscover original meanings or discover new ones, departing in
> every respect from the well-known and well-trodden syntactical or semantic
> paths, exploring whatever territory remains unknown on either side (118).

Implicit within Brink's definitions of social and literary language is the notion that literary discourse constitutes some sort of critique of the conventions that afford social language its meaning, whether that critique is overt or implied. For Brink this characteristic of literary discourse—that it is critical of conventional systems of belief as they are reflected in the meaning of social discourse—is integral to the identification of literary discourse as art. In part three of the essay he goes on to claim that *"All significant art is offensive"* (119), and develops what may be termed an aesthetics of response based on this proposition.

For Brink, the novel, as an artistic act of communication, is dependent upon its ability to provoke offense:

> 'Offend', 'offensive' is used here in the original sense of the etymology of the word
> as it is given in *The Shorter Oxford English Dictionary*, namely 'OF. *offendre* [*sic*] to
> strike against . . .' The element of resistance, of some form of obstacle is essential
> to the notion of offense. . . . [T]he aesthetic object does not communicate to its
> public in a purely passive state but only by dint of encountering, or arousing, and
> eventually overcoming an initial resistance (*Mapmakers* 119).

According to Brink the work of both the writer and the reader is initiated by their experience of offense. This quality of offensiveness, the element of resistance, is the response to her or his environment that prods the author to write;[5] it is also experienced by the writer in the production of the literary work through her or his attempt to transform social language into literary language. This transformation, the genesis of literary discourse, involves a critique of the values on which the meaning of pragmatic discourse depends. According to Brink, it is to this questioning of commonly held social values that the reader responds (at least initially) with offense.

As Brink describes the author's response of offense to her or his world, and the reader's response of offense to the fiction, both constitute responses to some form of perceived violation. Brink has made it quite clear that his novels have been written out of his sense of horror at the condition of apartheid; and he intends them to provoke a similar sense of horror in his readers. There are, however, two related questions that raise themselves with regard to Brink's aesthetics of response, questions that shed some light upon the limits of his fictional projects in as much as they constitute the faithful praxis of Brink's theory of offense. The first concerns Brink's "writer"; the second, his "reader."[6]

The first question is a basic but revealing one. How, one may ask, does Brink's totalitarian society produce his "writer"? What enables "the writer"—socialized as she or he inevitably is in the language of convention and consensus—to make that initial recognition of a practice of the society in which she or he lives as "offensive," the recognition that will lead to her or his transformation of pragmatic discourse into literary discourse? If "the writer" diagnoses the sickness of the state, as Brink argues, then J. M. Coetzee poses the relevant question: "Is diagnosis carried out from inside or outside the body? . . . If from outside, how did the organ find its way out of the body?" ("Brink and Censor" 72). "The writer" here begins to appear in a secular version of his traditional Afrikaner role—as prophet, as the witness to the truth. But who anoints him as prophet, except himself, and later, his readership? In the context of this question, the transformation of language conditioned by convention into the required literature of offense takes on the aspect of a transubstantiation, with its simultaneous eclipse of agency and claim to authority.

The opposition of the state and or society on the one hand, and "the writer" on the other, also renders Brink's concept of the "reader" problematic. His concept of "the reader" as it is employed in *Mapmakers*—one who "learns" offense from "the author's" word—appears to refer to a generalized reader. The question of whether the gender or race of a reader, for example, may result in different rather than commonly held social views, and whether readers may therefore respond with offense to different elements of a text—and, conceivably, not to those elements of the text that the author calculates that "the reader" will find offensive—is one that remains largely unanswered by Brink's theory. (His use of the masculine pronoun exclusively to refer to this generalized "reader" suggests an oversight of the question of differences in readership.)[7]

How, then, does Brink's theory inform his novels? What problems do his fictions try to solve—and there is an impressive list, one which reflects the violent, intractable nature of the South African context—and what problems do they create in the process? *A Dry White Season* provides us with a sense of what Brink has in mind when he characterizes the author, and subsequently, the reader as witness to the truth, and *A Chain of Voices* suggests what kind of truth the author is witness to.

2. THE BRINKIAN WITNESS TO VIOLENCE: *A DRY WHITE SEASON*

A Dry White Season, published in 1979, is the most appropriate of Brink's novels with which to begin a discussion of his critical and fictional writings, for in it Brink both deals directly with a dissident topic—police brutality—and represents the interaction between "the writer" and "the reader," the "world" and the "word," in fictionalized form, as he has outlined it in "Literature and Offense."[8]

In an interview with Jim Davidson recorded in 1982, Brink indicated that his work took a different direction after he returned from his second visit to Paris in 1968. Prior to this, Brink had been a founding member of the Afrikaner writers' movement known as the Sestigers, who were largely influenced by European existentialism and who had begun to find "the atmosphere here [in South Africa] so stifling and parochial that we started writing in the general European cosmopolitan way—existentialism and all that" (Davidson interview 27). Brink explains the shift that occurred in his work after 1968:

> For at least a decade I shied away from the real South African scene and the issues at stake here, and it was only after I came back from another stay in Paris towards the end of the sixties, in fact in 1968, in which I lived through the student revolt there, that I realized the enormous potential of what was here. . . . And so I started exploring that. It's not only that I can't, but there's no point in trying to compete with, say, a writer like John Fowles, or John Irving, or whoever it might be. One has to explore that particular bit of experience which is unique to oneself . . . (Davidson interview 27).

This privileging of South Africa as both geographic and political subject is indicated in the title of *A Dry White Season*. The title is taken from a poem by the black South African writer and activist, Mongane Wally Serote. The poem, reprinted as a preface to the novel, describes an arid landscape that functions as a metaphor for the political condition of South Africa. Responding to a query by Davidson, Brink has explained that, as is often the case with his novels, *A Dry White Season* is based on an actual incident:

> JD: To what extent is the starting point of any particular novel a real set of circumstances? When you began to write *A Dry White Season*, for example, was there a particular case that preyed on your mind?
> BRINK: Usually it takes something very specific to trigger it off. In this case there was a detainee who had allegedly hung himself near King William's Town—

Mohapi. The Mduli case in Durban also contributed to it, but it was mainly the Mohapi one which triggered it (Davidson interview 27).

The narrator of Brink's novel is an (unnamed) author, the fiction editor of an Afrikaans women's journal who writes "popular novels" (10).[9] He is approached by a former university colleague, Ben du Toit, who asks if he may send the writer-narrator a number of documents for safe-keeping, and tells the writer-narrator that he is to keep them until Ben returns for them; if something happens to Ben, the writer may use them in whatever manner he pleases, perhaps as the basis for a novel. Two weeks later Ben is "knocked down by a hit-and-run driver," as the newspapers have it (9). The writer-narrator, initially reluctant, decides to write a novel about Ben because "after twenty novels in this vein [Harlequin-type romances] something inside me has given up" (11).

Ben du Toit is portrayed as a school teacher who, during his university years, displayed a subversive streak; since then he has been leading the life of a well-respected Afrikaner family man. Over a number of years he has helped one of the groundsmen at the school at which he teaches, Gordon Ngubene, and has put his son, Jonathan, through school. One day Gordon and Jonathan appear at Ben's house: Gordon shows Ben that Jonathan has been whipped by the police for allegedly taking part in a brawl at a beerhall. Jonathan did not participate in the brawl, despite his increasing dissatisfaction with his lot, but was arrested nevertheless and sentenced to six "cuts" merely because he happened to be in the vicinity. Jonathan later disappears altogether during the Soweto riots.

The "six cuts incised on his [Jonathan's] buttocks like six gashes with a knife" (40) form the first of a number of descriptions of the violence through which Ben, and by implication the reader, retrace the paths of Jonathan and his father. By the time Gordon, with Ben's help, has elicited a response from the authorities concerning the fate of his son—a month after the riot—they are first informed that Jonathan has died of natural causes while in custody; they are later told that he was never in detention, that he died on the day of the riot, and that when no one came to fetch the body, he was buried in an anonymous grave. Gordon sets out to discover what has really happened to his son and where he is buried. Gordon is ultimately taken into custody himself and dies in detention, whereupon Ben undertakes to find out precisely what happened to Gordon. Ben alienates his family in the process and is finally murdered by a member of South Africa's secret police, the Special Branch, in what the narrator first hears is a "hit-and-run" incident.

Brink began to write *A Dry White Season* before the death of Steve Biko in detention in 1977. He suspended work on the novel for about a year after Biko's death, and then resumed writing because, he has stated, "I realised that it was also a matter of making sure the people knew about it, and were forced never to allow themselves to forget it . . ." (Davidson interview 27): The notion of the writer as witness to the evil of her or his times is clear in Brink's statement of his goal.[10] The story of *A Dry White Season* unfolds in a manner similar to the actual history of the Biko case, in that in both narratives the inconsistencies in official reports were/are brought to light through the presentation of physical medical evidence: Brink's primary strategy for bringing his "reader" to a sense of horror in *A Dry White Season* is through the description of various brutalities in a factual tone, and through the documentation of the growing significance of these brutalities for those who observe them—in this case, primarily through the unnamed narrator, "the writer."

As the trail of evidence consisting of a series of marks left behind by acts of violence brings us closer to "the truth" behind Jonathan's, Gordon's, and Ben's deaths, so we are encouraged to believe by the narrative tone that, despite the narrator's association with fiction-making, this is not a fiction of his own making, but testimony to a shocking yet indisputable series of events. At the beginning of the novel the writer-narrator questions his ability to present this evidence, implying that he is trying not to cushion the blow, as it were, by altering or embroidering the events to present a fiction: "I'm not used to this sort of stock-taking," he says, "and fiction still comes much more naturally to me than brute indecent truth" (21). The witness must be "true" to his calling; here the writer represented within a fiction–Ben–can only be a "proper" witness by (paradoxically!) eschewing fiction—or at least, by making his fiction appear to be the (that is, the [f]actual) truth.

Two elements of the fiction support its tone, that of the witness bearing some sort of testimony. The first is the indication that the writer-narrator is constructing his narrative from Ben's documents; the second, the function of various characters as witnesses in Gordon's and Ben's attempts to discover the circumstances surrounding the death of Jonathan, and in Ben's attempts to establish the details of Gordon's death. The nurse who informs Gordon and Emily that their son was admitted to the General Hospital with "his head swathed in bandages" and "his belly bloated" is the first of these witnesses (44). The next significant witness is Wellington Phetla, who was detained and questioned with Jonathan. According to the writer-narrator, Gordon persuaded the frightened Wellington to write down what he had to tell. The writer-narrator then tells us what Wellington had to say that he considers to be "of note," presumably "reconstructed" from the documentation given to him by Ben, including Wellington's original statement. The writer-narrator gives the Wellington's evidence in point form; what he considers to be notable is the abuse of Wellington and Jonathan. We are told that they were kept naked from the second day on; that they had been taken to "a place outside the city" where they were forced to climb barbed wire fences and were beaten with *sjamboks*; that they had been tortured in various ways; and that Wellington had heard Jonathan's cries of distress and then moaning: the next day someone had told Wellington that Jonathan had been taken to the hospital.

Brink describes the methods of torture in a matter-of-fact tone that takes advantage of a readership familiar with methods of torture and interrogation such as were used in the Biko case and have been documented elsewhere, and who would recognize many of the violations that he takes pains to enumerate. For example, point "c" of Wellington's testimony as it is reported by the writer-narrator reads as follows:

> c) that on one occasion he [Wellington] and Jonathan had been interrogated by relay teams for more than twenty hours without a break; and that for much of this period they'd been forced to stand on blocks about a yard apart, with half bricks tied to their sexual organs (50).

Despite the framing of the narrative by the writer-narrator, the inclusion of official documents (such as the statements of the witnesses at the inquest into Gordon's death), and of personal papers (such as the letters on toilet paper that Gordon wrote to his wife from prison and the prolonged extracts from Ben's journal entries, obviously written in the first person), obscures the presence of the writer-narrator character to a significant degree. The narrative takes on an omniscient tone that is sustained until the writer-narrator addresses the reader once again in the "Epilogue." This omniscient narrative voice, which inhabits the midsection of the novel, tells us of Ben's habits and states of mind in a factual manner entirely different from the hesitant tone of the writer-narrator's "Foreword," or the speculative one of his "Epilogue." We are told, for example, that while collecting evidence about Gordon's death, Ben

> rose exhausted in the mornings, and came home from school exhausted . . . only to lie awake again. School imposed a measure of wholesome discipline on his life, but at the same time it was becoming more difficult to cope with, more unmanageable, an anxiety and irritation, on some days almost anguish (262).

This omniscient tone adds to the overall realistic effect of the narrative—the "factual" nature of "the author's" testimony—which is an integral part of Brink's attempt to apply, through the creation of fictional narratives, the poetic of political conversion that he outlined in "Literature and Offence." This aspect of the narrative operates in a manner similar to that of a murder mystery, in that the reader is invited to accompany Ben in his quest to reveal the events that lie behind the abuse and murder of Jonathan and Gordon Ngubene—"the truth." This process leads to Ben's conversion, through horror at what he has observed, from ignorance to political awareness and involvement. The experience of reading the novel, according to Brink, is intended to have a similar effect on "the reader."[11] The writer-narrator is provided as yet another surrogate for "the reader" to emulate. He in turn is shocked by Ben's testimony and decides to use Ben's documents to reconstruct a history of Ben's conversion.

Ben and the writer-narrator are both "readers," Ben of the traces of violence that constitute "the truth" of the fiction, and the writer-narrator of Ben's documents that record those traces. They are also both "writers" in a context in which to create records is to expose oneself to severe occupational hazards. The secret police are after Ben because of the records he has made and those that he may yet produce. The writer-narrator inherits this risk together with Ben's papers. He becomes acutely aware of his potential surveillance when the letter Ben has written to him arrives suspiciously long after Ben has written it to him, and when mention is made in the newspaper reports that Ben was on his way to mail a letter when he was killed.[12]

In this light, both Ben and the writer-narrator become Brink's "writer": the writer as diagnoser of society's ills, as witness to the truth of its evils, as—to put him in his traditional Afrikaner role—the occasionally reluctant but always dutiful poet-prophet of the recalcitrant tribe. The narrator-writer's intention, as it is expressed in the "Epilogue," coincides with the stated intentions of the man who is in fact the writer of the novel, Brink himself:

> Perhaps all one can really hope for, all I am entitled to, is no more than this: to write it down. To report what I know. So that it will not be possible for any man ever to say again: *I knew nothing about it* (316).

Brink put it this way in his acceptance of the Martin Luther King Award for *A Dry White Season*:

> One function of the writer in a restricted society, I believe very firmly, lies simply in revealing to people *what is happening*: what they themselves allow to happen. Writing is one of the surest responses to the Nuremberg plea of ignorance. . . .
>
> I have a measure of cautious hope that Martin Luther King's way—the way of non-violent transition to a more just, non-racist society—has not yet been entirely closed. And writing, I firmly believe, is one way of keeping it open (*Mapmakers* 206–7)

However, the structure of Brink's *A Dry White Season*, when the narrative is viewed in its entirety, indicates that Brink is not unaware of the dangers of accepting the writer as prophet, as infallible witness. For *A Dry White Season* does not end simply with the recovery of information required to make sense of the deaths of Jonathan and Gordon Ngubene, the detention of Dr. Hassiem and the lawyer, and so on. Even to those unfamiliar with the operations of security officials in South Africa, the technical mystery of what is happening to the bodies of the victims does not remain a mystery for very long. Were this to be the driving force of the narrative, virtually all of Part Three of the novel would be redundant.

Part Three of the novel, as Ben du Toit remarks at the conclusion of Part Two, has him "on the edge of yet another dry white season, perhaps worse than the one I knew as a child" (163). This "dry white season," given emphasis by the title of the novel, is caused by a sense of atrophy or helplessness created by a circumstance that directly counters the impetus behind Brink's poetic of political conversion. In Part Three of *A Dry White Season*, Ben realizes that to be privileged with certain kinds of information—to have knowledge—does not, in this case, enable either the course of justice or a change in circumstances.

This element of *A Dry White Season* can be seen as an illustration of the problematic nature of bearing witness in the context of white liberalism. The final section of the novel raises two related questions. Can Ben bear witness adequately to the suffering of the black victims? And—a more radical question—what does it actually mean for him to do so? Faith in white liberalism as a tool for change has already disappeared, Stanley points out to Ben. Stanley speaks with a post-Soweto awareness of the suspicion with which the relationship between the two of them would be viewed. He explains to Ben that he will continue to find witnesses to testify to Jonathan's maltreatment,

"Even if my own people will spit on me if they knew I was here with you tonight."
"Why?" Ben asked, startled.
"Because I'm old-fashioned enough to sit here scheming with a white man. Make no mistake, lanie, my people are in a black mood. My children too. They speak a different language from you and me" (287–88).

One of the problems with white liberalism is implied, but not stated, by the narrative: ironically, the rhetoric of white liberalism mirrors the rhetoric of the security forces. When he tries to track down the details of the Ngubene story, Ben remarks that it is not "open hostility" that prevents his gaining access to the information he desires, but an ethos of protective conformity. "The real problem," he writes, is "this thick, heavy porridge of good intentions on the part of people obstructing you 'for your own good', trying to 'protect you against yourself'" (234). In the penultimate chapter of the novel—the last we read of Ben's narrative—Ben details his role in terms that echo those of the security forces: "I wanted to help. Right. I meant it very sincerely. But I wanted to do it on my terms" (304).

Ben goes on to examine the critical limits of his (white liberal) resistance:

> But I grasped so little, really: as if good intentions from my side could solve it all. It was presumptuous of me. . . .
> In their eyes my very efforts to identify myself with Gordon, with all the Gordons, would be obscene (304).

Yet Ben's voice retains its patronizing vocabulary, even in his very attempt to relinquish such habits of expression; and his narrative confronts, but does not resolve, the liberal paradox:

> Every gesture I make, every act I commit in my efforts to help them makes it more difficult for them to define their real needs and discover for themselves their integrity and affirm their own dignity. How else could we hope to arrive beyond predator and prey, helper and helped, white and black, and find redemption?
> On the other hand: what can I do but what I have done? (304)

Finally, we end up with a notion of sacrifice, "one that might, in the long run, open up a possibility, however negligible or dubious, of something better, less sordid and more noble, for our children" (305). Ben prefers this sacrifice, despite its danger of hubris, to the sacrifice of not doing anything at all. However, the danger of hubris is not negligible. Perhaps Ben is suffering delusions of grandeur when he speculates that everything he does prevents black self-expression, even self-knowledge; perhaps this is his last-ditch attempt to claim any sort of significance at all, albeit a negative one, for his own narrative of conversion. Such a paradoxical configuration of political implication marks that painful intersection between partial loss only of confidence in liberal intervention, and partial acceptance only of the possibility that the white gaze is irrelevant to black subjectivity.

That Brink's motives are exemplary, and that his sense of the relationship between private and public duty is informed by a consistent and admirable set of ethical prerogatives, are not in question. What is still at stake, however—and what is not only a problem for Brink's narrators, but also one which Brink himself, Breyten Breytenbach, and J. M. Coetzee have to come to terms with—is the question of the writer's credentials, her or his author-ity:

what is the basis of her or his critique of the society that produced her or him? Is it possible to tell the story "without embellishment," as the narrator-writer demands? Or to put it a different way, how does the writer remain uncontaminated by her or his own relation to the subject matter at hand?

In terms of the plot of A Dry White Season, it would appear that this problem comes back to haunt the writer: what are we to make of the series of "writers" (Ben du Toit and the unnamed writer-narrator) who set out to find the truth in Brink's novel—the truth of the violated bodies of Jonathan and Gordon Ngubene—and end up, in a sense, becoming the truth they seek (Ben is killed by the secret police; the unnamed narrator awaits a similar fate). The writer as interrogator of the violence of his society has become its victim. Where does this leave the dead bodies of those—represented by Jonathan and Gordon Ngubene—who are the ostensible subjects of this litany of violence, and does their position differ from that of Ben and the narrator? If the only way in which the writer can represent violence is to claim the experience of it, or at least the threat of it, as her or his credential, on what basis is this claim made? What are we to make of the substitution of the authority of the narrative voice for that of the bodies of the violated?

The questions that I wish to raise with reference to Brink's fiction, then, have to do with how the status of the author—the fiction of her or his authority—affects the presentation of violence and horror in her or his novels. What kinds of incidents does Brink's notion of the author enable the author to represent as horrific, or to use Brink's terminology, "offensive," and what kinds of violence might his notion encourage her or him to overlook? What constitutes the truth(s) that Brink's form of horror can—and cannot—recognize? To investigate this question further I shall discuss the treatment of violence in one of Brink's historical novels, since the representative logic of the historical novel depends upon the text's appeal to the authenticity of the historical event in order to persuade the reader of its own authenticity, its own authority.

3. Race, Sex, and Historical Narrative: Violence(s) in *A Chain of Voices*

Afrikaner Liberalism, the Fantasy of Miscegenation, and
Apocalyptic Liberation

Brink's novels, from *An Instant in the Wind* (1976) to *On the Contrary* (1993), provide examples of a number of couples who enact that—fictionally speaking—popular South African ritual of breaking the revoked but still notorious "Immorality Act," the provision that forbade sexual intercourse between members of groups classified as distinct under apartheid law, effectively branding interracial sex as miscegenation. The most famous couple of this type in Brink's oeuvre—due to the perverse notoriety generated by censorship—comprises, of course, Jessica Thomson and Josef Malan, of *Looking on Darkness*. Vernon February, ever astute on the subject of "coloured" stereotypes in South African literature, points out the function of exoticism in the relationship between the heroic Josef, bearer of his people's history of suffering, and Jessica, a "golden-haired tribute to white aestheticism": "The same undercurrent of sex which pervades the novels of white authors from Africa to America, when white women and "coloured" men are brought together, is noticeable here" (125).

Yet to brand Brink's attempt to portray such relationships a rudimentary example of orientalism, without investigating his fiction further, would be to simplify the matter considerably. *Looking on Darkness* did have South Africa "up in arms" over the interracial affair (February 57); February himself describes Brink's project in that novel as "ambitious," since Josef Malan does become "a gross historical (genetic) and political indictment against Afrikanerdom" (117). The connection between the concept of loyal Afrikanerdom and the betrayal of that notion specifically through an act of miscegenation is one that Breytenbach has had to deal with in terms of his own rather public private life; it is also a trope that repeats itself in the writing of the dissident Afrikaner. The trope involves both literary appropriation—the writer must give the black hero a history, in order to depict the hero's oppression and thus the evil of the taboo—and racial stereotyping: the black is sexual in a way that the white is not, and his object of desire is the white woman.

While critics tend to congratulate the author in such instances for conceiving of the black as having the potential to have a history, they do recognize the negative implication of the stereotyping. JanMohamed, for example, referring to *A Chain of Voices*, suggests that "to give a voice to slaves and particularly to their desire for freedom is no doubt a courageous and provocative act in contemporary South Africa" ("The Economy of Manichean Allegory" 91). Yet he comments that

> Nonetheless, the novel remains rooted in racial stereotypes/archetypes. The latter are not crude, for both the white and the leading nonwhite characters have depth. However, the only distinction between the two racial groups, other than the obvious one between masters and slaves, is that the whites experience severe sexual repression, while the nonwhites are obsessed with sex; indeed, some of the nonwhites can perceive themselves only in terms of sexual pleasure and fecundity (91).

There is, however, a specific connection between the presentation of the history of the relationship between whites and blacks, and the role that sexuality plays in the construction of that history, in terms of the Afrikaner liberal vision. Rather than accusing the exemplary text in question—-*A Chain of Voices*—of the sexual stereotyping that is an effect of its appropriative voice, or of the appropriation itself (which is the feature that allows for the expression of the idea of black history in the novel), I wish to examine the structural effects of the appropriation and their significance.

J. M. Coetzee's Eugene Dawn announces his own aspirations in terms that describe those of the dissident Afrikaner—"I have high hopes of finding whose fault I am," he comments (*Dusklands* 49). One of the ways of approaching this project would appear to be to search simultaneously for the origin of the violent, racial differentiation that informs Afrikaner nationalism (and its manifestation in apartheid), and for the reconciliation of that difference in the fantasy of sexual communion with the other. Not surprisingly, the dialectic between white and black in this project is a Hegelian master-slave one. However, while the all-important fiction in Hegel is that of the slave's recognition of the potential for liberation through his technological expertise, in the project I describe here, the Afrikaner dissident depends upon the fiction that the recognition of himself as both master and tyrant, will take place at the moment of sexual access to the body of the other.

Desire for the other, then, is reconfigured to express the desire to save oneself from becoming/remaining one of the tribe. Yet fascination with the origin of the self as master, even when it is phrased in order to understand and redesign that sense of self for a different future, complicates the very end to which it aspires. In practice, this results in a local literary history in which the Afrikaner dissident reads himself through the other, using the tropes of sadism ("I am master") and masochism ("I am guilty") in the context of an erotic encounter with that designated other. This encounter then constitutes the all-important scene of recognition, which is charged with the expectation of providing both the knowledge of the secret origin of the self as master—of the moment of racial differentiation that provides, or provided (since the event is viewed in the light of a historical origin) the superior identity of the self—and at the very same time, the apocalyptic consummation of the self as "liberated" in a Utopia of impossibly innocent nondifferentiation, manifest in the choice of the other as object of erotic desire. How does one evaluate the ethics of this trope? What kinds of violence does such a "history" recognize, and what kinds of violence can it itself exhibit?

Fiction and "The Truth" of Historical Narrative

Brink's second novel, *An Instant in the Wind*, and his fourth, *A Chain of Voices*, are both historical novels that include documents that provide a series of "facts" on which the fictions are based; and both, together with his most recent historical novel, *On the Contrary*, locate the potential for a dissident future for South Africa in fictions that reproduce acts of miscegenation as historical events, as keys to be rescued from the past and used in the present to work toward liberation. The eighteenth-century South African records with which *An Instant in the Wind* begins were fabricated in their entirety by Brink, although he has stated that the inspiration for the novel came from an episode that belongs to Australian history, the Mrs. Fraser story.[13] The transformation of Mrs. Fraser into a white South African woman, and the escaped convict into a male slave with whom she has a doomed affair, implicates the problem of race in the novel's investigation of the colonial past, placing it within a specifically South African context. For this reason, *An Instant in the Wind* constitutes an implicit but nevertheless obvious condemnation of the branding of interracial relationships as miscegenation by law in South Africa, and demonstrates the symbolic importance of breaking that taboo for Brink as the "author" who must affect, or even infect, his "readers" with his own sense of offense at the law. *On the Contrary*, which locates the source of the protagonist's dissidence in his guilt over his and others' abuse of a female slave, continues Brink's protest against the racism involved in the denial of interracial sex (through its stigmatization as miscegenation) and the violent implications of that denial.

A Chain of Voices constitutes a further exploration of the "original" determinants of mastery and slavedom, expressed in the novel as patterns of racial and sexual domination and submission. The fiction, like *An Instant in the Wind* and *On the Contrary*, investigates racial violence in the context of colonial history. The novel describes an actual slave uprising that occurred on the farms of two Afrikaner brothers in January of 1825. From then on the British government introduced a series of cautious reforms in the Cape. These reforms, which were unenforceable in practice, were calculated to demonstrate philanthropism without undermining the labor system that afforded Britain its colonial wealth (*Mapmakers* 155; Davenport 46). The rebellion of 1825 on which Brink's novel is based took place because the slaves, encouraged by the various measures that were supposed to have been in effect to ameliorate their situation, and by rumors that they were to be freed by Christmas Day 1824 or New Year's Day 1825, took up arms against their Afrikaner masters to achieve their freedom. The Afrikaners themselves were irritated by British rule, and in particular by the dictates from a foreign government on how to handle their slaves (this sentiment, as Davenport points out, is quoted by a number of historians as one of the primary initiatives for the Great Trek [46]). The rebellion inevitably failed and the representatives of the British crown at the Cape, while acknowledging a few of the harsh aspects of the slaves' treatment, sentenced most of the offenders to death and punished the others severely.

  Unlike the journal entries of the Larssons and the historical records in *An Instant in the Wind*, the "Act of Accusation" with which *A Chain of Voices* begins and the "Verdict" with which it concludes are, according to Brink, authentic extracts from archival documents that include documentation from the court proceedings and depositions made by the accused and the witnesses. However, the text constitutes an "imaginative reconstruction," as one critic puts it (Viola 67), as do *An Instant in the Wind* and *On the Contrary*, for the body of the text consists of the statements of thirty characters, each of whom gives an individual version of the rebellion and the events preceding it. These narratives form a fictional context for the "factual" documentation that precedes and follows them, supplementing the events described in the documents to such a degree that the documents and the narratives become the official and unofficial versions respectively of the same incident in the mind of the reader as the novel progresses. The reader is thereby encouraged not to distinguish between the rebellion as historical event and Brink's reconstruction of it, that is, the rebellion as narrated, or fictional event. Thus the juxtaposition of historical documentation and fictional narratives, while it nods in the direction of the recognition that the "facts" of a historical event are always "translated" by the perspective that narrates them, suggests nevertheless that such "facts" are still accessible to a Brinkian reader-witness, so long as she or he spends time on finding the most correct narrative voice or voices, the most "original" sources. In this context, the trial documents, even while they appear to "oppose" the witnesses that the fiction privileges as most reliable, nevertheless remain part of the novel's "fiction" of historical representation, a fiction in which author-ity is granted based on the belief that not only is access to the "truth" of the historical event possible; also, it is the author's duty to search for such access.

  The "Act of Accusation" and the "Verdict" frame what I shall call the individual accounts in such a way as to suggest that these accounts constitute testimonials of a sort. However, the tone of these accounts is too casual—they give the impression of informal oral communication—and the details given too personal for them to attain the official stature of the legal documents that have been incorporated into the narrative. It is perhaps this quality of informality that leads Andre Viola to describe these accounts as "interior monologues" (65). However, the adjective in this description appears to dismiss a major structural feature of the narrative of *A Chain of Voices*, namely Brink's characteristic development of the "implied reader," to use Wolfgang Iser's term, as a kind of witness to these various "testimonials." The individual accounts all give the impression of being addressed to someone, and that someone remains unidentifiable as a character within the text.[14] The first account, that of Ma Rose, employs the second person in its description of the landscape. Although this is a less obvious and more intimate form of address than the nineteenth-century "Dear Reader," it is similar in its rhetorical intention, that of drawing the reader into the narrative: "If you go towards Tulbagh and climb the highest peak, you can see a long way in all directions. You can see . . ." (23). In addition, the accounts include details that their "authors" would not be expected to include if the accounts were intended to approximate the diary form in orature, that is, if the persons addressed were intended to be the community of farm inhabitants themselves. Such information includes, for example, the details in the slave leader Galant's narratives of farm routines, or the Khoin earth-mother figure, Ma Rose's explanation of Khoisan deities. Similarly, the accounts include personal confidences that their "authors," by their own admission, are unable or unwilling to reveal to any of the other characters: Barend van der Merwe's confession of his inability to declare his love to his wife Hester, and his brother Nicolaas' confession of his deteriorating relationship with his slave Galant and his related attraction to Galant's lover, Pamela, are two examples of the numerous confidences that contribute to the "unofficial" aspect of these personal testimonies, whose structural function is to convince the reader of their ability to access the "truth," their author-ity, and so to constitute the reader as witness to the violence of the historical event. The problem is, of course, that (to use Brinkian terms) these accounts themselves bear witness to a metanarrative that appears to view its ability and authority to reproduce its historical subjects as absolute; it is a metanarrative that appropriates its historical subjects.

The "Act of Accusation" at the beginning of *A Chain of Voices* gives the official version of the rebellion and introduces the theme of violence; it was issued by "His Majesty's Fiscal at the Cape of Good Hope," one Daniel Denyssen. From this "Act" the reader first learns of a rebellion by a number of slaves, most of whom belong to the two farmers, the brothers named Nicolaas and Barend van der Merwe.[15] According to the "Act," the rebellion took place on the first and second days of February 1825 in the area of the Cold Bokkeveld. While Viola's description of the individual accounts that follow the "Act" as a "reconstruction" of the events described in the "Act" is useful up to a point, there are crucial discrepancies between the account of the rebellion given in the "Act" and those given by the individual "authors," such as the question of the slave Goliath's involvement in the rebellion. These discrepancies serve to illustrate that the "Act" itself constitutes a reconstruction of the events of the rebellion, based, we assume, on legal testimony not reprinted within the text.

Once again, this presentation of multiple and competing historical "voices" may at first appear to constitute the postmodern recognition of the impossibility of access to the historical event as anything other than a narrated "reconstruction," but there is a telling point of reconciliation between the "Act" and the voices that ostensibly "compete" with it for the status of "the truth." The continuity that does exist between the "Act" and the other accounts is provided by their agreement on the physical acts of violence that occurred during the rebellion. These include the wounding of Barend in the heel, and of Nicolaas' wife in the abdomen; and the deaths by shooting of Nicolaas, Hans Jansen (a farmer visiting Nicolaas' farm in search of a strayed mare), and Johannes Verlee (the newly appointed schoolmaster)—events that are marked by both "official" and "unofficial" testimonies as "true."

This privileging of the point of violence between master and slave as the locus of "the truth" about the origin of their relationship, produces the "meaning" of the rebellion in the localized "history" of racial relations that the novel attempts to relate. The rebellion comes to represent the point of origin of the violent racial differentiation that constitutes the Afrikaner as master (the slaves are punished, the rebellion as such "fails"), at the very same time that it projects the triumph of the slaves into the future (when the master's "true" nature as tyrant will be revealed). The master thus entertains the fiction of his having recognized his own tyranny in a fantasy that places actual liberation for the slave in apocalyptic time. This effectively prevents an end to the master's author-itarian sadism (it allows him to allay his guilt by fantasizing about his future imaginary sacrifice, the masochism he envisions for himself), and reproduces the slave, through simultaneous appropriation of the native and historical other—the appropriation that constitutes author-itarianism, the literary form of mastership—as subservient to the master's fantasy in a fictional trope of masochism that proves to be the necessary foundation of the fantasy.

The description of the incidents of violence, which enact the dual signification of mastery in the present and liberation in the future, dominates the "Act of Accusation," since the Act conforms to its legal purpose: that of establishing a case against the rebels. While the individual accounts do not resemble official depositions for the reasons noted above, they do constitute an inquiry of their own: the "authors'" motivation (although implicit) appears, as the testimony accumulates, to be to explain how the situation that brought about the violence described in the "Act"—the "crimes" that their testimonies bear out—developed. Once again, then, it becomes clear that the rehearsals of the prelude to the rebellion and of the rebellion itself contained in the personal accounts do not exist merely for their "authors'" personal satisfaction, but for the benefit of the implied reader as witness, or even more pointedly, judge. The "unofficial" testimonies that so inform the personal and privileged "independent inquiry" of the reader create a sociohistorical context for the rebellion, a fictional context that becomes increasingly important for the reader's interpretation of the acts of violence documented in the "Act of Accusation."

While it is true that the "flashback" structure of the novel (which Viola correctly identifies as a common feature of Brink's novels) "denotes that ordinary chronology or suspense cannot adequately lead to a revelation of truth" (64), it does not follow that the notion of truth, as it is expressed in this novel, is developed without an enduring respect for the authority of the chronological imperative of history; the fiction announces its authority as a legitimate investigation of the historical event through the invocation of a historical document and its adherence in the personal accounts to the "facts" of the violence related in that document. The personal accounts, despite the fact that the revelation of events which they offer to the reader is nonsequential, do not represent a rejection of the authority of a history in the determination of "the truth." On the contrary, they bear witness to a desire to supplement the official history, or at its most radical, a desire to create an alternative context for that history. The individual accounts emphasize a personal context for the death and destruction documented as fact in the "Act," but they do not attempt to suggest that these "facts" themselves are narrated, that they constitute a fiction in and of themselves: they do not attempt to replace "history" by giving the reader a sense of (any) history's inevitable character as fiction. In order to investigate properly the details of the structure and implications of this allegiance to the concept of "history" as truth—in other words, the belief that it is possible to access the truth of historical subjects—in a project that exercises its moral imperative by overlooking the partiality of any and all fictions including its own, we need to examine the nature of the sociohistorical context provided by the personal accounts of the acts of violence that constitute the rebellion.

Domination and Colonial Ordering

The vast majority of violent scenes recorded in the personal narratives involve the masters' (Piet van der Merwe's and his sons, Nicolaas' and Barend's) beating of their slaves and wives. Specific mention is made of at least ten beatings of slaves and three of wives, and numerous general references are made to similar occurrences. The purpose of these beatings is made clear as early as the second personal account, that of Piet van der Merwe: they are the means whereby the colonial social structure, in which whites dominate their black slaves and males dominate females, is maintained and entrenched. Piet describes how upon his return from the Cape, where he and his retinue heard rumors of emancipation for the slaves, he whips his slaves as a warning to them not to rebel against his authority. This task takes precedence over his greeting of his wife, Alida:

> I brushed Alida off when she came to greet me. There was something more urgent I had to attend to first. I ordered the *mantoor* [senior slave] to summon all the labourers to the yard. . . . Then, one by one, I had them tied to the front wheel of the wagon and flogged by the *mantoor*, every one of them, man, woman and child; thirty-nine lashes for each grown-up, and twenty-five for a child. The *mantoor* was last; I flogged him myself. Only then, after they'd all had their share, did I speak. "Let this be a lesson to you," I told them, "should you ever get it in your heads to rise up against me. Now go back to your work and finish whatever you were doing." Then I went into the house, and kissed Alida, and sat down to eat (39).

These relationships between master/slave and male/female, which exemplify, simultaneously, both the origin and maintenance of the practice of mastery, are characterized by the narrative in its use of patterns of dominance and enforced submission, patterns that are rendered complex by the interaction of colonial, racial, and sexual domination.

Colonial violence is represented in the novel in the portrayal of the British assertion of authority over the Afrikaners and, for all its philanthropic trappings, the British regulation of slavery evidenced in the "Act of Accusation" and "Verdict"; it is also represented by the description of the Afrikaner colonization of the interior, which is presented as their response in turn to British domination. Nicolaas, reflecting upon the rumors of emancipation, remarks that, although the prospect of losing his slaves is "bleak," the fact that this would be accomplished by British decree bothers him more:

> What really made me numb, *as if I'd been bludgeoned,* was the impotent rage that came from the rediscovery that our lives were held hostage by the whims and wishes of a distant adversary we didn't know and had no hope of influencing (229; emphasis added).

Despite the fact that the language of physical violence is used to describe the effect of British domination on the Afrikaner farmer, this language is employed in the form of a simile, indicating that its descriptive function is metaphorical, not actual. Indeed, the Van der Merwes' "colonization" by British authority is countered by the occasional effectiveness of their use of violence against that authority. The Van der Merwe property, the site of the slave rebellion, was originally staked out by Piet's grandfather, who trekked there after a quarrel with the *landdrost* (magistrate) in Tulbagh. He was summoned back, and when he failed to return, a detachment of dragoons was sent to fetch him. However, he managed to shoot them off the property. (This act of assertion, appropriately and ironically enough in view of the later slave revolt, gave rise to the name of the farm. According to Piet Van der Merwe, his grandfather told the dragoons "'In this place your word counts for nothing. . . . No one but I have the right to speak here.' And so he called the farm Houd-den-Bek, which means Shut-Your-Trap" [33]). A duplication of this event takes place when Barend is fined by the English *landdrost* for beating his slave, Goliath. When Goliath returns to the farm, having made his complaint to the *landdrost*, Barend whips him yet again. When the Commissioner comes to check on Barend's treatment of his slaves, Barend intimidates Goliath into accounting for his wounds to the Commissioner by telling him that he fell from his horse. The official is suspicious but unable to respond, and an escort of armed farmers leads him off the farm. As they do so, the farmers spot a herd of eland on the way, and the Commissioner is deliberately caught in crossfire. Although he is not wounded, he is literally "shot off" the farm.

The aggression between whites and blacks, and men and women (and, occasionally, adults and children)[16] that is depicted in the novel cannot be adequately accounted for by providing descriptions of the positions of the characters in the social hierarchy according to their race and sex—the male is always master; the white is always master—because both these factors interact simultaneously to produce the violent scenes described in the novel, and because the patterns of dominance are frequently reversed. For example, we know that Barend, a white male, is placed in a position of power over both his wife and his slaves, according to the dictates of the colonial society to which he belongs. Yet, paradoxically, his very need to maintain this position enables Hester, his wife, to stop his beating Klaas. "Barend"[17] describes this incident:

> At sunset she opened the door of the shed where we were working on Klaas, and came inside. At first I'd thought she'd brought me some coffee, for a flogging makes one thirsty. But she stood there empty-handed, trembling.
>
> "Will you stop this immediately?" she said. Right in front of the slaves.
>
> "Hester, you stay out of this. It's none of your business."

> "I tell you it's going to stop."
>
> I couldn't allow myself to be humiliated in front of my inferiors. Once again I raised the sjambok and brought it down on Klaas's shoulders. Suddenly she was beside me, grabbing the frayed end of the sjambok. . . .
>
> If I hadn't been so angry it might have amused me: I could have pulled her off her feet in one jerk had I wanted to. But to start a disgraceful tug of war with my own wife, with all the slaves looking on, was unthinkable.
>
> "Untie him," I ordered my helpers. "I hope he's learned his lesson." (163–64).

Hester's challenge renders his continuing the beating impossible: he cannot turn on Hester physically in front of the slaves, for that would reduce her position to that of the black slave Klaas, and reduce his racial stature by implication; nor can he allow the challenge to continue while he beats Klaas, for that would indicate to the slaves that he is unable to control his wife, thus reducing the stature of his sex.

This incident also illustrates the reversal of the pattern: Hester, who is dominated by Barend, is able here to control his actions. Once the slaves have left the scene of the beating, she prevents him from attacking her (temporarily) by implying that his need to subdue the slaves physically reflects his inability to command their respect, and hers. The beating becomes a sign of his weakness, not hers:

> Hester looked on in silence while they untied Klaas. After they'd dragged him out she said, without deigning to look at me: "Is this the only way you can be master to them?"
>
> "Hester, you're looking for trouble."
>
> "Are you threatening to beat me too?" she said.
>
> I grabbed her by the arm. . . . She didn't even groan. Suddenly I let go, turning on my heel to stride out of that shameful shed smelling of straw and hides, and of Klaas who'd pissed and shat all over the place (164).

The part that Hester plays in this drama exemplifies two consistent characteristics of the fiction's portrayal of the master-slave relationship. The first is that the slave does not (or cannot?) engineer his own liberation without assistance; and the second is that this assistance is provided by "his woman," who turns out, in the climactic scene of the novel, ideally to be white and the former woman "of" the (or in practice, a) master; for such is the "history" of the relationship between Barend and Nicolaas as masters, Galant as slave, and Hester as the pawn who negotiates the link between the two.

We are able, then, to approach the violent scenes in *A Chain of Voices* more readily through an examination of the variety of factors that contribute to the act of aggression than we are through merely classifying the characters' relative power according to their positions in the social hierarchy. The latter approach is both too linear and too static to account for the complex development of conflicts in the novel. For while the fiction "desires" the resolution of these conflicts—its message being that the master-slave relationship "must" be ended—it also exhibits the problem of trying to invoke resolution of the conflict in a form of narrative closure that claims the moral imperative of resolution as its own, while projecting actual resolution "out of" the narrative of present time: if the master's victory is temporary, indeed, temporal, the slave's liberation is nevertheless still apocalyptic, always in the future. It may be appropriate, then, to read the violent conflicts described by the novel not as annunciations of the collapse of relationships, that is, not apocalyptically—Hester does not cease to be Barend's wife when she challenges him; the slave Klaas still has to work for Barend after the beating—but rather as representative of the considerable role that aggression plays in the formation and maintenance of mastery.

The depiction of close relationships as violent rather than affectionate recurs throughout Brink's novel. Indeed, one of the most disturbing aspects of *A Chain of Voices* for its most observant reviewers is its portrayal of the violent as intimate, and therefore in some sense desirable.[18] The depiction of violent relationships as intimate is particularly evident in the beating scenes. Despite Galant's deliberate provocation of Nicolaas, the latter is reluctant to raise his hand against Galant. Only after Nicolaas has returned from the Cape to Houdden-Bek to find that Galant has killed more sheep than Nicolaas had allotted to the slaves, does Nicolaas bring himself to beat Galant. At first Nicolaas has Ontong, another slave, whip Galant; but when Galant challenges him by asking him if he is too scared to whip Galant himself, Nicolaas, who is known for his reluctance to beat his slaves, and Galant in particular, takes over from Ontong and virtually loses control. "Ontong" describes the incident:

> Straining to raise his head Galant looked round at Nicolaas.
> "Why you asking them to do it?" he said. "You scared to do it yourself?"
> "Ontong!" said Nicolaas.
> I brought down the sjambok on Galant's back. . . .
> "You scared?" Galant taunted Nicolaas again.
> That seemed to make him mad. He grabbed the heavy sjambok from my hand and started laying into Galant like a whirlwind, without paying much attention to where and how the blows landed. He went on and on until . . . the hippo hide started cutting into the bare flesh. . . .

"Kleinbaas," I said at last. I didn't want to go against the man but I was afraid something might happen if Nicolaas weren't stopped in time. He paid no attention, almost sobbing with rage with every blow. . . . I touched him lightly on the arm. "I think that's enough, Kleinbaas. You killing him." (199–200).

Notice the "history" given of the dynamic of the Nicolaas-Galant relationship. Initially, Nicolaas will not beat Galant, his favorite slave; finally, he beats him harder than he would any other slave because his special feeling for Galant—based on their childhood "friendship" (which, significantly, is also shared by Hester)—is betrayed by Galant's challenge to him. This linking of violence, intimacy, and desire is also expressed in the descriptions of sexual intercourse in the novel. The very early sexual activity between Hester and Galant, which belongs to the world of their childhood, represents the fantasy of an Edenic pre-history, an imagined origin of racial and sexual harmony in which there is no violent differentiation. This is the white liberal fantasy that Nicolaas shares with Hester, and which he "betrays" by beating Galant, but only, in his eyes, after Galant has betrayed it first—that is, Galant has not conformed to Nicolaas' fantasy of how he "should" behave, namely, masochistically. The nostalgia is not only Nicolaas', however; for if Nicolaas is presumptuous in his belief in the existence of this fantasy as a resource recoverable from the past so that he can live with a consciousness of the possibility of a nonracial future—how can he assume that Galant would share this fantasy to such an extent that he would be prepared to remain a slave in order not to betray the fantasy? Why should Galant "wait it out"? So too does the narrative itself appear to "desire," impossibly, such a "return" to the future. If the fiction of the access of "the truth" of the history—a process in which history as irredeemably other is deconstructed, domesticated—is marked by violence, so to is the narrative's own fiction of the possibility of access to those others of history, namely, the sexually other and the racially other, the woman and the slave, whose voices the metanarrative assumes that it can create, that it can "reproduce." What is the precise relationship, then, between the violence of domination as it is portrayed by the narrative, and the violence of domination that I am claiming the narrative itself exemplifies in its acts of appropriation? An examination of the fiction's depiction of violence can form the basis for a description of the narrative violence the fiction exercises.

It is not surprising that, following the logic of the lost Eden, adulthood brings with it desire for dominance, often expressed in terms of sexual dominance: many of the adult sexual relations described in the novel take on the aspect of rape. Although "Alida" indicates in her account that she agreed to elope with Piet, "Piet" describes her reaction toward his advances as reluctant ("[she] Tried to stop me" [35]) and to his absconding with her as defiant ("Alida sobbing in the wagon, hitting me with her small fists when I tried to comfort her" [36]). He and the slavemen are both described by "Ma-Rose" as raping Lys, Galant's mother, repeatedly. "Ma-Rose" indicates that Lys' very reluctance excites them:

> she had something about her that seemed to lure the men, as Ontong said, by saying: Come, bruise me. And they couldn't resist it—the way some people cannot enjoy a flower without plucking off its petals; the way they cannot pass a young anthill without kicking it to bits (27).

When Nicolaas, reluctant to have intercourse with his wife, Cecilia, finally consummates his marriage in an act initiated by Cecilia, his participation is described by "Cecilia" as an assault: "He tried to resist; then yielded to my more insistent caresses. In the end a wildness seemed to take hold of him and he crushed down on me in a frenzy" (122). Hester is taken by Barend to be his wife against her will, and "Hester" describes their sexual intercourse as "a fight of animals, nightly resumed" (139). Elsewhere "Hester" tells us that Barend often strikes her "in the rage of his efforts to gain entry into my body" (252). Galant lays claim to Bet (after Adonis, another slave, has approached her) by beating her and then entering her (133).

The Origin of Violence in Hegelian Narrative

In order to examine more closely this marking out of relationships through acts of violence—that is, the establishment of a context in which the expression of intimacy is conceived of as violent, not affectionate—it is helpful to remember the work of key documents of the Western philosophical tradition which explain the phenomenon of domination and submission in terms of the origin and truth of yet another history, namely the history of civilization. Both Hegel and Freud produce histories of civilization that suggest that violence, and the violation of individual will required to sustain it, are inevitable determining factors in human relationships.

In his *Phenomenology of Spirit* Hegel presents self-consciousness as absolute. Self-consciousness, he argues, exists only for itself; but the existence of self-consciousness depends upon another's recognition of that self-consciousness as absolute: "self consciousness exists in itself and for itself when, and by the fact that, it so exists for another; that is, it exists only in being acknowledged" (111). For Hegel this tension is unresolvable and inevitably disintegrates into a polarized relationship between its two aspects, the independent self-consciousness and the dependent self-consciousness. These abstract concepts, the independent and dependent self-consciousness, are manifest in the realm of social experience in the phenomenon of the master-slave relationship.

In *Civilization and its Discontents* Freud identifies human nature as essentially aggressive. The establishment of civilization is not accomplished in fulfillment of the will of human nature; on the contrary, it is an unnatural activity, the sole purpose of which is to control the individual desire to violate others. In this scheme nature and civilization form opposing poles, the relationship between which depends once again upon the exercise of domination; for civilization can only be established through the exercise of repression. This repression, Freud argues, is ultimately preferable to the unparalleled destructiveness that would be the inevitable result of its rejection. The cause of civilization is aided by the erotic instinct, which works against the death instinct in its motivation of the individual to obey those whom she or he loves.

Hegel's scenario of the fight to the point of death between master and slave, and Freud's understanding of civilization as an unnatural activity, accomplished only through the dubious but necessary benefits of the erotic instinct, both construct a universal history in which the violence of domination is controlled, a least initially in the case of Hegel, and permanently in the case of Freud, only by the desire to limit the domination of oneself by others.[19] Both narratives exhibit a distinctive Eurocentrism in their assumption of universality;[20] and both, especially Hegel's, look toward a time, necessarily apocalyptic, which would signal the end of violent conflict. Hegel enacts his specious closure through the fiction of the recognition of the slave of his own technical expertise; Freud, tellingly, also searches for an end to the history of conflict in knowledge—or in Hegelian terms, recognition (of its symptoms, analysis of its causes) but ultimately comes up, in a profoundly personal sense, against the immediacy of the phenomenon of Hitler, in view of which Hegel's fiction of recognition would appear to be absurd, and Freud's question, "how long shall we have to wait before the rest of mankind become pacifists too?" (362), takes on the aspect of a plea rather than a question about the timing of an event that is perceived to be inevitable.

The closure which Hegel imposes on his master-slave dialectic appears as doubtful as the progress Freud wants to attribute to the development of civilization. Hegel's and Freud's histories of the struggle between self-assertion and self-preservation are not persuasive models of a civilization which will reach its apotheosis in terms of an actual, future resolution of that struggle. Indeed, the struggle remains as a constant and fluctuating tension whose predicted resolution takes the form of fantasy. This requires looking more closely at the relationship between the will to dominate and the opposing desire for recognition of oneself from those whom one would dominate, which constitutes the dynamic of progress in Hegel and Freud, as it has been expressed in terms of the individual psyche.

The work of Jessica Benjamin, although she sometimes appropriates the work of Hegel and Freud for her own purposes in a way that simplifies their philosophies (and is thus also uncritical of their subconscious Eurocentrism), is useful for the self-same reason: it reproduces Hegel's master-slave dialectic, and Freud's tension between aggressive and erotic instincts, in the service of her own psychoanalytic practice. Thus her use of Hegel and Freud on and in her own terms emphasizes the ongoing dynamics of dominance and submission in the realm of interpersonal relationships, rather than stressing their role in a universal history that hopes to entertain apocalyptic significance.

In her book, *The Bonds of Love* (1988), Benjamin explores the point that Hegel, in his theory of self-consciousness and recognition, and Freud, in his theory of the instincts, set the individual's instinct or desire for self-assertion in opposition to a propensity for socialization. Benjamin rephrases this dilemma as the tension between the individual's need for self-assertion (expressed in Hegel as the independent self-consciousness and in Freud as our aggressive proclivity) and the need for recognition (Hegel's dependent self-consciousness, or Freud's erotic instinct). While she agrees that the tension between the need for self-assertion and the need for recognition is characteristic of human relationships, Benjamin argues that this tension, in successful relationships, is held in balance in the form of a paradox. Its disintegration into polarities is not inevitable. Disintegration becomes inevitable only when there is an inability to sustain the tension of the paradox; such disintegration is manifest in relationships of domination and submission, and manifests itself in adult form in terms of erotic domination and submission.

Using Benjamin's scheme and its vocabulary, we may say that erotic pleasure has its source in another's recognition and affirmation of the self. The tension between the desire for self-assertion and the need for recognition collapses when the desire for self-affirmation, the dependency on another for the enjoyment of the self, is viewed as an intolerable threat to the self: "[there is] a continuing fear that dependency on the other is a threat to independence, that recognition of the other compromises the self" (50). This insecurity, the inability to accept vulnerability as concomitant with, if not necessary for, genuine independence is evident in many of the characters: in Barend, who cannot tell Hester he loves her for fear of disclosing his vulnerability to her; in Hester, who views Nicolaas' initial generosity toward her as a threat to her independence; also in Nicolaas, whose attempts to recognize Galant as an ally and to get Galant to view him as such are undertaken within the economy of the master-slave relationship, and therefore cannot but prove that ultimately equality within such a structure exists only in the form of fantasy. Such refusal of vulnerability expresses itself in the form of the metanarrative as well: in its absolute mastery of its subjects, its appropriation of them, and in the fact that its acceptance of the moral obligation to terminate domination takes the form of its projection of that liberation either backward, into the fantastical Eden, or forward, into the desired, fantasized, apocalypse.

When the self can view its need for another only as a sign of its own weakness, the desire of the self to maintain its independence directs the self either to destroy the other, to violate the independence of the other, or to destroy itself, by giving itself up to the other in the hope of gaining at least a vicarious independence. In the first case, the self receives affirmation of its independence, the source of erotic pleasure, not from the other's recognition of itself, but from its own attempts to destroy the selfhood of the other. In the second case, the self receives its affirmation by making its desire conform precisely to the desire of the other: the self receives recognition vicariously, through the affirmation which its own erotic submission affords the other.

In both of these relationships to the other the context of eroticism is linked to that of violation. If the source of affirmation for the dominant self lies in the attempt to destroy the other, the physical expression of this desire tends toward sadism; the physical expression of the desire of the submissive self, that of becoming other by fulfilling the dominant other's wishes, tends toward masochism. Both these relationships express attempts at intimacy through violation: in sadism, the violation of the other constitutes the attempt "to break through to the other" (Benjamin 71–72); in masochism, the violation of the self is realized in the attempt to discover the self. In Benjamin's words,

> The masochist's wish to be reached, penetrated, found, released—a wish that can be expressed in the metaphor of violence as well as in metaphors of redemption— is the other side of the sadist's wish to discover the other (73).

The structure of *A Chain of Voices*, when viewed as the expression of white liberal desire, can be seen both to reflect and complicate Benjamin's concepts in literary form. The desire to be recognized as (having been) master, and as (potentially) liberated from mastery, creates a fiction in which the master exhibits sadism in the present, but depends upon forgiveness for his mastery by perceiving himself as submissive in the future. Consequently, the fantasy dictates that the other—who is primarily black, and only secondarily female—is perceived as masochistic in the present. The slave is thought of as having an intimate connection to the master by the master, because the slave will be liberated by the master's "recognition" (which he thinks he has already made) of the immorality of his mastery, this "recognition" to be realized when the slave is liberated by the master in some other time, Edenic or apocalyptic. The master's sadism is justified retroactively by his fantasized past or future submission; and the slave has the fiction of his own masochism imposed on him.

The Engenderment of Dominance and Submission

The patterns of dominance and submission described above recur in the metanarrative's characterization of relationships. There is perhaps only one character who, at a certain point in the narrative, is portrayed as desiring voluntary submission in a manner that corresponds to the precise terms in which Benjamin describes the behavior of the masochistic self. I am referring to the extremely disturbing figure of Bet,[21] who is perhaps prefigured in Lys and Lydia. However, the violent scenes in the novel can be read as representations of sadism in the sense that Benjamin describes the phenomenon because of the specific social context that Brink provides for each act of violence. Barend's physical penetration of Hester expresses his attempt to force her to conform to his desire to dominate her. The night after Hester manages to stop Barend's beating Klaas, "Barend" tells us that "That night I subdued her in another way. But once again she uttered no sound, no groan, no whimper of pain or delight. She was dry. Unyielding and dry, sterile as hate" (164). We are given to understand that Nicolaas' repeated and violent beatings of Galant represent a similar, perverse attempt to communicate with him. In one of "Nicolaas'" accounts, which details the one occasion when he, as an adult, is forced to acknowledge his dependency on Galant, "Nicolaas" gives his reason for abusing Galant as the desire to penetrate him, in much the same way that "Barend" describes his desire for Hester:

> that night, I realized that this had been at the root of my outbursts against him: this urge to force a response from him, to move him, to prise him out of that passivity in which he was untouchable, a smooth intractable surface of rock which one could scale or explore without finding any fissure. The very wounds I'd torn into his body might have been efforts to get inside him, to break through that surface; and indeed the skin had broken, but there were membranes of the mind which kept him forever inaccessible (219–20).

There is a striking similarity in the depiction of Barend's desire to gain recognition from Hester and Nicolaas' desire to be recognized by Galant, in that both relationships are represented as sadistic. These relationships form one of many examples that demonstrate the similarity of the fiction's treatment of racial and sexual oppression. The linking of intimacy and violence within sadistic relationships is underscored by the persistence of the structure of the perverse "love" triangle. This pattern of relationships is used to represent both sexual and racial domination. The "triangle" is created by one character's attempts to communicate with another by abusing a third character. The third character is perceived by the aggressor as related to the other in some way. This third character thus both represents the other to the aggressor, but is not that other. For this reason the third character, the "interloper," as it were, becomes the object of sadistic aggression in the first character's attempt to affect the other by violating that which is allied with the other. Within this structure desire is represented as synonymous with violence. Rape and flogging become substitutes for one another.

The triangular relationships between Nicolaas, Pamela, and Galant on the one hand, and Cecilia, Lydia, and Nicolaas on the other, demonstrate the characteristics of this structure. The two sets of relationships reflect one another in their representation of sadistic relations between white master and black slave, male and female. Cecilia beats Lydia, the slave girl whom Nicolaas abuses and rapes, in an attempt to provoke a response from him. Similarly, Nicolaas' habitual rape of Pamela, Galant's lover, constitutes as much an attempt to communicate with Galant as does his abuse of Galant. "Nicolaas'" account provides the following explanation of the motivation for his sexual assaults on Pamela:

> I was shocked to find only lust when I contemplated Pamela. Perhaps not even lust for herself? But a lust derived from the agony of knowing her closeness to Galant. She was the only possible means for me still to touch him. . . . This woman, this body had known him; knew him. Through her I groped towards that terrible closeness to him . . . (282).

Cecilia takes to beating the slave woman, Lydia, once she has discovered that Nicolaas deserts her in the evenings for Lydia. Her beatings of Lydia are described in blatantly sadistic terms. That she is excited by her abuse of Lydia is portrayed unequivocally in "Bet's" account of the assaults. In this account of the floggings Cecilia appears as Nicolaas does in "Ontong's" account of Nicolaas' beating of Galant. "Bet" relates that she is out of control: "Only after Lydia's screams had changed from the sound of a woman in labour to the whimpering of a dying puppy would the beating stop" (147). Lydia is also stripped naked during the abuse: "Sometimes the clothes were beaten to shreds; mostly they were just torn from her in rage" (147). Galant takes Bet away from the stable where the beating takes place, but she returns to see

> Lydia coming out naked. But it was the Nooi [Cecilia] herself I couldn't help staring at. Her face flushed a deep red, her hair all dishevelled and damp with sweat, her cheeks streaked with tears; and she was panting. It might have been of tiredness, it was enough to wear anyone out, even a woman as strong as the Nooi . . . but my first thought when I saw her was that she looked like a woman who'd been with a man all night (148).

On this occasion Cecilia succeeds in getting Nicolaas' attention temporarily. She later complains of Lydia's nakedness, whereupon Nicolaas, rather than admitting to his sexual relationship with Lydia by refusing to take action, gives Lydia yet another flogging.

In her study of intersubjective relations, Benjamin, as we have noted above, claims that the attempt to establish independence lies, paradoxically, in the recognition of other as other. This recognition is one that relationships of dominance are calculated to avoid, because such a recognition is viewed by the dominant self as an admission of vulnerability and therefore as taboo. For this reason Benjamin describes the attempt of the dominant self to establish her or his independence through domination of an other, instead of recognition of an other, as symptomatic of "false differentiation" (76).

This aspect of dominance, that is, of false differentiation, is represented in the two triangular relationships that I have outlined. Not only is Nicolaas unable to recognize Galant as another, independent individual without risking his own sense of independence, he is also unable to relate to Pamela as anyone other than Galant's wife. He is interested in her only because she represents an access to Galant. Similarly, Cecilia is depicted as unable to differentiate between Lydia and Nicolaas' abuse of Lydia. In her beating of Lydia she is simultaneously attempting both to eradicate Lydia from the equation and to ally herself with Nicolaas.

However, the representation of Cecilia's abuse of Lydia as similar to Nicolaas' abuse of Galant proves to be problematic when the larger context— that of the power relationships dictated by the society which Brink takes pains to depict and the structure of the metanarrative's interests as a whole—is taken into account. Where Nicolaas' struggle for assertion over Galant is sanctioned by this society (it is considered to be in keeping with his birthright), Cecilia's attempts to gain recognition from Nicolaas and thereby assert her independence from him, are not. Her range of options is more limited than his; her actions are curtailed both by the patriarchal character of the society in general and of Nicolaas in particular. Cecilia, as her father's only child, wishes to take over her family's farm as a male child would have done, but her father laughs at this notion. The only courses of action open to her are to remain with her father, who continually mourns the fact of her sex, or to marry. In her marriage to Nicolaas she exchanges one kind of patriarchal dominance, that of her father, for another, that of her husband. Her desire to obey the dictates of her position prevents her from confronting Nicolaas directly with his adultery. Only once he has ordered Pamela to stay in the farmhouse overnight so that he can demand sexual intercourse from her, does Cecilia object; and she does so by using an authoritative voice that is not her own, that of the Bible. Nicolaas responds to her protest, according to "Pamela's" account, by saying that he is master in his own house (277). What is obscured, then, in the parallel depictions of Hester and Nicolaas within these triangular structures, is that Cecilia herself is subservient to Nicolaas:[22] the Cecilia-Lydia-Nicolaas triangle is created as a direct consequence of Nicolaas' domination of his wife and Lydia.

The fiction clearly seeks to affirm the slaves' attempts at liberation: those slaves who seek to survive through allegiance to their masters, such as Klaas and Moses, are portrayed in a particularly unfavorable light. Given the fiction's support of the slaves, it seems incongruous that Cecilia, the only female character who actively seeks to assert herself, receives a distinctly negative treatment by the narrative; furthermore, this negative portrayal is accomplished through the narrative's depiction of her aspirations to the male domain as unseemly, and through the implicit and unfavorable comparison of her to the other women in the text, particularly Hester. Her physique is described as powerful, "tall and large" in comparison to Hester's, which is "thin and dark"; and her strength is never portrayed as an asset, but rather as unnatural. Her beating of Lydia is depicted as shocking not simply in its abuse of Lydia, but because it represents an assumption of the male role: "It usually happened as soon as the Baas [Nicolaas] had gone off to the veld; and *the Nooi would take the strap herself*. . . . it wasn't proper the way she did it" (147; emphasis added). Hester, when she wants to punish Klaas for getting Galant into trouble, gets Barend to flog him for her.

The fiction does make an effort to portray some women as independent: Hester is consistently resistant to those who make the effort to affect her in some way, particularly men. However, this attempt to illustrate the potential of women to exercise their own will tends to backfire, because the fiction itself participates, albeit subconsciously, in the practice of male domination, which is such a pervasive feature of the society it attempts to depict. Apart from Cecilia, who is depicted as abhorrent, and Lys and Lydia, who are depicted as "soft in the head," the women gain their recognition through their service to men. Their "independence" in Benjamin's terms, or in literary terms, their differentiation as characters, is ultimately dependent upon their allegiances to the men of both races whose action determines the central conflict of the novel.

That the depiction of women as independent is compromised is evident in the character of the women's attempts at self-assertion. Ma-Rose, who is of the Khoi and therefore not technically a slave, describes herself as the only free woman on the farm, and is described by Alida as free; but she is constantly in demand by men of both races for sexual intercourse. She is depicted in the service of men repeatedly: she even soothes the child Galant by fondling him (41–42).[23] Alida, despite her determination to keep Hester from Piet's influence, nevertheless tries to persuade Hester that Piet did not contribute to her father's death. Galant threatens to beat Bet if she refuses to steal newspapers from the farmhouse for him. Her refusal indicates her unwillingness to join his cause; and so we are not surprised when Pamela replaces her as Galant's lover, and Bet later tries to warn Nicolaas about Galant's plans to rebel. Pamela, on the other hand, is devoted to Galant to the point of self-abnegation; her self-confessed desire is to "have him and submit to him" (268).

The sexual intercourse between Hester and Galant is described in such a way as to indicate that it commands some sort of preeminent significance as an act of liberation in which the taboos that prevent interracial sex are broken; it is portrayed as the culmination of the revolt, and is described by Hester and Galant as a moment of freedom (505; 507). In her criticism of this "conclusion" to the revolt, Jane Kramer points out that this supposed mutual liberation is problematic if the novel is attempting to affirm racial equality:

> Bet shares his [Galant's] pain in slavery, but she cannot restore him. The black woman cannot satisfy the black man's longing. (Another white fantasy?) Her warmth, her surrender, is a mirror of his own submission. Galant recoils from Bet, and later from Pamela, the slave who replaces her as his lover. Sexual healing is the province of the white woman (9).

The problem, however, goes further than this: Hester's "liberation" is described by her account using language that suggests rape, and by "Galant's" account using the language of possession. Both these contexts suggest that Hester is not only the replacement of Bet and Pamela, but is also identified with them in that she is yet another female figure who offers herself up to a man in the attempt to achieve her freedom. Hester's own account describes her as receiving her identity from Galant during their sexual intercourse:

I'm crushed by his full weight, my legs helpless and apart, kicking to find some hold; the surface of a back gnarled and marked with seams and welts, calluses, old scars. This must be the end . . . as he pushes down on me, crushing me, breaking me, giving me a being, a name, an inseparable existence, . . . excruciating fulfilment. He lunges, cleaving me . . . and slaughtering me, setting me free forever, unbearably (504–5).

The scene in which she washes Galant's wounds after Nicolaas has beaten him, a scene that may well suggest the context of the crucifixion to the reader (she kneels in the straw on the barn floor and washes him as he hangs from the crossbeams, supported by a box she has placed under his feet), contributes to this image of her as giving herself up to Galant. Like the Virgin Mary, she is a female character, subservient to a dominant male character in a narrative in which she has no say; if she were to refuse to support Galant, she would be "blacklisted" by the fiction, just as Bet is.

Galant's narrative, which frames Hester's (her account of their intercourse is sandwiched in between two of his), suggests that he complements Hester's submission with an attitude of dominance. His intercourse with her is described as being important not because of his love for her—then it would have been "*no more* than a man-and-woman thing" (507; emphasis added)—but because in it he claims the right to "own" the woman that he loves, despite the fact that she is white and that he will suffer the consequences:

in that moment when, in the silent loft above the thundering house, I found *the woman who had always been mine*, I freely took up the burden of yesterday as I chose tomorrow for myself (508; emphasis added).

The linguistic context that we are given in the description of the intercourse between Hester and Galant conforms to Benjamin's description of the sadomasochistic relationship in which complementarity replaces mutual independence through the entrenchment of patterns of dominance and submission. The episode is an actualization of the sadomasochistic fantasy of Bet. Hester is portrayed as gaining her identity through her submission to Galant, just as Bet envisions gaining hers through submission to Nicolaas. This incident is given exceptional prominence in the structure of the text, both chronologically (it occurs at the height of the rebels' success) and in terms of its narrative sequence (the three accounts—Galant's, then Hester's, then Galant's once more—are the last three before the "Verdict" with which the novel concludes).

The text attempts to demonstrate the capacity of women to be independent, but ultimately succeeds only in depicting them as dependent. This suggests that the text is guilty of a kind of "false differentiation" of its own, in which women achieve recognition exclusively through their service to men within the narrative framework of the text; in addition, the structure of the text itself recognizes them only within their capacity to serve as foils to the men, whose actions within the text and portrayals by the text dominate the narrative.

Conclusion: "Treating" Racial Difference, "Mastering" History

The questions of dominance and submission, mastery and slavery, that the text raises are not answered simply by remarking upon the problem of sexism. To do this would be to forget Vernon February's point: that to depict the breaking of the miscegenation taboo (by portraying the interracial relationship in its most common fictional form, that which comprises the black man and the white woman), may represent the immorality of the taboo, but it simultaneously suggests that the black man proves his equality with the white man by having intercourse with the "white man's woman" (125). From this perspective, Galant may be dominant within the context of male/female relationships, but with respect to the structure of the novel as a whole, his "dominance" becomes less assured: does not the metanarrative of the novel confer his freedom upon him by having him ally himself with Barend's wife and Nicolaas' true love, the coveted white woman, the prize? Is this not perhaps further evidence of the persistence of the white liberal master's fantasy? The triangular structure of sexual domination in *A Chain of Voices* can be used to shed some light on the metanarrative's manifestation of a similarly triangulated structure of racial dominance.

In its dependence upon the eclipse of female assertiveness for the representation of the racial conflict as preeminent, the structure of the novel mirrors the structure of male dominance delineated by Benjamin in her interpretation of Pauline Réage's *Story of O* as a fantasy of erotic domination. The triangular relationship between Rene, Sir Stephen, and O corresponds to a degree to that between Nicolaas, Galant, and Hester. While Hester is not commanded by either Nicolaas or Galant to the extent that O is by Sir Stephen, she is depicted as surrendering herself to Galant, and Galant is depicted as taking her not for herself, but to demonstrate his equality with, if not superiority to, both Barend and Nicolaas. Similarly, Nicolaas is depicted as taking Pamela because of her "closeness to Galant" (282), and Galant, on the nights that Pamela slips away from the farmhouse to come to him, is said to want to ask her, *"Was he with you again? This wetness in you, is it his?"* (299).

This narrative framework, in which the women "go between" Nicolaas and Galant, corresponds to the triangular relationship depicted in *Story of O*, in that the women become the means to an end determined by the men; the homoeroticism of both novels is the effect of this exclusion of the female. The narrative of O reflects the way in which the dominance of the Nicolaas-Galant relationship excludes women through its use of them: "What each of them would look for in her," the narrative says of Rene and Sir Stephen, "would be the other's mark, the trace of the other's passage" (83). Benjamin, quoting from the text, points out that "O realizes that the two men share something 'mysterious . . . more acute, more intense than amorous communion' from which she is excluded, even though she is the medium for it" (59). Within such a narrative structure women can only be represented as peripheral, despite the text's attempts to do otherwise. Their only entry into the text depends upon their alliances with men. Those who have no such stable alliance, namely Lys and Lydia, are exotic versions of the mad woman in the attic, and as such are inevitably written out of the narrative. The figure of the outcast Bet, trying in vain to get back into the favor of the narrative by persuading Nicolaas to recognize her submission to him, can be seen as emblematic of the only position afforded women by the exclusive structure of the narrative.

We would do well to remember, however, that it is not only sexual otherness, but also racial otherness, that plays into the figure of the mad woman in the attic; Bertha's stigmatization in *Jane Eyre* depends partly upon intimations of racial "taint." I wish to argue, then, for a crucial difference between the way in which Benjamin describes the relationship between the Rene and Sir Stephen, and the relationship between Nicolaas and Galant. To accept Galant's desire to locate his actions in terms of Nicolaas, either as childhood friend that may yet still be adult comrade, or as the defiant opponent whose freedom is registered by possession of the woman Nicolaas covets—that is, to accept the place which the metanarrative appears to create for Galant in these terms—is to overlook the danger that the metanarrative risks in assuming access to the historical, native subject and his desire, even while recognizing the text's appropriation of female desire in compliance with its own ends. For the novel can be read as a white liberal fantasy, in that it exhibits the elements of that fantasy which I have outlined. Just as the figure of the woman is used in service of the narratives of male intercourse, so the figure of Galant is used as the racial other whom the master—be it Nicolaas, or the reader, or the author—can appropriate in order to exhibit mastery and claim integrity based on a vision of future "recognition" of her or his present immorality. Note that here the triangulation allows the master to keep the fiction of the balance between his own assertion and submission (Benjamin's scenario of a "successful" relationship) alive through his use of, his appropriation of, the native voice in a history that appears to negotiate between black and white subjects to the benefit of both, but that can also be proven to be essentially solipsistic—a literary example of Benjamin's "false differentiation."

The argument that I have been making, that the structure of *A Chain of Voices*—ironically—falls into polarities of dominance and submission in its very attempt to portray relationships that are based on such polarities as destructive, depends upon the recognition of the context provided by the novel for the acts of violence it portrays as fictional. This recognition is not easy to sustain, because the form of Brink's novel, as I suggested at the beginning of this discussion, works against the distinction between "fact" and fiction: the reader is encouraged not to recognize that the historical is always fictional, that the claim of originality is not a solution but an exercise in appropriation. This obscuring of the metanarrative of the text is an attempt to present its "evidence," in the form of apparently unmediated monologues, to "the reader," who is constituted as witness or judge. However, in employing this narrative strategy, whose structure inhibits the reader's recognition of the metanarrative's apparent impartiality as a fiction, the text exhibits the propensity to violate its own desire for integrity, both moral and formal. The appropriative gesture whereby the fiction "provides" a history of oppression of the native subject, and its contingent representation of the oppression of the female subject, is exercised, unquestionably, in the fiction's attempt to convey the violence of racial dominance; but through the use of it the fiction itself can be seen to be dominant: a "master"-narrative.

So we arrive at a paradox. The text privileges its subject—violence—over the structure or form of its representation in order to promote the experience of horror and the recognition of violent acts as violent by the reader. Yet because of its commitment to representing violence as the "truth" of a "history" whose "origin" is always potentially accessible, because of its neglect of the fictional nature of history, the text does not accommodate the potential difference of that very same reader whom it is seeking so earnestly to convert. By overwriting its ontological status as fictional, the novel can be seen, paradoxically, to deny the creative possibilities offered by its own ethic. That is, the novel overlooks the potential of fiction to create readers who may develop alternative fictions about the status of history to that which assumes the validity of its (apparent) conformation to a predetermined "truth." The next question now presents itself. What form could a fiction—one that seeks both to mark and exploit its own representation of violence as fictional—take?

NOTES

1. J. M. Coetzee's response to a question about "the South African writer" illustrates his wariness of that concept:

> Q: Did you conceive of the novel [*Michael K.*] as in any way a task presented to you by history—the history of South Africa specifically?
> A: Perhaps that is my fate. On the other hand, I sometimes wonder whether it isn't simply that vast and wholly ideological superstructure constituted by publishing, reviewing and criticism that is forcing on me the fate of being a "South African Novelist." (Morphet interviews 460).

2. J. M. Coetzee has this quality of Brink's work in mind when he discusses the history of Brink's run-ins with the Publications Control Board, the body responsible for censorship in South Africa. Coetzee's article, "André Brink and the Censor," has much to offer in terms of its explication of Brink's concept of the role of the writer and her or his relationship to the state; while Coetzee concentrates on Brink's essays, however, I look at Brink's essays—and Coetzee's comments on them—as a prelude to a discussion of the way in which Brink's concepts of the writer and the state reflect upon the form his fiction takes.

3. André Brink writes his novels in both English and Afrikaans, and insists that the English is not merely a translation of the Afrikaans:

> It started with *Kennis van die Aand* [Looking on Darkness], where intrinsic motives (the urge to attempt 'saying' the novel in a new language medium) as well as extraneous ones (censorship) combined to create the challenge . . . [of] not 'translating' the work, but rethinking it in the framework of a new language; even more important, perhaps, re-feeling it (*Mapmakers* 113).

Subsequently Brink has used both English and Afrikaans to write his novels. He explains this process with reference to *An Instant in the Wind*:

> The few preliminary passages written to get the 'feel' of the book . . . were all in English. . . . But . . . when I actually sat down to write, it happened in Afrikaans. That was only the beginning, though. Using the first draft as a guide, the whole book was then reworked in English. In the process some episodes contained in the Afrikaans draft simply fell away; a couple of new ones emerged quite spontaneously. After completion of this draft I spent some time working on both: some of the new 'English' episodes were incorporated in the Afrikaans text, but one or two . . . simply didn't 'work' in Afrikaans. (The opposite was also true in a few cases.) The novel was then completed in English—and from that text a final Afrikaans version was prepared. There are still differences between them, and to my mind there is nothing to be done about that: the novel exists in two languages, but each language imposed its own demands on the final shape of the work (*Mapmakers* 114–15).

4. In 1973 *Looking on Darkness* was banned because both the Censorship Board and the Supreme Court in its appeal decision censored the novel for being "porno-graphic, blasphemous and Communistic." *A Dry White Season* was published clandes-tinely in 1979 by Taurus. Three thousand copies were distributed before the authorities discovered its existence and banned it (*Mapmakers* 243). In 1979 *A Dry White Season* was unbanned, together with Gordimer's *Burger's Daughter*, "because they were found to be so badly written as not to fool or offend anyone," whereas a 1980 "Committee of Experts" under Professor van der Merwe Scholz reinforced the ban on *Looking on Darkness* by "finding it wholly devoid of literary merit" (*Mapmakers* 242). In May 1982 *Looking on Darkness*, banned on four previous occasions, was conditionally unbanned.

5. J. M. Coetzee points out that this argument takes a peculiar form when it is made specifically in the context of state censorship; for if the writer is prodded to write by her or his sense of offense at censorship itself, writing and state censorship take on a symbiotic relationship. If "without the heretic, the rebel, the writer, the state crumbles [*gaan tot niet*]," as Brink argues in an article entitled "*Heerser en Humanis*" ["Ruler and Humanist"] from *Literatuur in die Strydperk* (165), then, Coetzee points out, "one might equally say that, once caught up in the dynamic of blaming, the writer cannot do without the state and its denunciatory organ, the censorship [the Publications Control Board]" ("Brink and Censor" 72; I use Coetzee's translation of the Brink quote here).

6. I use quotation marks to refer to Brink's writer and reader in order to indicate that these are specifically Brink's concepts of the writer and reader, and not my own.

7. One of the ironies that Brink's construct of "the reader" creates, is that his generalized reader starts looking very much like the concept of "the likely reader" developed by the Publications Control Board, Brink's arch enemy (see Louise Silver on "the 'probable' reader"). This particular irony bears out J. M. Coetzee's point—that the dynamic of censorship creates a discourse of paranoia in which the author and censor, ostensible enemies, start to mirror one another in mutual responses that take on the aspect of an automatism ("Brink and Censor" 71–72).

8. Unlike those of his novels that are historical (*An Instant in the Wind*; *A Chain of Voices*; *On the Contrary*), or those that employ a foreign geographical setting (*The Wall of the Plague*; *The Ambassador*), *A Dry White Season*, like the recent *An Act of Terror*, is set in contemporary South Africa.

9. Brink has been editor of the fiction page of the Afrikaans weekly *Rapport* (Ross interview 56).

10. Brink explained the reason for his temporary suspension of the work on *A Dry White Season* to Davidson:

> I was knee-deep into the novel when Biko died, and that put me off it altogether for almost a year. I felt it would be obscene to ride on Biko's back as it were, and use him to write a novel about a person dying when a real person—and such a person—had died so close to Grahamstown. In fact the whole thing started when the Security Police arrested him here. It was only after I lived through that whole

traumatic thing that I realized that it was also a matter of making sure people knew about it . . ." (Davidson interview 27).

11. That Brink believes in the potential of literature to effect such profound changes in its readers is reflected not only in his stated purpose for writing *A Dry White Season*, but also in his critical writing. In an essay entitled "Imagining the Real" in *Mapmakers* Brink explains the didactic function of literature as he sees it, once again invoking the concept of a generalized reader:

> It is of little value simply to state certain truths: without living and experiencing them, they remain if not invalid at least inactive. *Life must be lived in order to be understood* . . . literature . . . when it is most true to itself, achieves this by immersing the reader in a variety of experiences he may otherwise have missed. Vicarious experience it may be, but none the less profound. . . .
>
> [The reader] is taken out of himself by entering into the new world of what he is reading; and eventually he is restored to himself and to his world, enriched by what he has drawn from that experience. He has glimpsed the possibility of a new significance in the world he inhabits (219).

12. In this respect the narrator-writer is "related" to Brink, the writer, in that Brink was aware, during the writing of *A Dry White Season*, that he would attract the unfavorable attention of the authorities through his publication of the novel.

13. Mrs. Fraser survived the shipwreck of the *Stirling Castle*, a British brig homebound from Sydney to London, on May 21, 1936, and endured two and a half months of captivity at the hands of the aborigines of Great Sandy Island—now Fraser Island—before being rescued and returned to Moreton Bay. Although the manner of her rescue is disputed, in each of the two versions her rescuer is supposed to have been a runaway convict who had taken to living with the aborigines after his escape.

It is relevant to this discussion to note that Brink's first encounter with the Mrs. Fraser story was not through reading histories, but through Australian artist Sidney Nolan's paintings depicting Mrs. Fraser and the convict in various landscapes. In Brink's novel, in a transposition suggested perhaps by Nolan's changing landscapes, the interior becomes that of the Cape, and Mrs. Fraser becomes the Cape-born wife of a European naturalist and explorer, Larsson. Larsson undertakes an exploration into the Karoo, which Elizabeth Larsson alone survives. She is discovered by Adam Mantoor, a slave who has escaped from the Cape. Their delayed but inevitable return to the Cape signals the end of their relationship and the recapture of Adam; Elizabeth, who had promised to protect Adam upon their return to the Cape, leaves him waiting outside the city in a field to which she never returns.

The Australian novelist Patrick White's version of the story was published in the same year as Brink's *An Instant in the Wind*. In White's *A Fringe of Leaves*, the issue of class plays an equally important, if not superior role, to that of race. For a comparison of the two fictions see A. J. Hassal.

14. That this narratee is not named by the text causes Andre Viola, whose critique of the novel is generally favorable, to comment that "the novel does not always satisfactorily handle the problem of the addressee, in the sense that at times some voices tend to hang in the air" (65).

15. One free man, Joseph Campher, is also among the accused.

16. We are told that both Piet and Alida hit children: Piet frequently beats his sons (73), and Alida slaps Hester after the girl has returned from one of her unauthorized wanderings (77).

17. The accounts, or "voices," are attributed to various characters by the text in a way that differs from the mode of characterization within a novel that utilizes some sort of explicit unifying feature, such as a narrator who appears throughout the text and employs a single voice. I have attempted to indicate this difference by placing the names of the characters, when they are used to signify the individual accounts, in quotation marks.

18. This aspect of *A Chain of Voices* is discussed in particularly strong terms by Francis King in his review of the novel:

> As the masters wield their sjamboks, with their wives often looking on in panting excitement, the floggings eventually become almost pornographic in their repetitiveness and in the feeling of disgusted satiety which they induce in the reader. . . .
>
> As, repeatedly, one or other of the masters takes forcible possession either of his white wife or of a black concubine, the narrative again veers towards a pornography of sadomasochistic violence (23).

Jane Kramer also comments on this aspect of *A Chain of Voices.*

19. In "Why War?" Freud suggests that something other than fear of the physical consequences of war is at work in pacifism, what he calls "a *constitutional* intolerance of war"; nevertheless, he adds "justified dread of the consequences of a future war" to this pacifist constitution to total the two factors that "may result within a measurable time in putting an end to the waging of war" (362).

20. The Eurocentrism to which I refer in Freud is evident in passages such as the one quoted below. Note that the description of the "primal period" of civilization suggests that the situation in which few share the benefits of society and the rest live in slavish suppression is allocated to the past; and "primitive peoples" of today are described as disadvantaged. There is no awareness in this passage of the history of colonization and its attendant international economic effects, which afford Europe—and afforded Freud's Germany—its creature comforts, its "civilized" pursuits:

> In that primal period of civilization, the contrast between a minority who enjoyed the advantages of civilization and a majority who were robbed of those advantages was . . . carried to extremes. As regards the primitive peoples who exist today, careful researches have shown that their instinctual life is by no means to be envied

for its freedom. It is subject to restrictions of a different kind but perhaps of greater severity than those attaching to modern civilized man (306).

The life of "modern civilized man," then, has its disadvantages; but "primitive peoples," Freud assumes, certainly would have nothing to offer him by way of a solution, being themselves even further disadvantaged.

Hegel's history of civilization allies itself even more closely with imperialist thought, a factor evident in his notorious assertions that Africa lies outside of "history" and that it exhibits no "culture" (*World History* 174–76). What is notably missing from Hegel's description of the slave freeing himself by mastering nature through his work for his master is, once again, a sense of the economic basis of political power. In addition, the *Phenomenology of Spirit*, in which phenomenology and necessity are indistinguishable, would seem to depend upon and also justify paternalistic periods of domination based on the perceived incapacity or immaturity of the other to achieve the Hegelian "true" mastery, namely ultimate self-consciousness. J. N. Findlay's analysis of the text puts it this way:

> Hegel thinks that the discipline of service and obedience is essential to self-consciousness: mere mastery of things alone would not yield it. Only the discipline of service enables the conscious being to master himself, i.e. his finite, contingent, natural self. Without this discipline formative ability would degenerate into a narrow cleverness placed at the service of personal self-will. (Hegel suggests that a period of subjection to others is essential to the highest magisterial rationality. Not to have undergone such discipline results in a trivialization of self-consciousness which never rises above petty finite interests. *It would seem that the permissive bringing-up of children is implicitly condemned, and that "imperialism" and "colonialism" at certain stages of development are given a justification.*) (Findlay in Hegel's *Phenomenology* 523; emphasis added).

21. After Nicolaas has beaten Galant's and Bet's baby, David, to death in a rage after an argument with his wife, he comes to Bet in a fit of remorse and asks her if there is anything he can do for her. "Bet" describes her response as follows:

> I pressed my head hard against his knees and grabbed him by the legs. I couldn't let go again. I felt I was drowning. I was thinking of Lydia. *Lie down there.* The way he went back to her the same night [after he beat her upon Cecilia's request] to abuse her torn body. I understood nothing about it all and still don't. I knew I'd lost Galant. . . . But that wasn't what shook me as I knelt there holding his legs and groaning like an animal, the sound Lydia made when she was beaten, like a dog, a bitch in heat. That was it: an emptiness growing and expanding inside me all night so I felt like crawling out to the yard to howl under his window like a dog.
>
> That was it: and from that day I couldn't let him be. I lusted after him day and night. I followed him wherever he went, begging with my body to be taken. He paid no attention (154).

22. Despite the fact that Cecilia claims that through Nicolaas' "use and abuse of my body a peculiar power of my own over him had been asserted" (122), Nicolaas still ultimately dominates her; he abandons her for Lydia, and later for Pamela.

23. This causes JanMohamed to comment: "The undiscriminating sexuality of Ma-Rose, the slave earth mother, is endowed with an ill-defined liberatory quality . . . ("The Economy of Manichean Allegory" 92).

BREYTEN BREYTENBACH'S PRISON WRITINGS

> The violence I want to express is the
> violence of philology. . . .
> The term here refers to any act of
> interpretation that is based on the
> assumption of the existence and knowability
> of a certain *intrinsic* property of objects of
> discourse in general which is named truth.
> The violence of philology consists precisely
> in its enacting a reconstructive project, in its
> proposing the possibility and the necessity of
> a restoration, presented as a reconformation
> to an origin(al). The violence of philology,
> that is, resides in its inventing the narrative
> or myth of a beginning in order to legitimize
> or even naturalize some kind of intervention
> on an object constituted as other.
>
> —Lucia Folena, "Figures of Violence"

1. INTRODUCTION

Like André Brink, Breyten Breytenbach is an Afrikaner dissident of some repute; he and Brink have been friends since their university years in Paris in the sixties. However, these are not the only grounds for discussing the work of Breytenbach alongside that of Brink and Coetzee. Breyten Breytenbach represents Afrikaner dissidence in a way that no other person could due to his standing as a renowned Afrikaner poet who was then incarcerated for treason; the English prose works of Breyten Breytenbach, *Mouroir* (1983) and *The True Confessions of an Albino Terrorist* (1984), were written during and after his imprisonment, and offer a unique opportunity of examining texts that were written not only to

60

represent violence, but also to combat it, in terms that constitute an extraordinary response to both private and public prerogatives.

Breytenbach, born in the small-town Afrikaner community of Bonnievale in the Eastern Cape in 1939, made a name for himself as an innovative poet of his native language early in his writing career.[1] In 1959 he moved to France, and in 1964 he married a Vietnamese woman, who would have been considered *anderskleurig*, or "of another colour," within South Africa. Breytenbach's antiapartheid sympathies and activities ensured that he was labeled as the black sheep of his family and his nation.[2] In 1975 he returned to South Africa in disguise, carrying a passport that identified him as Christian Galaska.[3] He was working underground for "an unofficial offshoot of the African National Congress" named Okhela (Breytenbach, "Not an Afrikaner" 4).[4] The South African security police were apparently tipped off as to Breytenbach's arrival by an informer stationed in Europe (J. M. Coetzee, "Poet in Prison" 30; Breytenbach, "Not an Afrikaner" 4; *TCAT* 80). They kept him under surveillance for a few days, then arrested him in August 1975.[5]

Breytenbach's family chose lawyers to act for him who had no experience with political trials and who, according to Breytenbach, were "far too closely integrated into the Afrikaner establishment" to design a strategy for a political defense even if they had wanted to do so.[6] Such was the agreement with the prosecution that they ultimately negotiated for him:

> In return for my pleading guilty, and in return for my not insisting on making political statements from the dock, and in return for the freedom of the other arrested ones [those arrested for assisting Breytenbach], the State graciously agreed to alter the charge sheet so as to delete any reference to violence, to not attempt to have me convicted under the Suppression of Communism Act, and it was agreed that the prosecutor would ask for the imposition of the minimum sentence, which was five years (*TCAT* 61).[7]

Breytenbach admits that the lawyers "advised particular caution—perhaps seeing the real dangers more clearly than I then did. And I went along" (*TCAT* 63). He explains the circumstances under which a "confession" of sorts was composed:

> I was asked to prepare a short statement. Without being political it was an attempt to explain how I got to be standing where I was, without rejecting my convictions. Read it—you will also hear the insidious voice of the controller in it. This was in the hands of Huntingdon a week before the trial commenced, and Vorster himself [the Prime Minister] had it on his desk before it was read in court (*TCAT* 63).[8]

On November 25, 1975, he was sentenced to nine years' imprisonment under the Terrorism Act. He served seven of the nine years. For the first
two years he was incarcerated in solitary confinement in Pretoria Central
prison. He was then transferred to Pollsmoor prison in the Cape. During his
incarceration in solitary confinement Breytenbach wrote "what would later
become" *Mouroir: Mirrornotes of a Novel* (*TCAT* 161), which was first published in French translation in 1983, then in English in 1984.[9] *The True Confessions of An Albino Terrorist* was published in 1984. The *Confessions* deals with
Breytenbach's victimization by telling, with some disruption, the story of his
imprisonment and, as Egan points out, it does so "from the certainty of a
known end" (90). *Mouroir*—in keeping with the time of its composition—
offers no certainty of any kind with regard to the identity of its subject(s), nor
any evidence of a beginning or ending: it exhibits no his-story.

My interest in Breytenbach's prison texts stems from their analysis of
structures of violence, and an attempt to confront those structures, by a person
who was in a position of extreme violation at the time of their writing; indeed,
Breytenbach cites this circumstance as the very reason for his writing of the
texts. In my reading of *Mouroir* and the *Confessions*, then, I concentrate not on
the details of the physical conditions of inmates in South African prisons, but
on that aspect of his prison writing which Breytenbach regards as so important: its capacity to help him endure his experience of extreme isolation and
deprivation. To demonstrate the importance of the relationship between text
and context to a discussion of violence in reference to *Mouroir* and the *Confessions* as autobiographical writings, we need a more detailed sense of that
context: what was the discursive position in which Breytenbach found himself
at the time of their writing?

Breytenbach's position during his incarceration can be divided into
its personal and public components. I will discuss first the relationship between detainee and interrogator which Breytenbach documents from the personal perspective of the detainee; and second, the way in which this
relationship represents and replicates the rhetorical attempts of nationalist
ideology to dictate the nature of interactions between the state and its subjects.
With this context in mind, we can then move on to an analysis of the representation of these structures of violence in *Mouroir* and the *Confessions*, which
I shall introduce with a discussion of the relationship between confession and
autobiography—a relationship that is based on the violence of interrogation.

The Relationship Between Detainee and Interrogator

Although the "observation period" for a political prisoner was usually
three months, Breytenbach was kept under observation and interrogation for

almost the entire two years in which he was held in solitary confinement (*TCAT* 129). During this time he had no contact with other prisoners, and his guards were instructed not to converse with him except to convey orders.[10] His only substantial contact during this period was with his interrogators. He expresses his disgust at his need for them: he depended on them not only for human contact, but for his life. The prisoner's mortification lies, he explains, in that he[11] is forced to participate in his own undoing: "it becomes possible for one ultimately to be like the rabbit assisting open-eyed and without kicking at one's own eating" (*TCAT* 51). Even more difficult to confront than his own weakness is the prisoner's awareness of having viewed the tormentor as a confessor, or even a friend: "This development is so profoundly unnatural that it makes him [the prisoner] sick of himself" (*TCAT* 343).

Yet Breytenbach points out that, paradoxically in view of their over-whelming power, the interrogators are dependent upon the prisoner to justify their existence.[12] More specifically, they are dependent upon the success of their efforts to force the prisoner to conform to their image of who he is. Breytenbach documents the desire of his interrogators to have him admit to their various hypotheses about what kind of underground activities he was involved in and which organizations he worked for. One of his principal interrogators was a man whom Breytenbach refers to in the *Confessions* as "Blue Eyes" or "Jiems Kont."[13] Breytenbach explains that "Jiems Kont" was "so sure that he'd brilliantly stumbled across the master spy of the century that he could hardly contain his own excitement" (*TCAT* 40):

> as the interrogation unfolded . . . I, after having been successively (unsuccessfully) a French, British and Israeli agent, would end up being accused of working for the CIA (*TCAT* 18–19).

The interrogators are dedicated to the "truth" of their hypotheses, despite all evidence to the contrary. This is illustrated further by the interrogators' response to certain fictitious characters portrayed in Breytenbach's pre-incarceration writings. A passage in *A Season in Paradise*, describing the Breytenbachs' departure from South Africa in 1973, refers to a "hanger-on" accompanying the Security Police (but not one of them) as "a lap dog." The interrogator referred to in the *Confessions* as Colonel Jan Snaaks (*snaaks* meaning "funny," but also "vicious") demands to know from Breytenbach "how I dared call him a lap dog" (*TCAT* 47). A similar incident occurred involving a character in a 1971 piece entitled *Om te Vlieg* [In Order to Fly], in which Breytenbach describes the attempts of an absurd figure named Panus to learn how to fly. Within that narrative Panus "dies" in a number of different ways. In one of the less "realistic" sections of *A Season in Paradise* Breytenbach "resuscitate[s]" Panus, and describes a meeting between himself and Panus in which he comments on how old Panus has become and "how pathetic and bare his wings" are. Breytenbach describes "Jiems Kont's" interrogation concerning the figure of Panus:

> In this weird world of ours many things are possible, Mr Investigator, but it still came as a surprise to me to be interrogated by Jiems Kont about Panus. 'Who is he really?' he wanted to know. And especially, 'What is his political orientation?' No way could I convince him that this personage 'twixt prick and bunghole was simply an outgrowth of my imagination (*TCAT* 49).

The blindness that Breytenbach's interrogators display with regard to recognizing the difference between their fundamentalist notion of "the truth" and, in this case, Breytenbach's fiction, is not so much funny as dangerous. Breytenbach, of course, cannot convince his interrogators of the impossibility of any of their fantasies being realized, least of all those in which they conceive of him as a master-spy, a double agent, or all the other activities (often mutually exclusive!) of which they accused him. Any attempt he makes to define himself as something other than what they believe him to be, is an enterprise fraught with danger:

> They're [the interrogators] dangerous. One always had the feeling that one had to placate them. Later on, with the prison warders, I had similar experiences. One was not so much afraid of the harm they might do you on purpose, but that they may lose control of themselves and maim or exterminate you, as it were, by accident. . . . One was always trying to calm them down, not making any untoward gestures, not saying anything that would infuriate them (*TCAT* 48).

The relationship between the interrogator and the interrogated which Breytenbach describes reflects to some extent the perverse mutual dependence of the dominant and submissive selves found in sadomasochistic relationships. In this context the interrogator appears in the role of the sadist: he fulfills the desire to assert his independence by destroying that which he views as a threat to himself, namely that which is he has determined to be other—the interrogated.[14] Breytenbach describes this relationship in his "Note on the Relationship Between Detainee and Interrogator:"

> There is the struggle for domination—to have the other do what you want him to do . . . there is the effort to destroy—because the opposing forces are irreconcil-

able, or because there is the pathological human curiosity for killing, for altering permanently, . . . or because the dismantlement has revealed vis-à-vis, a brother-I, . . . or only a miserable human-conditioned pile of flesh and faeces which is unbearable and needs to be done away with; there is . . . the blind desire to force a resolution to and a resolution of the irreducible contradictions—precisely because you cannot accept the (self)-image revealed to you, nor the knowledge that never the twain shall meet (*TCAT* 341).

Breytenbach's portrayal of the psyche of the interrogator proposes that the interrogator, like Jessica Benjamin's sadist, receives self-affirmation, the source of erotic pleasure, from his attempts to destroy the interrogated, who is the other. Elsewhere in the text Breytenbach describes this form of erotic pleasure in terms that are virtually identical to those used by Benjamin:[15]

they [the interrogators] tend to become very violent in an unconscious effort to blot out and perhaps to surpass the[ir] uneasiness. However strange it may sound, Mr Eye, I am convinced that some of the people they have killed in detention probably died when the interrogator was in a paroxysm of unresolved frustrations, even that the interrogator killed in an awkward expression of love and sympathy for a fellow human being (*TCAT* 50).[16]

As in Benjamin's analysis, this description of the sadistic relationship manifests a strange propensity for reversal due to its complementary characteristic (Benjamin 48). This aspect of the relationship, its complementarity, is expressed by Breytenbach in his description of the reasons for his interrogators' erratic behavior toward him. The aggression they direct toward him is, perversely, an attempt to erase their identification with him: "there is . . . the tendency to identify with the other (and the roles can be inverted)" [*TCAT* 341]. The propensity for reversal would seem to suggest that the interrogated, Breytenbach himself, plays the role in what he terms "this macabre dance" of the masochist (*TCAT* 341), the one who gives herself or himself to the other in a desperate attempt to gain at least a vicarious independence. Yet there is a crucial distinction to be made between Benjamin's masochist and the position of the interrogated in which Breytenbach finds himself. Breytenbach does not desire the position of the dominated: he is forced into it by the manipulations of those who work to procure the "security" of the state. This distinction in and of itself points to the danger of eradicating the broader field of political implications from an analysis of personal subjectivity—an old fallacy, that the political does not impinge on the private, which has been, not coincidentally, one of the longstanding myths of the apartheid regime.

The Violence of Nationalist Discourse

The "view of reality" to which the interrogators are "fanatically com-mitted" (*TCAT* 46), then, is not a manifestation of intersubjective complemen-tary relationships simply at the level of the individual. The violent confrontation between the interrogator, "Jiems Kont" or Huntingdon, or whomever it happens to be, and the detainee, Breytenbach, is a situation authored by the controlling ideology of the nation state. This ideology, the foundation upon which concepts of nationalism and state "security" rest, sub-sists by replicating and propagating the notions of self and other found in the relationships of dominance and submission which Benjamin describes in the context of interpersonal relationships, but which Hegel, tellingly, posed as the origin of "civilization." That this cult of domination is tied, dangerously, to racist conceptions of the "ethic" of national unity was the problem Freud had to confront, when faced with anti-Semitism in the guise of patriotism. The power of such nationalist rhetoric, which identifies the state as the true "self" and all those whom it deems to be a threat to the state as "other," is witnessed yet again in the event of Breytenbach's forced submission. He is made so conscious of the pervasiveness, the tyranny of this ideology, that he fears to trust those who are provisionally sanctioned by the state to "challenge" the state, namely his defense lawyers:

> I was numbed. To my mind the whole world was hostile (expressions of support were carefully kept from me, and the offices where I could consult the lawyers were bugged)—*legal gown and policemen's uniform blended.* All I wanted was to please. . . .
>
> One wanted to have it over and done with. I felt quite passive. I can under-stand how the mouse is paralysed although still alive whilst being eaten by the snake—celebrating with open eyes its own death (*TCAT* 62; emphasis added).

Breytenbach describes the ideology of the state using vocabulary that suggests that such ideology propagates, or more precisely, both constructs and exploits, the dominant/submissive pattern of complementary relations that characterizes his relationship with his interrogators. The sadist, it is proposed, gains self-affirmation or recognition from the destruction of the other, since she or he conceives of the other as a threat to the self. The use of rhetoric in which the self is defined through the construction of the other as a threat to the self—what we may provisionally call sadistic rhetoric—is a strategy we can identify as one upon which the creation of both the nation and its state depends. Lucia Folena makes this point in her essay on Reaganite rhetoric, an essay that explores the relationship between America's Central American policy making and its domestic policy.

In "Figures of Violence," Folena goes back in history to Jacobean England and the Scottish witch hunts to illustrate the use of rhetorical strategies to uphold the concept of the nation as unified and to accrue power to those in authority over the nation. Reagan's renaming of the Sandinistas as "Stalinistas" and his claim that "the struggle [in Nicaragua] . . . is not right versus left; it is right versus wrong" employ similar strategies. Such rhetoric "displace[s] politics into ethics and provide[s] the gestures of the culture with a metaphysical foundation" (230). This rhetoric informs the attempt to constitute the nation as a unified self through the creation of a binary opposition between self and other, providing, simultaneously, the rationale behind imperialism, and the justification for the violence that it perpetuates.

The existence of empire is justified, such rhetoric argues, in its attempt to resurrect the other to the privileged position of the self (or in Folena's vocabulary, the "Same"). Yet the imperialist project begins with and depends for its continuation upon the identification of that which it presents as potentially recuperable as the self, as fundamentally "other." The tautology that this argument manifests indicates once again that the "hidden agenda" of the project is the creation and maintenance of the imperial power as the dominant nation, through the projection of a self unified against an "other." The imperial power has absolutely no interest in the other on that other's own terms. The "other" here is purely a metaphysical construct:[17] "The Other is only a figure in the discourse of the Same: shaping the Other becomes a cultural priority" (221).

That there is no substantial recognition of the "other" as other—that is, without reference to the self—in this rhetoric, suggests that what is important to the upholding of the nation state as a unified subject is the structure of the imperialist binary opposition. Who or what is identified as other, and therefore as adversary, is not important; it is only necessary for there to be such an other. This is illustrated in André Brink's discussion of the development of Afrikaner nationalism. Brink points out that the Nationalist movement has always functioned in opposition to another group, which may be identified by the terminology we have been developing as the "other." The entity that occupies the position of the "other" has not been stable; rather, it comprises a series of substitutions.

Brink identifies four "moments" that, according to him, forged Afrikaner nationalist consciousness. Each of these "moments" represents the temporary unification of a disparate group, the Afrikaners, against an "other" and each "moment," it could be argued, is more violent than the one that preceded it. The first of these "moments" consists of the struggle of the Dutch settlers and French Huguenots against the representatives of the Dutch East India Company at the Cape in the early eighteenth century (specifically, against Governor Willem Adriaan van der Stel); the second was the rebellion of the settlers against the British authority at the Cape which resulted in the Great Trek in the 1830s; the third was the resistance against British occupation of the Boer Republics during the Anglo-Boer War (1899–1902); and the fourth was the election of the National Party in 1948, with its policy of apartheid and its institutionalization of the concept of white supremacy (*Mapmakers* 15–17). Brink, writing in 1983, criticizes the attempt to employ these "moments" as evidence of a historically proven (and frequently theologically defended) fundamental Afrikaner unity:[18]

> the widespread notion of 'traditional Afrikaner unity' is based on a false reading of history: strife and inner division within Afrikanerdom has been much more in evidence than unity during the first three centuries of White South African history. It is precisely because today's Afrikaners are so aware of what it means to be divided that dissidence in the present circumstances is viewed with such alarm and rage. Apartheid, which defines Afrikaner unity since 1948, needs an image of historicity, preferably of eternity for its success; dissidence exposes it for what it is. And the reaction becomes even more vicious if one takes into account that dissidence, this time, implies a revolt not against some foreign power but against the Afrikaner power base itself (*Mapmakers* 17).

Breytenbach's imprisonment and interrogation can be seen as one of these violent "moments" in which the attempt is made to maintain and to demonstrate Afrikaner unity simultaneously. Breytenbach must be punished both because he is a dissident and to demonstrate the state's intolerance of that which it has designated "other." Herein lies the distinctive character of Breytenbach's "crime," as it is perceived by his jailers. His dissent is all the more disturbing for having come from "within." That is to say, he is not merely the "other" who is to be converted to the rhetoric of Afrikaner patriotism and white dominance; he is the "self" who has become "other," and therefore needs to be converted back to his "original nature." His "crime" is not the lesser one of simply being "an-other;" it is the grosser one of being a traitor.[19]

    The upholding of the nation state as a unified subject against the "other," as Folena has pointed out in her analysis of Reaganite rhetoric, has as its primary goal the constitution of individual subjects as unified "consciousnesses." These subjects participate in the construction of the nation state because they "recognize" it to be to their own benefit. In this respect nationalist discourse, like any other discourse, functions ideologically; as Catherine Belsey puts it, nationalist discourse "discourages a full understanding of . . . [real] conditions of existence and the ways in which people are socially constituted within them" (57). The "sell job" of such discourse is to convince people that they are "autonomous individuals, possessed of subjectivity or consciousness which is the source of their beliefs and actions" (58). The basis of this "sell job" has a direct correlation to the belief underlying white liberalism: the assumption that one can undertake to liberate the black other, neglecting to take into account one's own status as subject of and subject to the apartheid state, bears witness to the success of this "sell job" in one of its less obvious South African effects.

In nationalist discourses the presentation of the self, or subject, as autonomous is spurious, because the definition of the subject in such discourses always depends upon the artificial designation of "others." The presentation of the subject as "autonomous" in and by nationalist discourse functions as a cover for its own undercover operation. The veiled activity of such discourse is not to describe, but to produce, the subject:

> I say: the category of the subject is constitutive of all ideology, but at the same time and immediately I add that *the category of the subject is only constitutive of all ideology in so far as all ideology has the function (which defines it) of 'constituting' concrete individuals as subjects* (Althusser, *Lenin and Philosophy* 171).

Breytenbach, with the heavy irony of the prisoner of conscience, but also with the clarity of vision of a Lucia Folena, describes the constitution of the subject as the undercover operation specifically of democracy:

> It can be said that we have to do here with real democracy. . . . You [the citizen] are a twinge of Conscience. And the Conscience, the great Justification, is the State. . . . And Minister Krüger said, 'The highest good is the security of the State.' (*TCAT* 215).[20]

This production of the individual as a unified subject by the rhetoric of nationalism becomes apparent, paradoxically, when the ideological machinery fails; that is, when the subject refuses to participate in the discourse of "self" and "other" as it has been defined by the state. The "failure" of the subject to conform to the established nationalist discourse can result in the state's implementation of violence to impress, physically, its notion of the self on the subject.[21] The state cannot acknowledge that the ideological operations that maintain its sovereignty are faulty. It must therefore place the blame for this "failure" of the individual to conform to its definition of her or his subjectivity on that individual. As Breytenbach puts it:

The State lives inside you. You are its condition. Except that the State is pure though jealous. Thou shalt have no other idols or urinations or blots. There will be no dissidence. You shall not prostrate yourself before any other idea. Who else will be able to punish you? . . . There is no freedom . . . there can only be guilt in its million convolutions and revelations (*TCAT* 215).

The reason why the Breytenbach case received so much press and became such an embarrassment to the Afrikaner establishment (and ultimately the government itself) now becomes clear. Breytenbach is determined not to be the liberal—in the sense of one who works against apartheid largely within the parameters of its law—hence his act of treason (participation in Okhela to raise money for arms to be used against the apartheid government) and the paradox that it represents. Coetzee explains Breytenbach's positioning of himself like this: "to repudiate white South Africa I have to be a white South African; or to repudiate evil I have to embody evil" ("Breytenbach and Censor" 67). Breytenbach represents a failure in the discursive politics of "self" and "other," because the Afrikaner nationalist rhetoric structured around those poles fails to account for his subjectivity as it is demonstrated by his actions. According to this rhetoric's definition of self and other, he represents the impossible, for he represents both "self" and "other;" he is Afrikaner by "virtue" of his birth and poetic talent; yet his political allegiances render him a traitor.[22]

One of the "indulgences" granted to Breytenbach in prison was permission to write. It is quite conceivable that this permission was granted, as J. M. Coetzee indicates, in the belief that Breytenbach is "bearer of a talent that he cannot, despite himself, betray" ("Poet in Prison" 73). His reputation as an Afrikaner poet in a tradition in which to write in Afrikaans is already to have aligned oneself with the forces of Afrikaner nationalism, then, precipitates the irrational discourse in which Breytenbach's politics represent an aberration from his "true" poetic self, the essential Afrikaner. It is necessary, then, for the Afrikaner establishment to invoke a kind of schizophrenia in conceiving of Breytenbach as a poet on the one hand and a "terrorist" on the other, if the construct of the essentially patriotic Afrikaner is to be maintained:

Hence the notion that the 'terrorist' in Breytenbach can be incarcerated and punished while the poet in him can be left free. By acting as though Breytenbach must be a radically divided personality, one self a poet to be saved, the other self a traitor to be damned, the greater Afrikaner family preserves its belief (and perhaps does so sincerely and in good faith) that the language, the mystical nation-essence, is greater than the fallible vessels who bear it ("Poet in Prison" 30).[23]

It is important to note that the concept of Breytenbach having a split subjectivity—of his being both a talented Afrikaner poet and an enemy of the Afrikaner nation—cannot be expressed in terms of the split subjectivity exhibited by postmodernism.[24] In postmodernism, the representation of the subject as split or fractured is conceived of as a liberatory performance; it is seen to constitute the postmodern subversion of the unified subject, of that which is produced by, rather than produces, ideology. Unlike the postmodern notion of the fractured subject, the splitting of Breytenbach's subjectivity is not an authorial choice. Breytenbach does not have access to a number of options from which he can choose fragmentation as a mode of performance, as an author chooses from an array of tropes. To represent it as such—to call his prison writing "postmodern"—would be to extract the political context of the writing of his autobiography from its literary classification, which would consequently be rendered "postmodern"—an example of the imperial tendencies of theoretical classification systems. Breytenbach's split subjectivity is an imposed and oppressive consequence of—not his choice to uphold—the adherence of nationalist discourse to the concept of the unified subject. The schizophrenic subjectivity is imposed on Breytenbach in the service of this ideal, in which the subject is constituted as patriot by being defined as unified against an-"other." This split subjectivity cannot be read properly, then, as an act of his free will. It is an imposition that is accomplished with what one would like to think of as an extraordinary use of violence—namely, the violence of interrogation.

Introduction to the Texts: Confession, Autobiography, and the Violence of Interrogation

In the eyes of the establishment and the system that supports it, the only way for the "aberration" that Breytenbach's political views constitute to be "cured," the only way for Breytenbach to be restored to his essential "true" self, is for him to recognize the folly of his "terrorism" ("Poet in Prison" 30). This recognition would take the form of a confession.[25] The importance of such a confession to the establishment—a confession that would acknowledge the justice of the system through its acceptance of personal guilt—is indicated by the establishment never giving Breytenbach the opportunity to occupy a legal position in which he could refuse to acknowledge his "guilt."[26] Indeed, the series of repeated attempts that were made by his interrogators to elicit confessions from Breytenbach form a history of his violation during interrogation.

The curtailment of Breytenbach's participation in his own trial, the limitations imposed on his self-representation, suggest judicial procedures that appear to have much in common with—and involve similar violations of the subject as—those of the medieval penal system documented by Foucault. In Part One of *Discipline and Punish* he describes this system:

> the penal investigation was a machine that might produce the truth in the absence of the accused. And by this very fact, though the law strictly speaking did not require it, this procedure was to tend necessarily to the confession (37).

The confession takes priority over other kinds of evidence because it is the most adequate proof that the accused is guilty, that is, that the subject position created by the investigation for the accused in her or his absence is valid. It also takes priority over other kinds of evidence because it represents the accused's acceptance of his or her guilt, and therefore represents also the accused's acknowledgment of the authority of the judicial procedure:

> To a certain extent, it [the confession] transcended all other evidence; . . . it was also the act by which the accused accepted the charge and recognized its truth; it transformed an investigation carried on without him [the accused] into a voluntary affirmation (Foucault 38).

The part that the confession plays in this legal procedure is riddled with ambiguities. As in Breytenbach's case, the confession, an effect of constraint, is nevertheless viewed by those who exercise the constraint as a "semi-voluntary transaction" (Foucault 39). The confession is also both the subject of investigation (because legally confession is not by itself adequate proof of guilt, although it is the most adequate proof), and simultaneously the proof that the investigation seeks to establish (Foucault 39).

The confession is not only an object desired by Breytenbach's interrogators in the form of a statement made by him. It is also, and perhaps more importantly, the controlling figure of the acts of interpretation to which they subject Breytenbach during his interrogation. As Folena implies, and as Foucault has suggested, the interrogator's desire for the prisoner to confess should not be mistaken for the desire to discover more about the speaker of the confession. Rather, the desire for the prisoner (or potential convert) to confess is rooted in the desire to force the subject to conform to the subject position that has been created for him or her, that of the guilty party, the transgressor. The prisoner, in effect, has no "voice": everything that she or he says will be interpreted in such a way that it constitutes evidence of her or his guilt.

In this context, Breytenbach is the victim of the interrogator's hypothetical fictional constructs. Such victimization indicates that violence may well be endemic to this kind of predetermined "reading" of texts. I use "text" here in the Derridean sense, not merely to denote "book," but as sign referring to the locus of the interaction between various discourses, in this case that of the interrogator's fiction of Breytenbach's "guilt" and the reality of Breytenbach's coerced position as the prisoner who is to confess in order to conform to that fiction.[27] Breytenbach is not in a position to convince his interrogators of their errors. He cannot force them to distinguish between different types of discourse, because they only recognize the one, that of interrogation and its manipulated responses. Breytenbach can say nothing that will not be used to create his guilt in this way.[28] This act of interpretation designates him as "guilty" in order to "restore" him through forcing him to participate in the rhetoric of confession.[29]

How does Breytenbach, as prisoner, "lose his voice" through being forced to confess? Emile Benveniste proposes that language constitutes "the possibility of subjectivity because it always contains the linguistic forms appropriate to the expression of subjectivity," such as personal pronouns (227). The specific speech acts in which these linguistic forms are used, structure subjectivity: "discourse provokes the emergence of subjectivity because it consists of discrete instances" (227).[30] The pronoun "I" represents a linguistic opportunity for the expression of subjectivity which is of primary importance to the discussion of autobiographical texts.[31] In specific speech acts, the expression of subjectivity by the use of the first-person pronoun (in this case, singular) depends upon recognition of the relationship between two distinct points of reference, namely the "I" who speaks, and the "I" who is the subject of the speech. This recognition, however, does not necessitate the complete identification of the "I" who speaks with the "I" who is the subject of the speech act. Indeed, such an identification would depend upon the validity of the concept of the unified subject, a concept that Benveniste proves to be a linguistic impossibility, and which (as noted above) Althusser among others has proposed is ideologically suspect.[32]

The confessional act of interpretation to which Breytenbach is subject does not depend merely upon recognition of a connection of some sort between Breytenbach as the "I" who speaks the confession, and Breytenbach as the "I" who is the subject of the confession. Rather, this act of interpretation depends upon his interrogators' assumption of a very specific relationship between the speaker and the subject—a relationship characterized by the complete con-fusion, the mistaken full identification, of the Breytenbach who speaks, and the Breytenbach who is subject of, the confession. This act of interpretation testifies to the potential power of rhetoric to constitute subjectivity because, in this case, the interpreters—the interrogators—have the power to impose their interpretation of Breytenbach's subject position on

Breytenbach:[33] he is forced to confess that he, the subject expressed by the formula "I, Breytenbach," is guilty.

Here the interrogated is forced to submit to the interrogators' interpretation of his self-expression. In this context, in which Breytenbach is forced to recognize "I," the speaker of the confession, as equal to "I," the subject of the confession, Breytenbach "loses his voice." To use Benveniste's terms, in this "discrete instance" Breytenbach's subjectivity "emerges" as his interrogators have constructed it for him, because of their power over him. "He" is not only the subject of the confession, but subject to it:

> The prisoner will inevitably end up confessing. There can be no doubt about that. His only leeway can be to hold out, desperately, for time. He may have to decide *when* to safely let go, about how long he can hold out. . . . [Nevertheless] *He will be raped* (*TCAT* 343; some emphasis added).

In order to counter the violation constituted by this erasure of his "voice," Breytenbach needs to distinguish between his interrogator's interpretation of "his" confessional voice, and his interpretation of it. In a position precisely contrary to that of his interrogators, Breytenbach considers his survival to consist of recognizing that the "I" who speaks the confession does not coincide with the "I" who is the subject of the confession and who is also therefore subject to the confession. The interrogated, we have been told, "will be raped." His survival depends upon his recognition of this: "[The prisoner's] problem is *to realize it*" (*TCAT* 343; emphasis added). The victim of this "rape," the interrogated, can only recognize this violation as a violation if he makes the Benvenistian distinction between the "I" who is the product of the forced confession, and the "I" who is forced to speak that confession.[34]

Both confession and autobiography are marked by their peculiar potential to express subjectivity through the use of the first person singular, the "I" that is crucial to both modes of expression. The confession constitutes a violation, because it reduces the subject, Breytenbach, to that which is represented in the confession. The autobiographical project may constitute a similar violation, because it proposes a correspondence between the author represented by the name on the title page of the autobiography, and the subjectivity represented by the first-person singular pronoun that populates its narrative. This is what Philippe Lejeune calls the "autobiographical pact" (3–30). Autobiography, then, would appear to be as predisposed to violate subjectivity as the confession. The crucial question presents itself: can Breytenbach manage to be simultaneously victim and autobiographer, without inscribing himself as victim of the autobiography?

Mouroir and *The True Confessions of An Albino Terrorist* are autobiographical texts that, in different ways, come to terms simultaneously with both the violation Breytenbach suffered as victim of interrogation and the potential violation that exists in subjecting himself to autobiography. These texts are autobiographical precisely because they are representations of the difference between Breytenbach's interrogators' interpretation of the "I" who speaks the confession to them, and his interpretation of that "I." As such, *Mouroir* and the *Confessions* constitute a re-cognition of the manipulation of subjectivity as personal violation. Their importance lies not merely in their representation of their subject, but in their construction of that subject— Breytenbach—as other than imprisoned, other than he who confesses and so contributes to his own subjection.

2. *Mouroir*: Producing His-Story Without Reproducing Violation

> *Mouroir* is the work of that rarity which
> Camus despaired of finding, an individual
> who has lived, as protagonist *and* victim,
> the central experience produced by his
> time and place and who possesses a
> creative ability equal to his experience.
> —Nadine Gordimer,
> "New Notes from Underground"

Mouroir: Mirrornotes of a Novel is the work Breytenbach wrote while he was actually in prison: most of it was written during the period in which he was in solitary confinement. The text, whose form is certainly obscure, has been described as a "disturbing series of prose poems" (Egan 90). *Mouroir* consists of thirty-eight pieces, which vary in length from one to seventeen pages. Certain names and images do recur in some of the "fragments" or "prose poems," but any attempt one may make to construct a sequential narrative from the pieces is abortive, due to the radical inconsistency of the text. This inconsistency is manifest in both the content and form of the work, and has led a number of critics to label *Mouroir* as "exceedingly difficult to read" (Ascherson, "Living" 23), or as J. M. Coetzee puts it, "of less general appeal [than the *Confessions*]" ("Poet in Prison" 31). Coetzee describes the problem:

> Certain of these pieces are linked closely enough for the reader to follow an erratic,
> dreamlike narrative through them. In the main, however, one is hard put to form

the pieces into the skeleton of any conceivable novel. One is better advised to read
the book as an assemblage of stories, parables, meditations and fragments . . . (32).

Many reviewers of the work (with the prominent exceptions of J. M.
Coetzee, Susanna Egan, and Nadine Gordimer) have dealt with the "difficulty"
of the text by assuming that the conditions under which it was written explain
fully its unusual form. Certainly, the circumstances in which Breytenbach
composed *Mouroir* were unusual. Breytenbach received permission to write in
prison provided that he did not show anyone his work and that he did not
attempt to smuggle it out. When he completed any part of a work, he was to
hand it in. He was not allowed to keep notes on any work (these were to be
destroyed). In return, Breytenbach was assured that the work would be kept
and handed over to him upon his release (*TCAT* 159; Coetzee, "Breytenbach
and Censor" 71–72).[35]

Another factor that contributes to the "circumstantial evidence," as it
were, used to explain—or more often, to explain away—the unusual form of
Mouroir, is that Breytenbach frequently wrote in the dark, after the lights had
been turned off. He describes this experience in the section of the *Confessions*
entitled "The Writer Destroys Time":

> In the dark . . . there is nobody to look over my shoulder. I am relieved! Then, like
> an irrepressible urge, there would be the need to write. In the dark I can just
> perceive the faintly pale outline of a sheet of paper. And I would start writing. Like
> launching a black ship on a dark sea. I write: I am the writer. I am doing my black
> writing with my no-colour gloves and my dark glasses on, stopping every once in
> a while, passing my sheathed hand over the page to feel the outlines and the
> imprints of letters which have no profile (*TCAT* 154).

This kind of writing, Breytenbach says, imposes a certain kind of continuity
on the writer; but this continuity is diametrically opposed to the kind of
continuity that characterizes a conventional linear narrative. The "night writing" (*Mouroir* 104), Breytenbach explains,

> makes for a very specific kind of wording, perhaps akin to the experiments that
> the surrealists used to make in earlier years. . . . Since one cannot re-read what
> you've written a certain continuity is imposed on you. You have to let go. You must
> follow. You allow yourself to be carried forward by the pulsation of the words as
> they surface in [*sic*] the paper. You are the paper. Punctuation goes by the board.
> Repetitions, rhythms, structures, these will be nearly biological. Not intellectually
> conceived (*TCAT* 154–55).

The extreme circumstances under which it was written do, inevitably, reflect upon the form *Mouroir* takes. For this reason, many critics of the work have accepted that an explication of the constraints under which it was written constitute a complete explanation of both its content and its structure—or perceived lack of structure. Such critics view these constraints as sufficient explanation of the text's "surreal" subject matter and the fact that, as Nadine Gordimer puts it, in *Mouroir* "narrative is an old railway line on which service has been discontinued" ("New Notes" 115).[36] However, to accept such explanations as adequate, is to relegate *Mouroir* to the status of a consequence of its author's victimization, rather than to explore the way in which the text confronts the fact of that violation.

In my discussion of Breytenbach's violation in the context of *Mouroir*, I do intend to take into account the circumstances in which it was produced, but I do not want to "explain" *Mouroir* as the "result" of Breytenbach's imprisonment. Rather, I wish to explore *Mouroir* in terms of the unique relationship between its ontological status and its literary form. By the text's ontological status, I mean its function as a support mechanism for Breytenbach during the period of his incarceration and its composition. In order to approach *Mouroir* as the trace of its author's violations and to view the curious nature of the formulation of this trace in the text, we need to define precisely how *Mouroir* constitutes autobiography.[37]

Many of the "narratives" in *Mouroir* are in the third person ("The Temptation in Rome"; "The Day of the Falling Stars"), or are addressed to a second person ("Tuesday"). In the latter case a first person is implied by the you-(I) opposition, but is not stated. Some do employ a first-person singular narrative voice ("And More"; "Wiederholen"). However, this voice—or rather, these voices—are not identifiable consistently across all the "narratives" that employ them as belonging to a single character, and may even change referents within a single piece (the "I" who begins "The Collapse" is clearly not identical to the "I" who concludes it, although they may—or may not—be related).[38] *Mouroir* cannot be discussed in terms of Lejeune's "autobiographical pact" then, since there is no "I" that inhabits the text that can be identified as corresponding to both its author and a single protagonist representing that author.[39] There is not even a way of reading the "I"'s employed by the "narrative"[40] as representing an inconsistent or qualified set of such correspondences (such as the narrative voice of the *Confessions* may be read).

Mouroir, then, cannot be considered autobiographical in the same sense that we consider, for example, Augustine's *Confessions*, or even Breytenbach's *Confessions*, to be autobiographical, because of the radical instability of the subject(s) represented by the personal pronouns in its "narrative."

This leads Egan to conclude that "in the long run, no one except Breytenbach can say for certain whether or not this work is autobiographical" (103). However, it is possible to move the question of autobiographical authenticity away from the context of the author's stated intention, and toward the nature of the reference made within the text to the author. This approach to autobiography allows us to concentrate on the relationship between the problem with which the autobiographer is presented—his violation by imprisonment—and the problems that he presents himself with in his writing. In other words, it allows us to discuss *Mouroir* both as an expression of Breytenbach's experience of violation in prison (albeit a less obvious one than the *Confessions*), and as an element of that experience.

In addition, this approach lends itself to the notion of a type of autobiographical writing that would accommodate, or perhaps even require, the use of the fantastic for its success. Such an autobiography would avoid the genre's traditional dependence on a division between reality and fiction, which poses as a symmetrical relationship between the two, in order to avoid replicating the violence experienced by its subject. Fiction would not "follow" reality, would not attempt to document, or re-semble, the subject's history of violation; rather, its validity as autobiography would lie in the degree to which the text came to terms with the violation re-presented by that history.

What I mean by a symmetrical relationship between reality and fiction may be explained further through an examination of the most persistent image in *Mouroir*, that of the mirror. Both its title and subtitle suggest the importance of the mirror image to the work. As Gordimer and Coetzee have noted, Breytenbach's polylingualism enables him to engage in extensive word-play, an activity that is reflected in the titles of this text. The original title (that of the bilingual edition) consists of the French word *mouroir*, with an Afrikaans phrase, *bespieëlende notas van 'n roman*, serving as a subtitle. In his English version of the work, Breytenbach leaves the word *mouroir* untranslated, but renders the subtitle in English as "mirrornotes of a novel." Gordimer remarks that

> Although *mouroir* is the word for "old people's home," it seems he [Breytenbach] has re-interpreted it as a dovetailing of *mourir* (to die) and *miroir* (a mirror) ("New Notes" 114).

This linking of the image of the mirror, or rather, the image in the mirror, with death alerts us to metafictional elements in *Mouroir* that suggest that a certain logic underlies the "difficult" structure of the work.

The mirror image in *Mouroir* plays a part in what may be described as the work's re-telling of the Lacanian mirror phase. This function of the image is demonstrated in the form of an allegory in the piece entitled "The Day of the Falling Stars and Searching for the Original Face." This piece tells of a "boy" who lives with a herd of gazelles and believes himself to be one of them. The "Academy," we are told, decides that he must be captured and returned to "civilization," for "they felt that it was the destiny of man to advance" (85). They continue to refer to their intended captive as "Boy," even though they have seen through their binoculars that he has a beard. They decide on the method of his capture, which is to flash a mirror at him. This strategy is chosen because "what was needed . . . was for Boy *to see himself* and . . . see the relatedness between himself and those wishing to capture him." In this way he would "become alienated from his mates" (87):

> The Academicians took out their mirrors and flashed them, flashed the authority of death which is the reflection of loneliness. . . .
>
> Boy saw. He advanced and he observed the deer he had always seen, but so distant and so small now. He also perceived among the gazelles something, a being, a creature resembling those standing behind the surfaces looking at him and making hawking noises. . . . He . . . advanced toward the pools of water held aloft as if by magic. He didn't realize that he was looking behind reality. He didn't know that these tongues could never be lapped up or integrated. He was not aware that he was to forgo for ever the taste of water (88).

This allegory rehearses the Lacanian model of the mirror phase. Between the ages of six and eighteen months, Lacan tells us, the subject differentiates between itself and that which is other. As Kaja Silverman points out, it therefore arrives at an apprehension of "its self *as other*" (157). This recognition is aided or precipitated by the child seeing itself for the first time in a mirror. The reflection exhibits a coherence to the subject which causes it, a child "still sunk in his motor incapacity and nursling dependence" (Lacan, *Ecrits* 2), to perceive the reflection as an ideal image in relation to which the subject sees itself as lacking.

The mirror phase manifests the process that Freud outlines in his description of the developing relationships between the id, and in particular, between the ego and the superego. However, the point that Lacan stresses, one that is of paramount importance to this discussion, is that the ideal image that causes the subject to experience itself as lacking is itself a fictional construct. This image is not a reflection of some sort of fundamental coherence that is attainable by the subject in actual terms. However, the subject interprets the image that way—as the goal that epitomizes self-mastery and independence— and the image structures the subject's desires accordingly:

> But the important point is that this form [the "Ideal-I" represented for the subject
> by the mirror image] situates the agency of the ego, before its social determina-
> tion, *in a fictional direction*, which will always remain irreducible for the individual
> alone (2; emphasis added).

The fictional status of the image in the mirror allows Breytenbach to use the image of the mirror metafictionally. In the Lacanian mirror phase, the relationship between the subject and the image in the mirror is structured by the goal of symmetry between the two: the subject desires itself to "match" the image in the mirror. In "The Day of the Falling Stars" "Boy" is captured by his seeing himself in the mirror (and, significantly, not in a pool of water, which is a substance that moves): he unwittingly "catches himself in the mirror." Breytenbach uses this image, that of the mirror image that "fixes" that which it reflects, to reflect upon the relationship between ideology and its subjects, and writing and its subjects. As his allegory suggests, Breytenbach sees in the specular nature of the image—be it the nationalist discourse's image of him or the image of himself he constructs in his own writing—a certain trap, or prison: a potential violation.

In the *Confessions* Breytenbach indicates that the kind of self-reflexive activity for which the Lacanian fable provides a juvenile origin is necessary; indeed, he indicates that in the case of his personal experience of imprison-ment, his survival depended upon it. He explains that he had the urge to write while he was in solitary confinement because, in the absence of human contact, he needed the writing as a kind of mirror, a reflection of his existence:

> Writing becomes for me a means, a way of survival. I have to cut up my environ-
> ment into digestible chunks. Writing is an extension of my senses. It is itself a
> sense which permits me to grasp, to understand, and to some extent integrate that
> which is happening to me (*TCAT* 155).[41]

Breytenbach indicates here that he needs to exercise some measure of control over his experiences by writing about them.[42] That this self-reflexive activity was key to his survival in prison is further indicated by his comments in the *Confessions* on the importance to him of the manuscripts that later became *Mouroir*. These writings are closely associated with his sense of his own iden-tity. He tells of how he spoke to anyone who visited him in prison about them, in order to establish their existence both for himself and to the external world, and speaks of the importance of obtaining guarantees from the prison officials that the material would be returned to him upon his release.[43] He describes how, on his way back to Paris after his release, the airport officials at Port

Elizabeth wanted to do a routine check of his briefcase for explosives, but he did not want to hand it over because it contained the manuscripts: "*They* were looking for bombs and *I* was hanging on to the fragmentary scenario of my identities" (*TCAT* 331).

I have gone to some trouble to establish the importance of these writings to Breytenbach in order to convey that, while Breytenbach expresses certain fears concerning the nature of the activity of self-reflection, he by no means suggests that this activity—one that he accomplishes by writing—should not take place. Indeed, he goes so far as to imply that existence without self-reflection is impossible. However, he is at pains to express his reservations about the type of reflection that demands absolute symmetry between the image and its subject.

Breytenbach raises these concerns in his expression of his own anxiety in writing the pieces that constitute *Mouroir*. For while this writing provided him with a means of control and therefore of escape, it also represented, paradoxically, the specter of imprisonment:

> I need it [writing] in the same way the blind man behind his black glasses needs to see. But at the same time I soon realize that it becomes the exteriorization of my imprisonment. My writing bounces off the walls. The maze of words which become like alleys, like sentences, the loops which are closed circuits and present no exit, these themselves constitute the walls of my confinement (*TCAT* 155).

As in his allegory, the words come to constitute an image of himself as a prisoner to such a degree that the image itself mesmerizes, or horrifies, him. By writing, then, he may come—like "Boy"—to imprison himself unwittingly, by "catching himself in the mirror":

> I write my own castle and it becomes a frightening discovery: it is unbalancing something very deeply embedded in yourself when you in reality construct, through your scribblings, your own mirror. Because in this mirror you write hair by hair and pore by pore your own face, and you don't like what you see (*TCAT* 155).

Just as Lacan's image in the mirror is external and inaccessible to the subject, and yet the subject binds itself to that image, so Breytenbach speaks of the image he creates of himself in his writing: "You don't even recognize it," he says, but "it won't let you out again" (*TCAT* 156).

This imprisonment, established by what may be called the hegemony of the image, Breytenbach associates with (as the narrator of the allegory puts it) "the authority of death" (*Mouroir* 88). When words construct, or are read as constructing, an image that commands such absolute symmetry, they invoke a stasis or fixity that Breytenbach expresses through images of death: images not of decomposition, but of sudden violent death, such as execution. In J. M. Coetzee's words, *Mouroir*

> is a kind of Ariadne's thread that Breytenbach spins behind himself as he advances through the labyrinth of his fictionalizing toward a meeting with something that is both the self beckoning from the mirror—Mister I—and the monstrous other who will not be recuperated into amity: Death ("Breytenbach and Censor" 79–80).

Although the concept of symmetrical representation by word images is linked with images of death throughout *Mouroir*, this connection is explicit in the piece entitled "The Double Dying of an Ordinary Criminal."

This piece is concerned with scenes and methods of execution.[44] The narrator of this section explains that in writing a description of the execution of the criminal, s/he performs a second "murder:" her or his re-telling of the event constructs an image that "traps" the victim exclusively as victim at/in the moment of her or his execution. This is one of the senses in which the criminal "dies twice." The narrator is anxious to point out that this second death is the responsibility of the writer who, according to the logic of symmetrical representation, repeats the violation without difference. "It is a literary phenomenon I'd like to point out to my colleagues," she or he tells us: "Reality is a version of the mirror image" (62).[45] She or he goes on to document the manner in which the act of writing effects a second death by documenting the first, thereby implicating the writer in the violation:

> I am part of the ritual. The pen twists the rope. From the pen he is hanged. . . . He hangs in the mirror. But where in reality he is separated—conceivably in spirit or vision and growth of flesh draped over humid bone—hanged, taken down, plowed under—each of these steps remains preserved in the mirror. The mirror mummifies each consecutive instant, apparently never runs over, but ignores as far as we know all decay and knows for sure no time. . . . He thus keeps on hanging and kicking in the remembrance (62; Taurus *Mouroir* 50).

This horrific catching of the writer in her or his own trap is illustrated in several episodes of the text that are characterized by a specific metafictional quality. An example of this is found in "Book, a Mirror." Susanna Egan's succinct summary of this episode not only alerts us to the level of metafiction we have been discussing—the relationship between the author and his writing—but also to the levels of metafiction created in *Mouroir* by the appearance of characters from other writers' works and the reappearance of Breytenbach's characters in a number of different episodes:

> In a remarkable section called "Book, a Mirror," the writer Angelo, in company with his disturbed friend, Gregor Samsa, who is director of a prison, is taken to an underground travelling library. Not only does Angelo find one of Breytenbach's titles by D. Espejuelo, but he also reads about the pope and the space travel that we have already encountered in *Mouroir*, and then finds himself reading the story of which he is now a part. Like Aureliano Babilonia at the end of *One Hundred Years of Solitude*, he reads ahead, ostensibly to discover what happens next, in fact to discover his own dissolution: "the visitor truly loses all sense and knowledge of his own suchness (*quiditas*), decomposes, becomes absorbed in" (*Mouroir*, p. 180) [Taurus *Mouroir* 165]. The quiditas that decomposes is the story, which fails to continue. It is also the writer, who is only a character and must read ahead in search of a conclusion. And it is the character who has no writer to provide a denouement (96).

Another illustration of the writer catching herself or himself in her or his own trap is presented in "And Move." In this piece the writer-narrator is persuaded by one of her or his two friends, Galgenvogel ("Gallowsbird") and Tuckverderber[46] (or Galgenvoel and Tuchverderber; as with many names in the text, these have variations) to write a conventional story. They accuse the narrator of being "prolix, verbose," and "weighty," which, she or he tells us in parentheses, "is exactly to the point" (121). (Breytenbach, it would seem, had foreseen the criticism his prose would receive on account of its "difficulty"!) The story they want him or her to write is in the realist mode; it is, as J. M. Coetzee puts it, "a conventional bourgeois tale of suburban adultery" ("Poet in Prison" 32).[47] Finally the narrator agrees to write such a story, attempting to ignore the fact that, as she or he puts it, her or his trousers are soaked in "the thin blood from bloated horses' heads" (121). The writer of the conventional tale, it would seem, will be overcome by the violence he cannot describe, or chooses to ignore. The outcome of this attempt is described by Coetzee: "he plods on . . . till the fictional world he has created turns nasty, takes on a life of its own, and rends him" ("Poet in Prison" 32). Tuchverderber and Galgenvogel ("one of them—or it might have been both") betray the narrator as character just as they have betrayed her or him as writer: at the end of the story they produce a ceremonial slaughter knife, "a steely white flash-tongue of all clarity and knowingness and simplicity," and plunge it "into the layers of my [the narrator's] dumbness" (126).

In texts published after the *Confessions* and *Mouroir* Breytenbach comments on the broader ideological implications of narratives that adhere without compromise to the principle of absolute symmetry between the image and its subject. In a piece entitled "Self-Portrait/Deathwatch" that concludes *Judas Eye* (1988), Breytenbach critiques the kind of ordering, or determinism, which *Mouroir* identifies as an assumption of the symmetrical approach to representation. In the section entitled "Black/White" he argues that such determinism is the hallmark of discourses—such as those of Calvinist Christianity, imperialism, and apartheid—that seek to consolidate their power by authoritarian means:

> Calvinists hold to the dogma of pre-destination. Essentially it means coming to terms with being part of God's embroidery. It means, I think, accepting the salutary relief of fatalism (125).

The order of religious fatalism is also that of adherence to the law, as in law and order:

> This order has its temporal translation. Our terrestrial masters have the God-given *right* to rule and the interests of the State are paramount. (The State is God incarnate among men.) Many roads lead to totalitarianism, the power malady, but the above conception constitutes, I dare believe, a short cut to the priorities of law and security, to the inviolability of property, to the entrenched privileges of the strong; to holy wars, capital punishment, torture, whiteness and charity (125).

This ordering, or determinism, issues from a firm belief that everything can be represented, that everything can be named. Naming, as Breytenbach argues in *Mouroir*, is an attempt to control: "Naming is taming. It is casting the arbitrary over the unknown" (84). Thus even those unruly historical, geographical, and psychological "territories" that remain as yet not fully "discovered" must be "mapped." Breytenbach collapses the distinctions between these kinds of territories, indicating to what degree they have become properties of Western notions of the "other":

> It [predestination] also implies assuming that there is an *order* . . . to all that quiver and copulate in the celestial spheres and down hither—even down into the past or into the murky subconscious which, of course, is the passage to India discovered by Christopher Freud (*Judas Eye* 125).

How can this order, this determinism, be ruptured? Or to put the question in its literary context, how does the writer or reader come to terms with the horror generated by the fixity of the images that he or she constructs? In the specific context of Breytenbach's autobiography, the question can be re-phrased as, can Breytenbach manage to be simultaneously victim and auto-biographer, without victimizing himself for a second time in his autobiography? How can he avoid the "double dying" to which he subjects the "ordinary criminal?" In his conclusion to "The Double Dying of an Ordinary Criminal," Breytenbach writes that at first there may appear to be no escape from this "death-trap," but then proceeds to suggest that the writer may be capable of re-presenting death as part of a process of resurrection, or re-creation.[48] This is an alternative "second death" to that of the mirror image:

> the writer just as the reader (because the reader is a mirror to the writer) can seemingly make nothing undone. He cannot reopen the earth, cannot set the snapped neck, cannot stuff the spirit back into the flesh and the light of life in the lustreless eyes full of sand, cannot straighten the mother's back, cannot raise the assassinated, cannot reduce the man to a seed in the woman's loins while a hot wind streams over the Coast?
>
> Or can he?
>
> Is that the second death? (62–63; Taurus *Mouroir* 50–51).

How can this alternative "second death" be realized? What form does Breytenbach suggest that this alternative would take?

In *End Papers* (1986) and *Judas Eye*, Breytenbach has theorized about the way in which the relentless logic of determinism may be "broken." He proposes that the fixity of the image can, or rather should, be compromised. The writer or reader, artist or viewer, can disrupt the power that the image wields over them as its potential subjects.[49] This strategy employs a way of reading or seeing that involves envisioning that which is absent, rather than recording that which is present.[50] This metaphysics of absence involves a rejection of the validity of appearance and an inscribing of that which is fantastic, or novel; it is fantastic not because it is to be forever impossible, but only because it is being represented in the confines of the present.

In "Self-Portrait/Deathwatch: A Note on Autobiography" Breytenbach argues that "History . . . is stained by the dead weight of what you have lived through" (*Judas Eye* 123). History, viewed as a discipline in which proof consists of the determination of a monological "truth," involves the violent eradication of options. This applies to the history of paintings or texts, as well as personal history. "'Completing' a work is simply a matter, step by step, of reducing the choices," a process that produces and simultaneously seeks to suppress a number of "murdered what-ifs" along the way (*End Papers*

140). Personal history is liable to replicate this determinism—and the violence of this determinism, which exists in its brutal reductionism—"because memory," operating as a function to reproduce as present that which is past, "is [also] a prison" (*End Papers* 87).

Breytenbach argues that in order to rupture this violent logic, to wake up "from the coma of cause and effect" (*Judas Eye* 125), one needs to view history differently; or rather, one needs to view history as difference.[51] One can create history, rather than being determined by it, if one sees history as "the mother of invention," not because the past defines the (a single) present, but because "it also delineates the absence of what you did not experience" (*Judas Eye* 123). One counters a fatal determinism, then, by re-inscribing the potential, re-presenting that which is always already "other": history is re-generated as story. These stories, although they cannot protect Breytenbach from the terror inflicted upon him, at least help him to recognize, and thus attempt to counter, his victimization.

Mouroir manifests this way of "seeing" or "reading" history in the literary context of autobiography. Through *Mouroir*, Breytenbach counters the prison of history erected by memory. By writing *Mouroir*, Breytenbach literally gives himself an alternative history to that of his victimization. This history does not erase or replace that of his victimization, but it allows him to be something in addition to, something other than, victim. He achieves this "interstice of freedom" (*End Papers* 146) by re-presenting himself in the text as other or/and other(s): herein lies the conjunction between the autobiographical and the fantastic in *Mouroir*.

In "Self/Portrait/Deathwatch" Breytenbach outlines a plan for writing an effective autobiography, a plan he has followed in *Mouroir*. He points out that an autobiography that attempts to construct an image of the self that is identical, or a symmetrical representation of, the self, is sabotaged by the fixity of the image of its writer before it is even begun: "If I do thus write about some id or other oddment it must be dead," he claims. "Therefore I cannot write about me" (*Judas Eye* 123). Breytenbach suggests an alternative form of autobiography, one which can be described as his attempt to "read" himself as he suggests that history should be "read." In this autobiography he attempts to re-invent himself through the documentation of that which is other. The "others" he mentions here are a series of his "characters" or alter egos, many of whom participate, as it were, in *Mouroir*:

> It would be more illuminating to trace the trajectories of Panus, Elephterià, King Fool, Don Espejuelo, Geta Wof, Jan Blom ["Flower"], Vagina Jones, Lazarus, Comrade Ekx, Afrika Aap ["Monkey"], Bangai Bird . . . To get *you* at the tip of my pen

and/or into the word processor: I the Other or/and the other Other. Or to be free to create the third persons (*Judas Eye* 123).

This form of autobiography, of which I am arguing *Mouroir* is an example, poses a relationship between images of the other and the self, of writing and reality, of survival and death, a relationship that is analogous to the relationship that Rosemary Jackson contends that the mode of fantasy holds in relation to the monological form of the novel.[52] Significantly, Jackson uses the concept of a mirror image that is reflective, but not symmetrical because it is "unrecognizable," to describe the relationship between the realistic and the fantastic. She also argues that the fantastic does not erase or replace the horrific effect of the real, but exercises a formative critical function in relation to it:

> The fantastic exists as the inside, or underside, of realism, opposing the novel's closed, monological forms with open, dialogical structures, as if the novel had given rise to its own opposite, its unrecognizable reflection. . . . The fantastic gives utterance to precisely those elements which are known only through their absence within a 'dominant' realistic order.
> . . . What could be termed a 'bourgeois' category of the real is under attack. It is this *negative relationality* which constitutes the meaning of the modern fantastic (25–26).

Mouroir functions in a position of "negative relationality" to the category of the real with regard to both its subject and its form. The terror Breytenbach was experiencing during its composition occupies the position of the text's subject in terms of Jackson's "negative relationality"; and the form of the text occupies an analogous position in relation to conventional literary forms, especially that of "realistic" autobiography.

Mouroir's persistent refusal at all costs to locate a "self" and an "other" results in a discourse concerned to re-present the potential, and not that of the real (the material, in the sense of what has already materialized). Because that which is potential is that which is not yet chosen. This discourse is characterized by multiplicity and an attendant lack of author-ity (distinctive features of Jackson's fantastic). Indeed, the only property of the *Mouroir* "narratives" that can be "characterized" is the nature of their re-presentation—their form— which is itself inconsistent. The "narratives" use forms as divergent as the allegorical, the dramatic, and the poetic. Their re-presentation operates according to the logic, or rather antilogic, of metamorphosis, not the logic of metaphor: "Metamorphosis, after all, 'manifests' or accomplishes itself from form to and into form" (*End Papers* 111); or, "the heart of the labyrinth is not attained. Instead, a new surface recurs at every turn, becoming a point of entry into yet another branch of the labyrinth" (J. M. Coetzee, "Breytenbach and Censor" 80). This results in the fluidity of the "narrative" that so many of *Mouroir*'s reviewers have found disturbing.

The attempt to re-present the potential as possible in narrative results in narrative forms that do play havoc with "the classical unities of space, time and character" (Jackson 46). That *Mouroir* is exemplary of such "novel" forms can be seen, for example, by the "narratives'" deconstruction of character. Because the "narratives" disable, rather than enable, the identification of their subjects', "character," in the sense of what Hélène Cixous terms "personage" or what we have termed "fixed image," does not exist in the *Mouroir*.

> By definition, a "character," preconceived or created by an author, is to be *figured out*, understood, read: he is presented, offered up to interpretation, with the prospect of a traditional reading that seeks its satisfaction at the level of a potential identification with such and such a "personage" . . . (385).

Instead, in *Mouroir* we get "characters" that may or may not be related, that drop out of the "narrative" altogether, or even metamorphose into other "characters." This instability extends to the author as "character," ensuring that the author is not violated, that he is not "offered up to interpretation." Cixous describes this form of "characterization," which renders "personage" an invalid concept, in terms of escape and invention. In using these terms, Cixous' explication describes Breytenbach's disappearance as "Breytenbach = victim" both through (the writing of) and in (as "character" of) *Mouroir*.

> In texts that evade standard codes, the "personage" is, in fact, Nobody—he is that which escapes and leads somewhere else. . . . Fortunately, even when Nobody is dubbed with names of "characters," when Nobody is alive, there is still part of his subjectivity that remains unassigned, on which the code has no hold, which disorganizes the discourse, and which produces itself (it is not produced or reproduced or reproductive, but inventive and formative) ("Character" 387–88).

Mouroir constitutes an act of defiance against violence which is not simply personal. As Frederic Jameson ("Magical Narratives" 133–63) and Lucia Folena (among others) have argued, the naming of the other is an ideological act: "the identification, the naming of otherness . . . is a telling index of a society's religious and political beliefs" (Jackson 52). The refusal to identify that which is other, and the desire not to "fix" notions of the self which that refusal implies, is also an act of significant ideological proportions, and a subversive one at that.

Mouroir's refusal to employ the conventional machinery of characterization constitutes an attempt to undermine the notion of the fixed, unified subject. The concept of the unified subject is crucial for the kind of ideological "sell job" with which Breytenbach's captors attempted to terrorize him. For if the subject is to see itself as failing to conform, it must see itself as failing to conform to an image of itself which it believes to be "right" or "natural." The discourse of power can only utilize the opportunity to present the image of the subject which it requires for its own perpetuation to its subjects, if it conceals the "constructedness," the artificial nature of that image by presenting that image as "fixed"; that is, as the only one conceivable:

> The machine of repression has always had the same accomplices; homogenizing, reductive, unifying reason has always allied itself to the Master, to the single, stable, socializable subject, represented by its types or characters ("Character" 389).

This subversive move, the dismemberment of the concept of the unified subject, can also be seen as a recognition and rejection of the Althusserian subject of the state—the "end product," in this particular case, of the Afrikaner nationalist attempt to constitute individuals as subject to its dictates, to "father" patriots. In this context Breytenbach's resistance can be conceived of as one that questions, rather than describes, the histories of "civilization" given in the genre of Western philosophy and psychoanalysis. If, for the sake of example, the Freudian family, or its equally dubious relation, the Lacanian symbolic order, contributes to form the medium in which a society's image of itself is constructed, it also plays a part in the medium that enables terrorization of those who refuse to conform to that image. Fanon recognized the cultural limitations of such myths in his emphasis on the necessity of replacing Freud's Oedipus complex with the confrontation of the white as the founding scenario of black colonial psychic development; Breytenbach makes a similar recognition in his comment, that predestination assumes an order "even down into the past or into the murky subconscious which, of course, is the passage to India discovered by Freud" (*Judas Eye* 125)—history, the colonies, literature, the subconscious—these have all become the realms of imperialist dogma.[53] The formative myths of "civilization" cannot escape their genesis in ideological assumptions of one sort or another, and resistance can only be effective if it recognizes the effects of those assumptions:

> what, concretely, is this uncriticized ideology if not simply the 'familiar,' 'well known,' transparent myths in which a society or an age can recognize itself (but

not know itself), the mirror it looks into for self-recognition, precisely the mirror it must break if it is to know itself? What is the ideology of a society or a period if it is not that society's or period's consciousness of itself, that is, an immediate material which spontaneously implies, looks for and naturally finds its forms in the image of a consciousness of self living the totality of its world in the transparency of its own myths? (Althusser, *For Marx* 144).

The extent to which these ideological discourses are tyrannical depends, once again then, on their capacity to instil the belief that subjects are unified. For if a subject can be fully named or "fixed," it can also be controlled or repressed, terrorized into the paralysis of either conformity or disempowered horror: the "naming is taming" phenomenon. The "characterization" which is not characterization that we find in *Mouroir* is an attempt to take advantage of the fact that "Being several and insubordinable, the subject can resist subjugation" (Cixous 387); or that, in Breytenbach's own words, "Metamorphosis . . . has no truck at all with repression" (*End Papers* 111).

Paradoxically then, the autonomy of the subject—its power to resist violation—lies in the de-stabilization, not the assertion, of the concept of the unified subject. This de-stabilization is evident in many recent novels, in particular those belonging to the postmodern tradition. *Mouroir*, which I have tried to consider as an example of a postcolonial approach to examining violations of subjectivity, has elements in common with, but is radically distinct from, this postmodern project. The point of difference lies in the relationship of the author to his or her text. The "breaking of the mirror" in the literary context may appear, particularly in postmodern fiction and its closely allied critical tradition, as the consequence of an aesthetic or political choice. In the case of *Mouroir*, Breytenbach has indicated, the deconstruction of the "I," the image of the ego, was necessary for the purpose of immediate survival.

In the *Confessions*, Breytenbach argues that he did not survive in prison in the way that many of his supporters think of him as having "survived." He does not evaluate his living as a prisoner as a form of resistance:

> People say, *but prison is a clear instance of opposition, of resistance.* I say, *resistance, if that is what you want to call survival, is made up of a million little compromises and humiliations, so subtle that the human eye cannot perceive them* (258).

For Breytenbach such survival constitutes a form of submission; it is a condition born of the necessity to conform to the mirror image created for him by his captors to ensure, to the best of his limited ability, his own physical survival. Thus, he claims, "I did not survive. This is important to point out" (*TCAT*

308). Breytenbach privileges resistance of a different kind, that which involves the dismemberment of the ego, in the struggle against violation. A death of sorts does take place, but only to inaugurate the possibility of survival without compliance, survival without self-violation:

> It is important that you consciously (I'd be apt to say 'personally') assist at the putting down of the I. That is if you wish to parry destruction, to unsurvive. . . . The I not only as a concept of (para)physicality, as a screen of illusions, as a hole-ness—but in its most mundane manifestations (*TCAT* 308).

This task—that of raising the possibility of survival without ignoring violation by employing a rhetoric of (impossible) recuperation—is one that Breytenbach associates with writers who are in one way or another exiles, or individuals "torn from [their] 'natural background,'" such as James Joyce, Julio Cortazar, Jean Genet, and Withold Gombrowicz. In his discussion of the work of these authors, he can be seen to describe his own literary project of survival, the contestation of violation in the writing—and reading—of *Mouroir*:

> Exile becomes a confrontation with the I, leads to a mating with the phantom ego. The destruction of the ego-perception, that *deus ex machina*, opens the way to the kaleidoscope of creation. We have the (desperate) communications of the disintegrating seer coming to grips with his broken vision of an incomplete reality in and through a language going to pieces (*End Papers* 153).

It is in—and from—this context that Breytenbach claims that "Art is the matter of survival" (*End Papers* 146).

3. The Relationship Between Confession and Autobiography in *The True Confessions of an Albino Terrorist*

The True Confessions of An Albino Terrorist was dictated by Breytenbach to his wife, Yolande (Hoang Lien) Breytenbach, in the weeks immediately following his release. This was done in an attempt to "purge" himself of his prison experiences, a move that was impossible for him when he wrote *Mouroir*. The project of the *Confessions* is, consequently, an urgent one: "Now I must get rid of the unreality. I must vomit. I must eject this darkness. . . . You must allow me to regurgitate all the words, like the arabesques of a blind mind" (*TCAT* 27).[54]

Because it was dictated by Breytenbach's need to tell the story of his imprisonment and interrogation, the *Confessions* offers the reader more in the way of linear narrative than *Mouroir* does. The text may appear at first to provide, as Egan argues that it does, "all the usual advantages of valuable auto-biography, the authority, the perspective, the ability to make sense for others of what is already intelligible to the narrating self" (90); in other words, all the attributes of conventional autobiography. Yet the *Confessions* is, ultimately, not a conventional autobiography; if anything, it is a parody of that convention.

The narrative tells the history of the violations that Breytenbach ex-perienced in prison, particularly the violence of interrogation. The representa-tion of this violation in the text repeats or "mirrors" that violation, to the extent that it employs a measure of consistency in the treatment of subjects and their histories. That is to say, the *Confessions*, at least when it is compared with *Mouroir*, would appear to represent a more conventional notion of his-tory: one that renders history accessible and nameable. In this respect, the *Confessions* risks being read as if it were a text that represents a "fixed" truth for all time—and risks the violations attendant upon such a reading—in a way that *Mouroir* never does, or rather, never could.

The narrative takes the necessary risk of documenting several horri-fying incidents, such as the attempts at self-destruction by prisoners (230–31); the prevalence of sodomy, accepted as a fact of prison life by the warders (270); the occurrence of murder and cannibalism among prisoners (272); and the pervasive, endemic violence of the warders in the system. But, as Breytenbach identifies and despises the voyeuristic response of the warders such as Huntingdon to his own misery, he recognizes and attempts to avoid tempting his readers to participate in an analogous voyeurism.

This reluctance to encourage voyeurism in his readers is evident in the narrative. For example, having listed a number of methods of suicide, Breytenbach abruptly concludes the paragraph, stating that "this [discussion] opens up the whole chapter of suicides proper, which perhaps need more atten-tion" (231). If more attention is given to the topic of suicide in the *Confessions*, it is not given in the form of direct observation as it is, briefly, in the passage that precedes this disclaimer. In another, more obvious example, Breytenbach chastises his reader for assuming that the murder and cannibalism that he documents among the prisoners is attributable to the secret and incestuous world of either the "prison" or the "tribe"—assumptions in which both collec-tives become voyeuristically constructed as exotic, othered spaces by the reader:

> These men eat human flesh as rats will devour each other—for similar reasons—
> and not because it has ever been 'traditional' anywhere. Don't try to shrug it off

by saying 'they' are not like 'us'. Don't go and look for so-called Cultural so-called
Differences . . . When you decide to release these confessions, Mr. Investigator,
you will have smoothly combed prison spokesmen denying *en bloc* the veracity of
what I'm telling you. They will be sitting in smart offices, far away from the
stinking death lying in the cells, and their civilized mouths will produce bureau-
cratic appeals to your 'understanding'—how frail is human nature!—by admitting
to exceptions which have all been investigated, with the guilty ones punished. Will
you be taken in? I'm telling you that what I am describing is *typical* of that mirror
which the South African penal universe holds up to the Apartheid society—and
that it is *inevitable* (272–73).

Here Breytenbach attempts to prevent a voyeuristic reading of his text by
pointing out that the horrors he describes are an inevitable consequence of
apartheid and its effects on the lives of black prisoners, not the result of an
essential cultural tendency of either inmate life, or black identity (a familiarly
racist conceit), or both combined.

    Both statements made in the *Confessions* and the structure of its
narrative attempt to avoid the situation in which readers would be tempted to
view Breytenbach as he fears the victims of the apartheid prison system will be
viewed, or as Huntingdon views him—with an attitude of fascinated horror,
which simultaneously fixes the victim as a victim for all time, and offers the
viewer the safety of distance and the opportunity for voyeuristic sadism.
Breytenbach constantly inserts *Mouroir*-like statements that suggest that he is
uneasy with the notion that the *Confessions* constitute an exclusively authoritative version of events, "the last word" on the subject of himself as a victim
of political terrorization. "I don't think there is any total objectivity ever," he
says (338). Readings that depend upon the fundamentalist concept of realism
associated with a belief in total objectivity as possible deny process and invite
the tyranny of the Lacanian mirror. "Nothing is as illusory as the real,"
Breytenbach points out (241): "Reality is that illusion that will be executed"
(239). And "The I is out. It is outside the walls [of words]. . . . If it can be
written about, it doesn't exist" (241). Autobiographical representation in the
Confessions then, while it repeats the story of Breytenbach's imprisonment and
interrogation, self-consciously attempts to avoid repeating the violation of his
subjectivity which that experience entailed. He refuses to write a conventional
history of his prison experience, one which would assume that his subjectivity
can be reduced to his status as prisoner. Such an assumption would force him
to relive, rather than to contest, his victimization in his writing of it.

    In the *Confessions* the confession is both an object sought by those
who violate Breytenbach, and the metaphor that he uses to describe the precise

nature of that violation. Breytenbach invokes the form of the confession to convey his victimization during interrogation: the narrator and narratee replicate to some degree the positions of confessing subject and confessor. Unlike the narrators in *Mouroir*, there is an "I" who speaks the *Confessions* who can be identified with its author, Breytenbach; and the "confessions" are, for the most part, addressed to a "Mr Investigator," who is occasionally referred to as "your Honour" or "Mr Eye" (as is evident in some of the quotations I have already drawn from the text).

Because the "I" that inhabits the narrative of the *Confessions* can, at many points in the narrative, be identified with Breytenbach, it is tempting to assume that the *Confessions* as a whole invokes Lejeune's "autobiographical pact." This would enable the reader of the text to interpret the series of correspondences between the author, the narrator, and the protagonist that the autobiographical convention invokes as a series of complete identifications. In this case the narratee, the "you" who is (following Benveniste) always implied by the enunciation of the "I," recognizes the identity of the author of the autobiography as coincidental in her or his entirety with both its narrator and its protagonist. If this scheme for reading Breytenbach's post-prison narrative is followed, Breytenbach as writer of the *Confessions*, Breytenbach as the assumed narrator of the *Confessions*, and Breytenbach as character in the *Confessions*, become exactly coincidental with one another. However, Lejeune's model for reading autobiography proves to be inadequate to this particular text. For even if we overlook the fact that the "I" who speaks the "confessions" is not always readily identifiable as Breytenbach, there is still the problem of the narratee: why does Breytenbach address his narrative to a number of persons, chief among which is not a "Dear reader," but a "Mr Investigator"?

The reason for employing this form of address is that the binary opposition confessor/confessing subject reflects and therefore describes the interrogator/interrogated opposition. Both oppositions serve to consolidate and further authorize entrenched positions of power through their deployment of the rhetoric of self and other. If this rhetoric were employed without disruption, however, it would re-present the type of violation of subjectivity effected by the interrogators' act of interpretation in Breytenbach's autobiography, since it would reduce the subject to the author's representation of himself in the text.

The autobiography has the potential to replicate the self/other opposition found in the confession as it is represented in Breytenbach's *Confessions*. This is the case not only because the autobiography expresses subjectivity by using the same grammatical construct as the confession, but also because the autobiography itself can constitute an interrogation, in that it is an investigation of the self. If the autobiography were to undertake this exploration of the self through positing a series of subject-positions that conformed exclusively to the self/other binary opposition, Breytenbach would fall victim yet again to what we have termed the violation of subjectivity, this time within his own narrative. If he were to see himself exclusively within the terms of such a structure, he would be disabled in that he would fail to identify the effects of that structure upon himself. He would not, as he puts it, "survive," because he would not be able to recognize the violation of himself as a violation. Breytenbach reflects upon the self-replicating nature of structures in his comments about the South African system here, but his observations apply in the context the argument I am making about the danger of accepting the self/other structure as "real":

> the System is historically defined and conditioned, and people come like words from the belly of the System. It cannot change by itself. It is impossible for those who are bred from it to modify the System significantly from within. The structure must be *shattered* (239).

How, we may ask, does Breytenbach's autobiography constitute a "confession" and yet simultaneously perform the critique of the hermeneutic of confession necessary to express the violation he experienced? How does Breytenbach "survive" this autobiography? Although Breytenbach exploits the potential of the confession to replicate the self/other paradigm of the interrogation, he also attempts to critique that paradigm. He dislocates the hegemony of the self/other mode of perception by treating the confessor/confessing subject relationship ironically. The title of the work, *The True Confessions of An Albino Terrorist*, indicates the text's ironic invocation of the confessional mode within its autobiographical context. The ironic distinction between the confessional "voice" and the autobiographical "voice(s)" is accomplished through the parody of the interrogator/interrogated relationship effected in the narrative.

In *A Theory of Parody* Linda Hutcheon approaches parody through a discussion of intertextuality as a recurring phenomenon across a variety of art forms. She proceeds to identify the major formal operatives of parody to be "ironic versions of 'trans-contextualization' and inversion" (37). Hutcheon's comments are useful to this investigation, in that the parody of the interrogator/interrogated relationship can be expressed in intertextual terms. This parody may be said to operate between Breytenbach's formulation of that experience within the mode, or "text," of confession (where interrogator = confessor and interrogated = confessing subject), and his contextualization of this confessional formulation according to the demands of his larger autobiographical project.

The points at which Breytenbach speaks as the victim of detention and subject of interrogation in his autobiography—I have quoted examples of this element of the narrative in order to describe the interrogator/detainee relationship—are fairly straightforward and express the helplessness of his situation. However, the continuity of this perspective, in which Breytenbach speaks of himself as a victim in opposition to the interrogators who dominate him, is disrupted by his frequent ironic adoption of the interrogator's "voice." In such instances, the "I" in the autobiography, which we assume to be related to the subjectivity of Breytenbach, the detainee, is nevertheless also related to the subjectivity of his (former) adversary, the interrogator. Through this ironic inversion Breytenbach "interrogates" the interrogator who is, for a moment, presented as confessing himself to Breytenbach.

In this perverse identification, Breytenbach recognizes the interrogator as a sadist who requires a complementary victim—Breytenbach—in order to extract recognition of himself from one who is dependent upon himself, rather than from an independent other whom he, a sadist, would regard as a threat to the self. The desire of the interrogator for this sadomasochistic relationship is expressed through the association of images of dominance and submission, and mirror imagery:

> I must know (he says). . . . I must *prove*. Therefore I must ask. . . . Don't you know its necessary? That it can *never* be any different? That it has been like this from the beginning of time—you and I entwined and related, *parasite and prey? Image and mirror-image?* . . . Here we are today, still today, still this interminable dark day, days and days forever. I am with you. I never let go of you again. You are programmed. I cleanse you. I break you in. *I break you down* to the pure outcome of spontaneous confession and give-away and self-oblivion. Since I love you so (57; some emphasis added).

This inversion, in which Breytenbach is represented as confessor and the interrogator as the confessing subject, takes place within the larger context of Breytenbach's autobiography. In this larger context, the alliance between self as confessing subject and other as confessor undergoes not only an inversion (in which self = confessor and other = confessing subject), but also a disruption. The self/other opposition of interrogation as confession is "trans-contextualized" (to use Hutcheon's vocabulary) in its representation within the context of the autobiography. This "trans-contextualization" subordinates the structure of the self/other binary to the alternative prerogatives of the autobiographical discourse, creating a breakdown of the symmetry of the distinction

between self and other, a rupture in the logic of unified, and therefore identifiable, subjectivity. Breytenbach has learned, says J. M. Coetzee, "that I and
You need not stand for fixed positions" ("Breytenbach and Censor" 76).

Breytenbach "interrogates" or investigates the interrogator then, not
to construct the interrogator as "other," but rather to discover the effect of
the interrogation process upon himself; that is, in order to discover and
recognize himself as victim. In this case Breytenbach expresses himself as
victim of the process of interrogation and the rhetoric that sustains it, rather
than the victim of the interrogators as individuals. For *The True Confessions
of an Albino Terrorist*, Breytenbach tells us, is above all an investigation of the
"I" who speaks it, a confession by the self to the self, as his occasional addressing of remarks to "my dear dead I" suggests (*TCAT* 255). The narrative "had
to become the reflection of a search for what really happened, and for the
identity of the narrator" (*TCAT* 338); more specifically, it had to become an
inquiry after an identity for the narrator which had been (at the time of the
interrogation/coerced confession) and is (at the moment of speaking/writing
the autobiography/voluntary confession) not constructed by the self/other
opposition, but obliterated by it.

In the context of Breytenbach's autobiography, then, the figure-ing
of the interrogator is repeated with difference in the Breytenbach who inhabits the "I" of the narrative: the interrogator is reflected in Breytenbach the
investigator. A similar rupture in the self/other logic of identification is per-
formed in the narrative's structuring of the relationship of its subject to its
narratee. As I noted above, the narrative is addressed to "your Honour," who
is also "Mr Investigator" or "Mr I" or "Mr Eye." This form of address alludes
to the interrogator (and the interrogator as judge), but a distinction is made
between the interrogator and the "person" addressed or narratee, since
Breytenbach on one occasion begins by addressing the interrogator and then
corrects himself: "In any event I am trying to describe to you . . . Mr Interrogator—sorry, Mr Investigator" (101). This form of address suggests that the
narratee has a similar curiosity to that of the narrator as investigator-of-the-
self: the narratee is on one occasion referred to as "you old voyeur, you" (329).
"And who is the interrogator?" J. M. Coetzee asks, quoting from Breytenbach's
Confessions in his answer:

> In a sense, the reader who wants to read what Breytenbach has to say; but also the
> self that writes itself. 'Mr Investigator[:] you know that we're always inventing our
> lives. . . . You and I entwined and related, parasite and prey[,] image and image-
> mirror.' ("Breytenbach and Censor" 78).

This voyeurism is common to both the narrator and the narratee. The narrator and the narratee (the latter, we recall, is also referred to as "Mr Eye") both "watch" that which is potentially "other." The narratee is "other" than the captive Breytenbach whom she or he "investigates";[55] and Breytenbach, the speaker of the autobiography, is other than Breytenbach, the subject of it, whom the former Breytenbach "investigates."

Yet, not surprisingly, this voyeurism is also associated with the activity of self-discovery. Breytenbach, speaker of the autobiography, is reflected in Breytenbach, subject of the autobiography, through the autobiographical pact expressed in the use of "I," although the two are not identical. The narratee is similarly reflected in the self who speaks/writes the autobiography, since in it Breytenbach is in effect "reading" himself, resurrecting himself through the reader who is implied by the narratee.

The structural features of the narrative described above represent intersubjective relationships as playing reflexive or mutually interdependent, rather than complementary, roles in the constitution of subjectivity. To illustrate these structural features I have made use of a diagram, in which the grid expresses relationships of reflection, but not the fait accompli either of completely positive identification (identification with "self"), or of its complement, completely negative identification (identification of self as against "other"). To this end the lines in the diagram represent not divisions, but double-sided mirrors, images of which recur throughout Breytenbach's narrative.

SELF	OTHER
"I" who speaks the confession	"You" who are interrogator
"I" who speaks the autobiography, the narrator	"You" who are the investigator, the narratee
"I" who am the subject of the autobiography	"You" who are implied reader

By means of these structural features the narrative seeks to prevent the reader from reading the intersubjective relationships represented in the novel as relationships of complete identification, either positive or negative. This strategy employs, or rather deploys, the potential of the narrative to disrupt the reader's desire to recognize the subjects represented in it as fully represented by it. In this way the narrative tries to provoke the reader into recognition of the narrative's own partial-ity in its representation of subjectivity. It attempts to limit simultaneously the violation of its own subject, and that of the reader's subjectivity.

The genre of the autobiography is representative and constitutive of the self to the extent that it takes specific advantage of the potential of language to express subjectivity. *The True Confessions of an Albino Terrorist*—the peculiar autobiographical project in which Breytenbach inscribes, rather than describes, himself here—depends upon a representation of subjectivity that dislocates, rather than locates, identity. The narrative attempts to represent the intersubjective relationships that it investigates—the alignments of subjectivity around the poles of self and other—as reflections, not complete identifications, of one another. *The True Confessions of an Albino Terrorist* seeks to convey notions of subjectivity by representing the potential of language to describe subjectivity, since it is anxious to represent the violations of subjectivity endemic to the experience of incarceration and interrogation. Yet the text is equally anxious to represent that experience without repeating the violation of subjectivity attendant upon it, so it also presents the implications of the nonrecognition of the limitations of textual descriptions of subjectivity: a dangerous belief in total objectivity, a denial that subjects are always in the process of change, and the structural totalitarianism that is the reification of such a commitment to stasis.

J. M. Coetzee, as usual, poses the ultimate question: "Can we go so far as to say that Breytenbach has found a way out of violence *tout court*?":

> The answer must remain suspended. But if we consider the fate of the literature of self-reflexiveness from Rousseau's *Confessions* to Beckett's *The Unnamable*, it seems all too likely to be No. Turning the gaze from the window to the mirror has never been a *way out* or a *way past*: it has always proved to be what Breytenbach in *Mouroir* discovers it to be: a diversion ("Breytenbach and Censor" 83–84).

My conclusion is, I think, fundamentally different from that of Coetzee. *Mouroir* and *The True Confessions of an Albino Terrorist* demonstrate the horror of imprisonment, where the victim's "fixing" by both physical incarceration and the hegemony of an image cannot be separated; as a consequence, these texts also demonstrate—from a position of "negative relationality" to it—the privilege of perspective. Bearing this in mind I would claim that, although Breytenbach's autobiographical attempts, for some of his readers, may constitute simply "a diversion," to reduce them to that status is to forget that they also comprise a complex and vital act of self-defense.

　　　　　Despite his criticism of *Mouroir*, Coetzee is well aware of the fact that he has never been forced to write for survival in the way that Breytenbach has. This much is evident in his identification of Breytenbach as one of the few Afrikaners who have earned the right, as it were, to disassociate themselves from the implementation of apartheid. Breytenbach, Coetzee has said, "may have the power" to "withdraw from the gang"; *"but only because he first paid a price"* (*Doubling* 343; emphasis added). Yet Coetzee's fictions, which form the focus of the next chapter, also constitute a kind of self-defense, even if it is of a very different kind. Coetzee's form of self-defense is calculated to vitiate the seductions of spectatorship, the dangers of which have been illustrated in Breytenbach's descriptions of sadistic voyeurism. Coetzee deploys a number of remarkable narrative strategies in an attempt to manage the implications of his own, potentially spectacular, subjects.

NOTES

　　1. As J. M. Coetzee puts it, "he came to be seen as the leading poetic talent of his generation" ("Poet in Prison" 29).

　　2. Breytenbach's political views are in stark contrast with those of his brothers. At the time of Breytenbach's writing of *The True Confessions of an Albino Terrorist* (hereafter cited as *TCAT*), Jan Breytenbach was a Brigadier-General in the South African Reconnaissance Units, the equivalent of the Green Berets; Breyten Breytenbach describes him as "a trained (and enthusiastic) killer, . . . a 'dirty tricks' expert for Military Intelligence." His other brother, Cloete Breytenbach, is described as "a reporter, a fellow traveller of the [Security Police], with decidedly fascist sympathies" (*TCAT* 68).

　　3. This was Breytenbach's second return to South Africa. In 1973 he received permission to visit the country with his wife. Despite his political views, he was still viewed as "the darling of much of the Afrikaans literary world." In his description of the Breytenbachs' return visit, J. M. Coetzee suggests the eagerness of Breytenbach's fellow Afrikaner writers to welcome him "back into the fold":

> Audiences at poetry readings gave him and his wife a rapturous welcome. The word in the air was 'reconciliation'. The prodigal son would yet return, the breach would be healed, and all would be well ("Poet in Prison" 29–30).

This was not to be the case.

　　Breytenbach's account of his 1973 visit is recorded in the autobiographical narrative *ń Seisoen in die Paradys* (1976), first published by Perskor, then translated into English as *A Season in Paradise* (published by Persea Books in 1980). It should be noted that the first edition, the Afrikaans one, is a censored version.

　　4. For more on the organization Okhela, see Breytenbach's "Not an Afrikaner" and *TCAT*, 77–81, 383–90.

5. In "A Poet in Prison" J. M. Coetzee suggests that, since his mode of return was so clumsy with respect to half-hearted disguises and so on, Breytenbach must at some level have desired to be caught: being caught was the only way in which he could attain notoriety, the recognition of his dissidence. Coetzee moves toward an explanation, or at least, an explication of this desire in his latest article on Breytenbach:

> The [Breytenbach] dilemma can be stated in the form of two questions. If the passion behind my denunciation is not the passion of a pure (idealistic) moralism, what is it? The answer to the first question is: my passion stems from the fact that I am implicated (historically, emotionally) in South Africa; insofar as the present day South African order is, and rests upon, a crime, that crime is part of me and I wish to purge myself of it. The answer to the second question is: I take the risk of reidentifying myself with what I could leave behind. I risk the European identity I have half-adopted by resuming a white South African identity I detest. Thus the paradox clarifies itself: to repudiate white South Africa I have to be a white South African; or to repudiate evil I have to embody evil ("Breytenbach and Censor" 67).

6. Sam Norval was a civil lawyer and Pieter Henning a corporate lawyer. With regard to his comment that they were "too closely integrated into the Afrikaner establishment," Breytenbach remarks:

> by this I mean that the political police—the State for that matter—were not natural enemies for them. . . . I believe that they tried, mistakenly but with such solicitude, to do what they thought best for my interests at the time, and the atmosphere of terror created by the powerful political police was such that they felt we ought to tread very lightly indeed. . . . I was aware that they were also having talks with the police and with the prosecuting team, but strangely, all of this was quite beyond me. I was not aware—I don't remember now—of a formal agreement being reached, or how it would affect my future (*TCAT* 62).

7. The length of Breytenbach's actual imprisonment suggests that the prosecution reneged on this deal (*TCAT* 61; Coetzee, "Breytenbach and Censor" 81).

8. When one of his interviewers challenged Breytenbach with having "made a pretty meek declaration to the courts," Breytenbach pointed out that it was in his lawyers' interest not to defend the case too vocally, and that both the security police and the Prime Minister had access to his court declarations before they were made. His response also included the following:

> If I were to abstain from making a political affair out of it, then I would be given the minimum sentence that the law on terrorism allowed: five years. . . . The security police asked me expressly to apologise to Vorster for the poem *Letter from abroad to Butcher* (dedicated 'to Balthasar', in which the then Prime Minister, Balthasar John Vorster, was described as a murderer). By means of this grovelling gesture they wanted to show the Prime Minister how much they had managed to achieve. I also submitted: under such circumstances one becomes the instrument of one's own destruction ("Not an Afrikaner" 5).

9. The Faber edition of 1984, which is the edition quoted here unless stated otherwise, claims to be the "original English text" (8). However it should be noted that a bilingual English/Afrikaans edition of *Mouroir* was published in 1983 by Breytenbach's publishers within South Africa, Taurus, and was entitled *Mouroir: bespieëlende notas van ń roman*. If a quote is taken from the English which is in Afrikaans in the original Taurus edition, a page reference for the Taurus edition is given. If the English rendition differs significantly from the Afrikaans, the latter is given in a note.

10. Breytenbach describes the effect of solitary confinement on the prisoner's mental state:

> all objectivity is taken away from you. You watch yourself changing, giving in to certain things, becoming paranoiac, staring at the wall, living with an ear to the door and yet cringing at the slightest noise, talking to the ants, starting to have hallucinations—without ever being able to ascertain the extent of these deviations or this damage precisely because you have nothing against which to measure it (*TCAT* 130).

11. I am using the masculine pronoun to designate the prisoner because the concepts relating to the experience of the prisoner discussed here are taken from Breytenbach's description. This is not to assume, however, that his version of the experience would not correspond, at least to some degree, to a female prisoner's experience under similar conditions.

12. Breytenbach explains:

> This much you, the detainee, will *know* in advance: that the interrogator disposes of a panoply of powers, which include the 'right' and the willingness to kill you (it is signalled clearly: not for nothing have well over seventy South African people over the last decade been done to death in cells by the security forces); the 'right' and the desire to maim you, because you must be destroyed; the 'right' to manipulate and to circumscribe your environment—physical or moral. . . . The interrogator's power is absolute and having the detainee know it is his most efficacious weapon, but ultimately it rots him utterly (*TCAT* 342–43).

13. Of this pseudonym Breytenbach writes:

> How he thought himself to be James Bond! I called him Jiems Kont in my mind. Excuse me for taking refuge in my own language. . . .
>
> Anyway, if you have the lack of respect or common decency of not wanting to call a Black man by his own name you call him by the generic name of Jiems, our Afrikaans version of 'James'; and 'Kont', well, it is just the untranslatable Cunt (*TCAT* 40).

14. The masculine pronoun is used here in references to the interrogator, because Breytenbach's interrogators were exclusively male.

15. Breytenbach writes about the pleasure Huntingdon (one of his jailers) took in watching Breytenbach collapse after the trial: "taking exactly the same line they [the jailers] did" (*TCAT*; 45; 181).

On another occasion, Huntingdon brought Breytenbach's elder brother, Jan, to him, in order (according to Breytenbach) to show Jan Breytenbach "taking exactly the same line they did" (*TCAT* 45; 181). Huntingdon is described as responding to Breytenbach's shock at his sentencing as follows:

> In my cell the implications finally hit me and I have what one could only describe as a nervous breakdown—with this monstrous man sitting there in a chair, hidden behind his dark glasses, watching me, finally reaching the apotheosis of his own search for satisfaction. He goes all white in the face. To him it must have been like an orgasm (*TCAT* 71).

16. The movement toward the resolution of tension in the sadistic relationship is always a move toward death, but not with the aim of death, since that would conclude the relationship: "Metaphorically then, and sometimes literally, the sadomasochistic relationship tends toward death, or at any rate, toward deadness, numbness, the exhaustion of sensation" (Benjamin 65).

17. In his exploration of the psychology of colonization, O. Mannoni makes this point:

> Psychologically, then, errors of perception in colonial matters may well be . . . the result of the projection on to the object of some defect which is properly attributable to the subject. . . . What we project onto the colonial inhabitant, in fact, is . . . our most elementary and deeply-hidden fears and desires, the primal Good and Evil, not as a philosopher might see them, but rather as they might appear to a child in a dream, or as Shakespeare and Daniel Defoe saw them (198).

Or, we might add, as James I or Reagan would like their "subjects" to see them.

18. Thompson and Wilson's *The Oxford History of South Africa* stresses the theological aspect of Afrikaner nationalism by referring to the constitution of the *Broederbond*:

> the constitution of the powerful and influential secret society, the *Afrikaner Broederbond*, states that the *Bond* 'is born of the deep conviction that the Afrikaner nation was put in this land by God and is destined to continue its existence as a nation with its own nature and calling' (2: 371–72).

19. As such, Breytenbach's "crime" ensures that he is treated with a contempt and often an intense hatred analogous to the pointed aggression reserved for those who "went native" in earlier colonial times.

20. Jimmy Krüger was Minister of Justice during Breytenbach's incarceration.

21. Clearly, the point at which the state determines that its subject has committed a "violation" of such proportions—when such a "violation" involves the subject's political affiliation—depends upon the degree of totalitarianism practiced by the state.

Breytenbach discusses the South African state and totalitarianism specifically in *End Papers* ("On the Ethics of Resistance as a Writer in a Totalitarian State" 184–94).

22. The strength of the definition of the Afrikaner patriot as "self" explains the mystification and curiosity of his interrogators concerning his motivation. The man who drove Breytenbach to Pretoria after he was arrested at the Johannesburg international airport displayed this curiosity:

> The he-man in front drove at a comfortable pace from Johannesburg, at least from the airport, to Pretoria, all the while shooting questions at me, wanting to know why, why, why do you people *do* this? *What* is it that motivates you? He said, '. . . I want to know what *causes* you to do something like this? *What* is the ideology line behind it? I want you to tell me all about socialism, I want you to tell me about Marxism, I want you to get to the gist of the matter' (*TCAT* 19).

23. The strength of this tradition is such that it leads J. M. Coetzee to comment on the fact, "impossible" from the traditional Afrikaner perspective he describes here, of the coincidence of revolutionary substance and poetic talent in Breytenbach's writing. Commenting on the *Confessions*, he states that Breytenbach's "writing characteristically goes beyond what one had thought could be said in Afrikaans" ("Poet in Prison" 74). This comment has less to do with Coetzee perceiving any limitation or essential inferiority of Afrikaans as a language for literary expression; rather, it is an observation about the assumption that Afrikaans is—always, already—the language of Afrikaner nationalism. Even were a poetry collection such as *Die Huis van die Dowe* (1967) to be read as "non-political," Breytenbach's subsequent collections, such as *Buffalo Bill* (1984), written while he was in solitary confinement in Pretoria Central, would defy the most ardent attempts of his nationalist following to separate the technical excellence the poetry exhibits in utilizing Breytenbach's native tongue from its blatantly subversive context and content.

24. See Linda Hutcheon's chapter on the "Subject in/of/to History and His Story" in *A Poetics of Postmodernism*.

25. J. M. Coetzee suggests that the jailers' view that Breytenbach has a potential for "conversion" explains the "insufferable intimacy" forced on him by his jailers, "in which compassion and cruelty seem at times pathologically intertwined" ("Poet in Prison" 30).

26. They despise him for his treachery; but they recognize him as a potential Afrikaner and a potentially loyal subject of the state. It would have been awkward, however, if Breytenbach had been given such an opportunity, since he did not feel he could defend his actions politically: Okhela was never granted the official support of the ANC (see *TCAT* 62).

27. In his response to Ann McClintock and Rob Nixon's critique of his "Racism's Last Word," Derrida protests against their narrow (and thereby incorrect, in his view) definition of his use of the word "text":

> *text*, as I use the word, is not the book . . . it is not limited to the *paper* which you cover with your graphism . . . there is nothing "*beyond* the text." That's why South

Africa and *apartheid* are, like you and me, part of this general text. . . . That's why the text is always a field of forces: heterogeneous, differential, open, and so on ("But, beyond . . ." 167–68).

28. J. M. Coetzee traces the evolution of the "voices" of Afrikaner nationalism and its dissidents in Breytenbach's pre- and post-incarceration prose and poetry. In "Breytenbach and the Censor," Coetzee uses the figure of the censor, both as state official and as internalized monitor, to describe Breytenbach's personifications of the voice of the state, which he constructed in order to counter the dictates of his own heritage.

29. This "restoration" is presented by his interrogators as being for his benefit, but it is in fact for their benefit and the benefit of the system that they represent. They perceive such a restoration to be a justification (or in Benjamin's terms, an "affirmation") of their task.

30. Here "discourse" in Emile Benveniste's scheme performs the function of "ideology" in Althusser's discussion of subjectivity.

31. Emile Benveniste's theory, grounded as it is in speech acts, is particularly appropriate to this discussion, considering the oral aspect of the composition of the *Confessions*.

32. See Emile Benveniste, "Remarks on the Function of Language in Freudian Theory" (65–75) and "The Nature of Pronouns" (217–22).

33. These interrogators represent the authority of the state: "The State *is* in reality the earthly shape and terrestrial abode of Him, the *Interstigator* (sic)" (*TCAT* 215).

34. In "Breytenbach and the Censor," Coetzee begins the section on Breytenbach's prison writings by stating that he will be "concentrating on hidden voices *against* which Breytenbach speaks" (71). Using Bakhtin's terms, Coetzee distinguishes between monologic and dialogic poems from Breytenbach's prison collections. In the monologic ones, "I" = accusing self = Breytenbach, and "You" = accused other = apartheid state or its representative(s). In the more complex latter form, Breytenbach "has learned . . . that I and You need not stand for fixed positions" (76). Speaking as the enemy, as "we the enemy," he points out, constitutes "a preemption of the enemy's speech" (75). Yet while I characterize this "slippage" as a defense—albeit limited—of considerable importance, Coetzee refers to it, ultimately, as "a diversion" (84).

It is worth pointing out in passing that Coetzee has a longstanding interest in the implications of the Benvenistian pronoun. See, for example, his essays on Achterberg and on confession.

35. Breytenbach did not believe that his jailers would honor their part of this bargain, and arranged to have material smuggled out of the prison. This was the only offense Breytenbach was found guilty of in a second trial, in which the prosecution once again attempted to prove him guilty under the Terrorism Act, and this time, also under the Prisons Act (*TCAT* 252):

> Material smuggled out in the early days was used as evidence during the second trial to validate the charge of my having used illegal means of communication with the outside world. After the trial . . . [a general] . . . told me it had been their intention to cancel my permission to write in the light of the abuses that came out

in court, but that they had been put under persistent pressure by the literary establishment to allow me to continue doing so (*TCAT* 162).

36. Sheila Roberts, for example, goes so far as to say that Breytenbach's "impulse" to record "the truth" of his experience was "distorted" by his attempts both to baffle and to evade the officials who collected and read his work:

> I cannot help but feel that his strong impulse to record the complex emotional truth of his prison experiences was modified, distorted perhaps, by a desire to confuse this initial police readership and their threatened censorship. . . .
>
> I am convinced that because he was writing *Mouroir* in prison, Breytenbach availed himself of greater subterfuges of form and style than he might have found congenial had he been a free man (309–10).

This assumes that language is to a greater or lesser degree transparent, if it is employed in a context unaffected by official censorship. Such an assumption is one, it seems to me, that Breytenbach frequently takes pains to deconstruct.

37. I have described *Mouroir* as the "trace" of Breytenbach's violation because, unlike the *Confessions*, it does not document Breytenbach's prison experiences directly, although it does contain many violent images related to imprisonment (such as the shooting in "Wiederholen," the gang rape in "The Collapse," and the hanging in "The Double Dying of an Ordinary Criminal"). For this reason, and because the work has a somewhat obscure form, "it may," as Susanna Egan points out, "seem positively perverse to explore *Mouroir* as autobiography" (94). Egan argues that *Mouroir* can be considered autobiographical because Breytenbach "is dealing with experience in ways that are common in experimental fiction but also drawing on a power that springs from an authentic claim on empirical truth" (103). Although I share Egan's interest in considering *Mouroir* in the light of autobiography, I wish to state precisely how I consider *Mouroir* to be autobiographical. What is the relationship between the text and the circumstances of Breytenbach's life—what Egan has referred to as "empirical truth?"

38. The "non-referentiality" of the individual personal pronouns employed in the narratives of *Mouroir* is made explicit by Breytenbach in the "*Apologie*" that prefaces the original bilingual edition of the work:

> In hierdie verslae is daar 'n ek en ekke, 'n ons, jye, hye, sye, hulles en julles. Maar dié ek is nie ék nie en die jy, geëerde leser, is nie jy nie; nog is die hy die sy die hulle of die julle jý of júlle.

> In these accounts there is an I and I's, a we, you's he's she's, they's and you's [plural]. But the I is not I and the you, honoured reader, is not you; nor is the he the she the they or the you you or you [plural] (Taurus *Mouroir* 1; my translation).

39. In other texts, such as *End Papers*, it becomes relatively clear that Don Espejuelo, to whom the bilingual edition of *Mouroir* is dedicated, is a form of alter ego for Breytenbach. However, the status of this "character" within *Mouroir* remains typically unclear.

40. Because the writings in *Mouroir* exhibit this radical inconsistency, I shall use the term "narrative" within inverted commas in reference to this particular text.

41. This strategy for survival seems to have been, incredibly considering the circumstances, somewhat effective. J. M. Coetzee, in his review of *Mouroir* and the *Confessions*, comments upon Breytenbach's remarkable psychological resilience: "He [Breytenbach] spent two years in isolation in Pretoria Central Prison, a spell from which he emerged with his sanity miraculously unimpaired. . . ." ("Poet in Prison" 30).

42. J. M. Coetzee identifies the motivations behind *Mouroir* and the *Confessions* as including both revenge and "a more cautious project," one that has to do with control, and aims to "incorporate the censor figure"—who represents both external and internal resistances (prison warder, guard, literary censor, as well as Breytenbach the Afrikaner)—"into himself (calling it the figure in the mirror, calling it the I) and *manage* it in that way" ("Breytenbach and Censor" 81).

43. Breytenbach writes that:

> I had to try and get some recognition from someone, somewhere, admitting that these things [texts] did in fact exist. I kept note of whatever I handed in to them and informed Yolande accordingly. We soon tried to get them to recognize the fact that they had these by asking my lawyers to approach the authorities with the request of obtaining copies of the work, using the pretext that we were worried about what would happen if, say, the prison burned down. Sure, we knew that there was no chance of their granting the request, but in the process we at least had a confirmation in writing from them that they were indeed in possession of so many pages. It was then too, that they formally undertook to return all of the material to me on the day of my release (*TCAT* 161).

44. Sheila Roberts has describes this "narrative" as a "realistically detailed death by hanging" (309). If she means by this that the logic of representation in this piece conforms to what I have been defining as the logic of symmetrical representation, I believe that her reading ignores prominent clues that the "narrative" gives to the reader about its treatment of its subjects.

45. Dit is 'n literêre fenomeen waarop ek my kollegas wil wys: die ritueel moet in ons voltrek word. (Taurus *Mouroir* 50).

46. These two characters mirror each other in that they are interchangeable. The narrator tells us that "either Galgenvogel or Tuchverderber" challenged him (121).

47. The narrator relates that he received the following proposal from either Tuckverderber or Galgenvogel:

> Of an afternoon we sit chewing the fat and there they are munching their lips and gnashing their gums. "Why dontcha write a simple story?" one of them, either Galgenvogel or Tuchverderber, asks. "Why not 'boy sees gurl, gurl sees boy, boy *likes* gurl, gurl screws boy (or the other way around), alas gurl is already married, boy terminates husband with extreme prejudice, luckily the court finds it legitimate defence and they all live happily ever after'? To what purpose all this hum-hum muck ?" (121).

The narrator goes on to tell us that "The thin blood from bloated horses' heads has soaked into my trousers." He comments that Tuchverderber and Galgenvogel "think I'm writing for obscurity. Just jiggling around with *Kultur*. Little do they know. If at all" (121).

48. This "resurrection" is not the Christian Resurrection, but has more in common with the notion of resurrection represented by the Indian Shiva, god of destruction and creation: a description of Shiva follows the passage I have quoted.

49. Breytenbach is a painter as well as a writer, and he indicates that the theory he is proposing applies to the creation and reception of both writing and paintings.

50. This strategy is indicated in *End Papers*, in which Breytenbach, mimicking Borges, writes "Pierre Mesnard's Story," which Borges did not write but "would have written . . . had he not been so old and so weak" (87). He also writes a "Letter to a Figure in Manet's *Olympia*" on behalf of "Ka'afir." The letter is addressed to Ka-Ma, the black woman in Manet's painting: Ka'afir "you will remember" is

> the young man who was standing to your [Ka-Ma's] right and just behind Victorine's left shoulder in that painting where she is lying naked. . . .
> True, he was then later effaced from the work (*End Papers* 160),

51. For an excellent discussion of repetition as the production of difference in history and autobiography see Michael Sprinker's discussion of Vico, Kierkegaard, Nietzsche, and Freud in "Fictions of the Self: The End of Autobiography" in *Autobiography: Essays Theoretical and Critical*.

In this essay Sprinker traces the relationship between the concept of repetition as a function of memory in Vico, and analyzes Kierkegaard's *Repetition* as an autobiographical text. Following Lacan's advice, he then proceeds to analyze Freud's "The Interpretation of Dreams," concluding that the text "enacts the process it describes by tracing and retracing the paths of its own discourse" (341). He concludes:

> The writing of autobiography is a similar act of producing difference by repetition. Just as dream interpretation returns again and again to the navel of the dream, so autobiography must return perpetually to the elusive center of selfhood buried in the unconscious, only to discover that it was already there when it began (342).

52. Rosemary Jackson uses Bakhtin's term to mean the novel form characterized by the "notion of realism which had emerged as dominant by the mid-nineteenth century" (25).

53. Kaja Silverman raises this issue specifically in connection with the genesis of the Lacanian mirror phase. Lacan states that the mirror stage occurs before what he terms the subject's "social determination," thereby suggesting that the image in the mirror is ideologically neutral. Yet as Silverman points out, Lacan also tells us that the child's identification of the image takes the same form as subsequent identifications with images that are socially determined, such as the male child's identification with an ideal paternal representation during the Oedipus complex. Silverman concludes that

"The question we are thus obliged to ask is whether the mirror stage is not in some manner culturally induced" (160). Fanon and Breytenbach would both answer, "Yes!"

54. Breytenbach explains how *The True Confessions of An Albino Terrorist* came about:

> I had to write it. That is, I dictated it. The document itself took shape from the obsessive urge I experienced during the first weeks and months of my release to talk talk talk, [*sic*] to tell my story and all the other stories. It must have been rather horrible for him or her who happened to be victim to my vomiting. So I was advised to talk it into a tape. . . .
>
> My wife typed the tapes. I used her transcripts as 'rough copy'. These I would blacken, add to, delete from, change about—and she would type a clean version for me to go over again if needed. Without her it could not have been done (*TCAT* 337–38).

55. Breytenbach satirizes the voyeurism of the narratee, suggesting that her or his curiosity is analogous to that of the interrogator, since it is structured by the desire to dis-cover Breytenbach's "essential" self:

> Mr Investigator, the public play is not really the part of the story which interests you the most, is it? Do you want to dance? I think you'd rather like to know about what was happening behind the walls. (Are you also one of those that believe that the unsaid must be more truthful?) (*TCAT* 63).

Forms of Violence in J. M. Coetzee's *Dusklands* and *Waiting for the Barbarians*

> Imaginative fiction should have
> an element in it in which you
> begin to sense the unbearable
> notions of reality.
>
> —Wilson Harris, "Interview with Wilson Harris"

1. The Gun as Copula: Colonization, Rape, and the Question of Pornographic Violence in *Dusklands*

The concern to avoid fictional representations of violence which have a tendency to seduce both author and reader through a fantasizing activity marked by its pornographic interest—that is, to avoid the kind of fictional representation I have discussed in reference to Brink's *A Chain of Voices*—is evident in Coetzee's novels. Coetzee rejects the model in which a writer-narrator constitutes the authoritative witness to and judge of his subject, who is regarded as having an ultimately representable history: the model exemplified in the fiction of Breytenbach's trial, judgment, and incarceration. Implicit in Coetzee's rejection of this modus operandi, which will prove to be a denunciation of it, is the desire to re-present the acts of violence that constitute a recurring subject in his fiction, without participating in the process of violation which those acts exhibit. Coetzee's renunciation of this model also enables him to engage in a second project, one closely associated with the attempt to depict violence without inviting sensationalism. This project may be described as an attempt to counter history as a prison, one in which we are doomed to repeat without difference the contours of a violent past—a task that Coetzee

110

accomplishes through his refusal to structure his fictions as ones that function as representations of an "original" history, constructed through communal assent of the author and her or his "subjects," including, as in the case of Brink, narrator and reader. This past, fetishized by such fictional "treatments," is one that, Coetzee has argued, has ensured a present that remains essentially colonial, characterized by an inability to sustain itself except through repeated acts of violation.[1] Coetzee's first novel, *Dusklands* (1974), demonstrates both thematically and formally these two characteristics of Coetzee's fiction—its awareness of the propensity for a fictional "treatment" of violence to subvert itself into the form of a fantasy that is pornographic in its effects, and its concern to deconstruct the repetitive structures of colonialism.[2]

With *Dusklands*, Coetzee began his fictional exploration of colonization.[3] *Dusklands* investigates the relationships among the colonizer, the historian, and the writer of fiction. The work consists of two novellas. The first, "The Vietnam Project," deals with United States' involvement in Vietnam. The narrator of this novella is a mythographer with the ironic name of Eugene Dawn, whose job is to advise the United States military on propaganda strategies aimed at weakening the Vietcong. The second novella, "The Narrative of Jacobus Coetzee," consists of two narratives of "exploration" of the South African interior by a Dutch colonist, one said to have taken place in 1760, and one in 1761–1762. These "explorations" consist of a series of brutal conquests of the native people of the interior, the Nama. Just as chronological ordering is upset in the narrative of *Dusklands* as a whole, by placing the Vietnam narrative before the narratives of Dutch colonization, so the later South African exploration is placed before the earlier one.

The reversal of chronological order and the juxtaposition of Eugene Dawn, the theorist of conquest, and Jacobus Coetzee (hereafter referred to as Jacobus to avoid confusing Jacobus Coetzee and J. M. Coetzee), the conquistador, suggests that the occupations and preoccupations of these men, though temporally distant from one another, are reciprocally mimetic. Both men are colonizers in a history that repeats itself in the rise and fall of successive empires; both are historians in that they interpret the past using the myth of self and other in its colonial context; and both are revealed, through the various levels of metafiction in their narratives, to be authors of their own fictions.

Eugene Dawn's narrative is a theory motivated by fantasy, a circumstance that he himself does not recognize. He is identifiable as a type of author not only because writing is a large element of his profession, but also because he corresponds to Coetzee's description of the author as voyeur ("Dark Chamber" 13). Eugene Dawn attempts to enter "the dark chamber" of a Vietnam that he refuses to visit, although he has been given the opportunity to do so. He authorizes his fantasy of penetrating the mythical Vietnam—the one that he creates in his report—by exploiting the form of that report. The fact that his text "leaks" out of that form on either side of the second section in which the report is given, as well as within the so-called report itself, indicates that Eugene Dawn's perpetual fear has once again been realized. Just as America is unable to subdue the Vietcong, a failure that his report is calculated to overcome, so Eugene Dawn's fantasy of complete mastery, in this case over his own narrative, is threatened. That the report is consumed by Eugene Dawn's autobiography is not surprising, for Dawn's report turns out to be autobiographical once he starts attempting to enact the fantasy that it outlines.

The argument of Dawn's report is that American propaganda will not be effective until the myth by which it attempts to control the enemy is one with which the Vietnamese are familiar and, also, until the myth used is one that circumvents the ability of the Vietnamese to interpret counterforce as an opportunity to defend their identity, rather than as a radical threat to it. What is needed for America to be victorious, Dawn argues, is not the physical violence of counterforce but cultural violation: the introduction of a countermyth. The voice of the divided self that is the West's heritage from Descartes, and which according to Dawn has been used to little effect in trying to undermine the confidence of the enemy, must be jettisoned in favor of a myth that recognizes the Vietnamese privileging of community welfare over the interests of the individual. Eugene Dawn describes the myth that needs to be revised as the Oedipal one of the sons' rebellion against the father. According to him, a form of this myth is prevalent in Vietnamese popular consciousness, and he quotes a (fictional) authority on this point:

> "The sons of the land (i.e., the brotherhood of earth tillers) desire to take the land (i.e. the Vietnamese *Boden*) for themselves, overthrowing the sky-god who is identified with the old order of power (foreign empire, the U.S.). The earth-mother hides her sons in her bosom, safe from the thunderbolts of the father; at night, while he sleeps, they emerge to unman him and initiate a new fraternal order" (II, pp. 26, 101) (25).

According to Dawn, the problem is that within the context of this myth, the father is by definition vulnerable. The father will be repeatedly replaced and overthrown, because

> The myth of rebellion assumes that heaven and earth, father and mother, live in symbiosis. Neither can exist alone. If the father is overthrown there must be a new father, new rebellion, endless violence, while no matter how deep her treachery

toward her mate, the mother may not be annihilated. The scheming of mother and sons is thus endless (26).

What Dawn proposes instead is the introduction of a father figure, represented by a father-voice on propaganda radio programs, who is presented as invulnerable. The medium of the radio is, according to Dawn, perfectly suited to this message. "Radio information . . . is pure authority," he tells us (14), and "the father is authority, infallibility, ubiquity. He does not persuade, he commands" (21). The success of such propaganda depends, Dawn argues, upon the acknowledgment of the United States' military to themselves that their use of force is not for the purpose of defense, but to demoralize the enemy, because "in limited warfare, defeat is not a military but a psychic concept":

> in practise our most effective acts of demoralization are justified in military terms, as though the use of force for psychological ends were shameful. Thus, for example, we have justified the elimination of enemy villages by calling them armed strongholds, when the true value of the operations lay in demonstrating to the absent VC menfolk just how vulnerable their homes and families were (22).

In this scheme the destruction of the protective mother-figure, represented by mother-earth, is crucial. Dawn points out that "we" no longer live by cultivating the earth, but by decimating "her," and that "we" should recognize that "we" have forsaken the earth-mother for the goddess of technology, daughter of "our" own making. Dawn uses the figure of Athene to represent the age of technology: "We have the capacity to breed out of our own head," he states (26). According to Dawn, the capacity of this self-made goddess as savior needs to be recognized. Thus he reprimands the military for having limited their use of PROP-12, a dramatic soil poison, and for finally discontinuing its use. Such self-hypocrisy, he argues, is self-defeating: "Until we reveal to ourselves and revel in the true meaning of our acts we will go on suffering the double penalty of guilt and ineffectualness" (29).

Eugene Dawn's mythographic prescription for Vietnam can be identified as the fantasy of the sadist, both in terms of Jessica Benjamin's definition of the sadist in *The Bonds of Love* and in terms of Susan Suleiman's profile of the "'founding' scenario" of the Sadean fantasy in *Subversive Intent: Gender, Politics and the Avant-Garde* (1990) (68). Benjamin defines the sadist as an individual who is incapable of accepting the paradox of mutual independence, in which the need for self assertion and the need for recognition of the self by an other are held in balance. The sadist perceives dependency on another's recognition of himself[4] as a threat to his independence. The sadist, then, can receive recognition of his own independence only through violation of an other. Since recognition of the self, according to Benjamin, is the source of erotic pleasure, the sadist experiences sexual satisfaction in his violation of an other. In the light of this analysis, Dawn's proposal—that America take on the role of the all-powerful father—amounts to a recommendation that America adopt the mentality of the sadist. The goal of this course of action corresponds to Benjamin's definition of the desire of the sadist; to reach the ideal (impossible in practice) of independence from recognition by an other of the self, or in other words, to achieve complete autonomy.

Eugene Dawn's fantasy also corresponds to its literary progenitor, the Sadean fantasy. In both Eugene Dawn's proposal and the Sadean fantasy, the other to be violated in the attempt at mastery is identified as female. In her discussion of Robbe-Grillet's *Projet pour un révolution à New York*, Suleiman, drawing upon Deleuze, argues that "the founding desire behind Sadean fantasy is *the active negation of the mother*" (68). Eugene Dawn's proposal contains a similar element: his goddess of technology, who is to be substituted for the earth mother, is born in the manner of Athene, bypassing the role of the mother. That the attempt at mastery in Sadean fantasy is made through the violation of the female, leads Suleiman to two related conclusions that are pertinent to the fantasies of both Eugene Dawn and Jacobus Coetzee. The first is that the gender of the fantasizer—male—is a determining factor in Sadean fantasy; the second is that the Sadean fantasy is in fact a fantasy of self-engenderment:

> In this context [that of the active negation of the mother] one can understand the Sadean hero's . . . refusal to accomplish the sexual act in a way that might lead to procreation. One can also understand why several Sadean heroes actually kill their mother. One such hero—Bresac, in *Les Infortunes de la vertu*—justifies his murder of his mother by invoking an argument at least as old as the *Oresteia*: the father alone is responsible for the creation of the child—the mother simply furnishes a resting place where the fetus can grow. *Here, surely, is something that can be called a predominantly masculine fantasy: that of a world where man is not born of woman.* Let us recall that in mythology the birth of heroes is rarely 'natural.' And not only in mythology: if Macduff is a conqueror, it is precisely because he is not 'of woman born.' *Woman, the irreducible Other, is eliminated to make way for engenderment of the same by the same* (68; emphasis added).

In *Dusklands* as a whole, Sadean fantasy operates within the context of colonization, in which it performs as a tool for a kind of narrative control that proves, ultimately, to be impossible, suggesting not only the impracticability of absolute mastery, but also the colonial and patriarchal limitations of the master-slave dialectic.[5] Coetzee's novellas illustrate the use of disguised forms of the Sadean fantasy to justify and perpetuate patterns of racial and sexual domination in a colonial context, demonstrating that such usage is capable of producing a breed of violence that is anything but fantastic. Both Eugene Dawn's fantasy, which masquerades as mythography, and the fantasies of the second novella, which masquerade as history, are narratives that depend upon the Sadean myth to engender the violence of colonization. This violence can be located in the colonist's desire to exclude, to eliminate, that which is other—an "other" marked as such by racial or sexual difference, or by both. The myth that drives the Sadean fantasy is that this violent exclusion offers its protagonist complete autonomy and absolute power.

Eugene Dawn's narrative shows the Sadean propensity to destroy that which he marks as "other." His application of the Oedipus myth to the project of maintaining American superiority over the Vietcong in "The Vietnam Project" indicates a collusion between patterns of racial and sexual domination which is evident in his autobiographical "project" as well. He confesses that he is excited not by sex with Marilyn, his wife, but by three photographs in particular of the many that he carries around with him. These are all photographs that "celebrate," as it were, American victories in Vietnam. One is of a large American sergeant copulating with a small Vietnamese woman, who may be a child; the second is of two sergeants, Berry and Wilson, holding the severed heads of three Vietcong; and the third is of a prisoner in a tiger cage on Hon Tre island.

Eugene Dawn's excitement at scenes of domination and his obsessive desire for absolute control are mirrored in the actions of Jacobus Coetzee. In this respect, Jacobus represents the fulfillment of Eugene Dawn's fantasy, for Jacobus is the Sadean hero victorious. Jacobus views the territories of both the native and the female in the same way. To him they represent only opportunities for mastery, areas for colonization. Just as Dawn is excited to the pitch of erotic fantasy by the photographs illustrating mastery, Jacobus tells us that the ideal condition for stimulating his erotic pleasure is rape. His ideal sex-object embodies both sexual and racial difference: a Bushman girl. Sex with Dutch girls affords no pleasure, Jacobus tells us, because Dutch girls embody property and therefore power, and are in this respect inviolable. Bushmen girls, on the other hand, can be used and left for dead. With a Dutch girl

> You lose your freedom. . . . Whereas a wild Bushman girl is tied into nothing, literally nothing. She may be alive but she is as good as dead. She has seen you kill

the men that represented power to her, she has seen them shot down like dogs. You have become Power itself now and she nothing, a rag you wipe yourself on and throw away. . . . She can kick and scream but she knows she is lost. That is the freedom she offers, the freedom of the abandoned. . . . She has given up the ghost, she is flooded in its stead with your will. Her response to you is absolutely congruent with your will. She is the ultimate love you have borne[,] your own desires alienated in a foreign body and pegged out waiting for your pleasure (61).

Jacobus' identification of this scenario as the source of erotic pleasure, and Dawn's of his vicarious source, namely the photographs, create a profile for both men which corresponds to Jessica Benjamin's definition of the sadist's mechanism for gaining recognition. Each enjoys the scene of violation of that which they have designated "other," because such violation represents to each the elimination of a threat to his independence, and the concomitant affirmation of his will.

What remains to be investigated is that even more complex feature of the fantasies of domination and submission in *Dusklands*, namely their masochistic element. If Dawn and Jacobus constantly seek confrontations from which they may gain sadistic forms of self-recognition, it is perhaps not surprising that these figures also illustrate the propensity for reversal between sadistic and masochistic components which Jessica Benjamin has identified as characteristic of the sadomasochistic relationship. Sadism and masochism, Benjamin has argued, are two sides of the same coin in that both are bids for recognition of the self. In masochism, this desire for self-acknowledgment expresses itself paradoxically, in the submission of the self to a dominant other's will in an attempt to gain at least a vicarious independence. Both Eugene Dawn and Jacobus Coetzee's fantasies of confrontation with an other, while they provide instances for occupation and therefore sadistic recognition, are also described in ways that suggest that Dawn and Jacobus also experience the masochist's desire to be "occupied," or in Benjamin's vocabulary, to be "reached, penetrated, found, released" (73). Thus there is a paradoxical disappointment on the part of Eugene Dawn and Jacobus Coetzee when the enemy—be it Vietcong or Nama or even occasionally woman[6] —fails to be dominant, fails to represent an appropriate resistance to the will of the colonizer. This disappointment lies in the failure of the enemy to provide the Americans (in the case of Eugene Dawn) and the whites (in the case of Jacobus Coetzee) with an opportunity for masochistic self-recognition through surrender.

For Jacobus Coetzee as well as Eugene Dawn, territorial aggression, exercised against a body that is racially or sexually "other," offers opportunities for sadistic and masochistic forms of self-recognition that are represented by the gun. Because aggression exercised to the point of virtual annihilation is the only form of intersubjective recognition in both sadism and masochism, the gun becomes a copula through which such recognition is achieved. Jacobus Coetzee gives us the sadistic version of this form of gun-worship in the course of his meditations, which are apparently induced by his physical illness:

> The gun stands for the hope that there exists that which is other than oneself. The gun is our last defence against isolation within the travelling sphere. The gun is our mediator with the outside world and therefore our saviour. The tidings of the gun: such-and-such is outside, have no fear. The gun saves us from the fear that all life is within us. It does so by laying at our feet all the evidence we need of a dying and therefore a living world. . . .
>
> The instrument of survival in the wild is the gun, but the need for it is metaphysical rather than physical (79–80).

The desire for absolute mastery that the gun represents takes in this instance its sadistic form: Jacobus receives self-gratification from the destruction of all that he determines to be other. In a reversal of sadistic and masochistic bids for recognition, the reversal that Benjamin identifies as characteristic of sadomasochistic relationships, the desire for absolute mastery also takes a masochistic form. In this case evidence of aggression inflicted upon the self is desired for its potential to be interpreted as self-recognition. This desire expresses itself as the perverse wish to be "shot," to be victim rather than victorious. Eugene Dawn's "history" of the American-Vietcong encounter reflects this desire. In it he refers to both colonization and rape as opportunities for masochistic self-recognition in which the "enemy" has failed America by proving itself to be vulnerable in the case of the fighters, and to be unresponsive (at least in the desired fashion) in the case of the women. The "failure" of the enemy lies in its unsuitability as an idol to command masochistic submission on the part of the invaders: "We brought them [the Vietcong] our pitiable selves," Eugene Dawn tells us,

> trembling on the edge of inexistence, and asked only that they acknowledge us. We brought with us weapons, the gun and its metaphors, the only copulas we knew of between ourselves and our objects. . . . We landed on the shores of Vietnam clutching our arms and pleading for someone to stand up without flinching to these probes of reality: if you will prove yourself, we shouted, you will prove us too, and we will love you endlessly and shower you with gifts.
>
> But like everything else they withered before us. We bathed them in seas of fire, praying for the miracle. In the heart of the flame their bodies glowed with

heavenly light; in our ears their voices rang; but when the fire died they were only ash. . . . If they had walked toward us singing through the bullets we would have knelt and worshipped; but the bullets knocked them over and they died as we had feared. We cut their flesh open, we reached into their dying bodies, tearing out their livers, hoping to be washed in their blood; but they screamed and gushed like our most negligible phantoms. We forced ourselves deeper than we had ever gone before into their women; but when we came back we were still alone, and the women like stones (17–18).

This refusal of the world to correspond to a metaphysical scheme that is essentially a fiction, is "read" by both colonizers, Dawn and Jacobus, as a threat to their respective identities. Even in the face of this incongruity they refuse to adjust their metaphysical scheme, the pattern according to which they "read" events. This refusal places them in the position of attempting to force the world to conform to that pattern through repeated acts of violation: such is the lot of the sadist. On what we may call the "internal" front however, this incongruity nevertheless amounts to a refusal on the part of the external world to offer the sadist the recognition he desires. Since their attempts to gain external recognition for themselves have always been sadistic, Dawn and Jacobus apply sadistic methods to gain the recognition that they desire from themselves. The external world having forsaken them, they turn upon themselves in what becomes a masochistic bid for self-recognition.

Eugene Dawn's one violent act demonstrates the proximity of sadism and masochism in this context. He stabs his son, Martin, to prevent his wife from gaining access to the boy. This act corresponds to the characteristics of sadism as we have defined them, including the fact that through this act Dawn aims to "preserve" Martin "undefiled," as it were, by the female "other" whose eradication Dawn persistently desires. Yet in the attempt to conform to his own notion of the perfect father (all-powerful) and the perfect son (entirely submissive to his father's will), Dawn mistakenly identifies completely with his son, literally con-fusing his own identity with Martin's. Thus the stabbing is also masochistic:

I am holding Martin very tightly around his chest so that he will not slide down; the fruit-knife is in and will not go in much further on account of the haft.

Amazing. I have been hit a terrible blow. How could that happen? . . . The only consistent thing in my experience is the smell of carpet. The smell of carpet: in which I used to lie as a child, of a hot afternoon, thinking. . . .

Now I am beginning to be hurt. Now someone is really beginning to hurt me. Amazing (42–43).

Jacobus' internal sadomasochism is evident in his discussions of the boil he develops on his backside. Jacobus' ideal, like Dawn's, is to be autonomous. Thus he systematically alienates those about him through repeated violent acts. He alienates the Nama, for example, by biting off the ear of one of their children, and later rejoices in his independence after having left Klawer, his manservant, to die on the first return to the colony. Yet he does create a substitute source for external recognition, by thinking of the boil he has developed on his backside as a kind of pleasurable invasion by a dummy "other." As Attwell points out, "the carbuncle is a blessing, for *self-inflicted* pain enables Jacobus Coetzee to reconstitute himself as object of consciousness" (*J. M. Coetzee* 52):

> I imagined the swelling in my buttock as a bulb shooting pustular roots into my fertile flesh. It had grown sensitive to pressure, but to gentle finger-stroking it still yielded a pleasant itch. Thus I was not quite alone (83).

Later, Jacobus lances the boil in a kind of rape of the self. The masturbatory imagery surrounding this enterprise suggests that he experiences erotic satisfaction from the masochistic form of self-recognition that this activity offers. He pinches the boil in "climax after climax of pain." Finally

> The skin must have been weakened by my exertions; for at once, with exquisite surprise, I heard, or if not heard felt in my eardrums, the tissues give way and bathe my fingers in a spurt and then a steady dribble of wet warmth (89).

Both Eugene Dawn's and Jacobus Coetzee's attempts to bring their sadomasochistic fantasies to life involve attempts at self-engenderment. Their fantasies correspond to Suleiman's description of the first essential of a fantasy of self-engenderment: the elimination of the sexual "other." Dawn and Jacobus both attempt to violate the female, particularly through negation of her importance as mother. Dawn identifies the problem with the original myth as being the fact that the mother, despite her "treachery" to the father, cannot be eliminated, and goes on to suggest that we need a new myth in which there is no place for maternal autonomy: neither her rebellion nor her capacity to give birth—a capacity that in and of itself represents a threat to the autonomy of the father—will be admitted. Jacobus' rape fantasy illustrates the enjoyment he takes in a similar violation of the status of women. Also, he too bypasses the role of the mother in his attempt at self-regeneration. He refers to his boil as his child. In the pain of attempting to pierce the boil, which does not give way easily, he refers to the fact that he takes "pride in . . . [his] offspring's stubbornness" (89).

The solipsistic self-engenderment illustrated by the content of Dawn's mythographic prescription and Jacobus' recalcitrant boil perform metafictionally, when the status of Dawn and Jacobus as narrators is taken into account. Both are caught within their fictions of autonomy—they are their own creators—and are thus unable to escape, as it were, their own narratives. Jacobus, despite the depths of degradation and ridicule to which he falls when he is sick among the Nama, is ultimately never shaken in his conviction that he is the god whom he believed the Nama would recognize him to be. In this context Jacobus' last words are ironic. It is no wonder that fear of death for him is "merely a winter story" or that he says "a world without me is inconceivable"; the only possible death for him—a character driven by his own narrative—is suicide, an act which Jacobus would find inconceivable (107). Similarly, Dawn clearly makes himself the victim of his own narrative; in an elaborate autobiographical project to which the Vietnam report soon falls victim, Dawn (re-)enacts his proposal for Vietnam by abandoning his wife and making off with his son, as pointed out by Peter Knox-Shaw (32). This is confirmed by the words he uses to describe the stabbing: "Holding it *like a pencil*, I push the knife in" (42; emphasis added).

This element of J. M. Coetzee's narrative—I mean the narrative of *Dusklands* as a whole—also has a metafictional function on a primary level, that is, with regard to Coetzee as fiction-maker. To the extent that Dawn and Jacobus are their own creators, as narrators they function as sadists, and as characters they function as masochists. Eugene Dawn himself makes reference to the sadistic character of narrative. "Print . . . is sadism, and properly evokes terror," he tells us. The reader who believes in print is a masochist: "Print is the hard master with the whip, print-reading a weeping search for signs of mercy. . . . Print-reading is a slave habit" (14). In this context both reading and writing are pornographic activities, since "Pornography is an abasement before the page . . ." (14).

If Dawn/Jacobus as narrators are sadistic and Dawn/Jacobus as characters are masochistic, is the writer always a sadistic colonizer, and the reader, at the mercy of the writer's images, always masochistically colonized? Coetzee's own fictional practice suggests ways in which the sadomasochistic model of reading and writing can be broken. The status of Dawn and Jacobus as characters and as reliable narrators is thrown into doubt by the metafictional elements of their narrative which suggest that, in the case of their narratives, both narrator and character are products of the tautological fiction of sadomasochism. In this very example Coetzee demonstrates that the sadomasochistic model of reading and writing is a failed model. Precisely because it refuses to recognize the fictional status of its myth, its method of reproduction is fatally solipsistic.

In *Dusklands* J. M. Coetzee takes pains to indicate the fictional status of his own narrative project, and to this extent both refuses to adopt the position of narrator as sadist, and encourages the reader not to adopt the position of masochist. The metafictional elements of the narrative to which I have referred perform the function of reminding the reader that all narratives, even histories (and this is Hayden White's point), are fictional. We are even reminded of the "character" of the author of this textual drama in *Dusklands*, since Coetzee gives four of the characters his own surname. In addition to Jacobus Coetzee, Dawn's boss has the name of Coetzee, the narrative of Jacobus Coetzee has a fictional editor named S. J. Coetzee and a "translator" named J. M. Coetzee.

The points in the text where there exists the largest propensity for the narrator to perform as sadist, and the reader to respond as masochist, are those that represent violence. Here in particular Coetzee takes care to mark the scenes of violence as representations of violence. Both the Vietnam photographs (the fact that they are photographs clearly indicates that this is a "frame-up") and the orgies of sadistic violence in which Jacobus indulges, display what Debra Castillo, using a Barthesian term, labels an "'over-constructed horror' . . . that prohibits empathy"—that is, the empathy necessary for a reading of these scenes to be pornographic. Thus Coetzee's narrative does not encourage the reader's involvement as participant in a pornography of violence, but rather points the reader to the fact that the violence that he represents lies elsewhere. Castillo's reading of the metafictional aspect of the photographs demonstrates this strategy:

> J. M. Coetzee's primary purpose in providing shock photos of an untenable reality is to release the silenced, unimaginable other, the pictorial "ghosts or absences of themselves," from the spectacle of horror that imprisons them (*Dusklands* 17). . . . The fictive surface, yielding to penetration as the tiger-cage does not, releases lacerating horror, bruising the reader, who can, finally, feel the point that description alone cannot provide, releasing her into a vigilance through or beyond the text ("Coetzee's *Dusklands*" 1114).

This exploitation of the "fictive surface" as fictive, wards against the pornographical readings invited by realist representations of violence. For the abasement of pornography before the page is, Dawn's narrative tells us, "such abasement as to convulse the very page" (14), that is, as to collapse the distinction between word and world. To the extent that *Dusklands* refuses to master the violence of which its narrative offers representations, that is, to the extent that it presents the acts of violence it describes as unimaginable, marking the fact that they "cannot satisfactorily be contained in interpretation" (Attwell, *J. M. Coetzee* 55), the text itself fails as pornography.

2: "Into the Dark Chamber": Colonization, Inquisition, and Torture in *Waiting for the Barbarians*

> There has been something staring me
> in the face and still I do not see it.
> —The magistrate, *Waiting for the Barbarians*

In an article entitled "Into the Dark Chamber: The Novelist and South Africa," Coetzee discusses the question of the representation of torture in South African literature. In this piece (which demonstrates his critical expertise), Coetzee explores the reasons for the novelist's attraction to the issue of torture and the problems it poses as a subject for literary representation. He argues that the torture room is of interest to the writer because it "provide[s] a metaphor, bare and extreme, for relations between authoritarianism and its victims" (13). Coetzee proposes that the pitfall of "erotic fascination" with the scene of torture into which many authors drop is a temptation posed by the very nature of the imaginative activity in which the novelist engages. Coetzee cites Irwin's *Doubling and Incest / Repetition and Revenge* in this context:

> The fact that the torture room is a site of extreme human experience, accessible to no one save the participants, is a . . . reason why the novelist in particular should be fascinated by it. . . .
>
> To Mr Irwin (following Freud but also Henry James), the novelist is a person who, camped before a closed door, facing an insufferable ban, creates, in the place of the scene he is forbidden to see, a representation of that scene and a story of the actors in it and how they come to be there (13).

The torture room, then, is not only a metaphor for the relationship between authority and its victims; it is also a metaphor for the act of fiction-making. Coetzee suggests that in this sense the South African state, because of its repression, created—perversely—a situation conducive to the novelist's work: "The dark, forbidden chamber is the origin of novelistic fantasy *per se*; in creating an obscenity, in enveloping it in mystery, the state creates the preconditions for the novel to set about its work of representation" (13).

This complicity between the conditions under which the writer in South Africa functions and the voyeurism inherent in the activity of fiction-making threatens the writer with the horns of a complex dilemma:

there is something tawdry about *following* the state in this way, making its vile mysteries the occasion of fantasy. For the writer the deeper problem is *not* to allow himself to be impaled on the dilemma proposed by the State, namely, either to ignore its obscenities or else to produce representations of them (13).

The first option, that of choosing not to deal with the relationship between the authority of the state and violation, presents the obvious danger of disassociation from political responsibility. The second option, that of choosing to represent acts of torture in fiction, presents the danger of committing further violations in the re-presentation of the scene of torture.[7]

Coetzee's third novel, *Waiting for the Barbarians*, can be seen as an attempt to come to grips with the dilemma he poses in "Into the Dark Chamber." In this fiction Coetzee chooses to deal with scenes of torture. The novel investigates the function of torture in the relationship between the authority of the state and those subject to it. However, Coetzee appears to be aware of the risk that such a fiction runs. For the narrative of *Barbarians* is structured so as to (per)form a caveat both to itself and to other fictions that attempt to represent the act of torture. This caveat consists of the suggestion, made by the metanarrative of the text, that the assumptions underlying the hermeneutic of inquisition—a hermeneutic that is taken to its extreme in torture—may well be adopted by the fiction itself in its attempt to investigate, to interrogate, the acts of torture it describes.

The location of *Waiting for the Barbarians* is the outpost of which the narrator, an imperial magistrate, has charge. This outpost is on the frontier between the Empire and the lands inhabited by the so-called barbarians. The location is remote from the center of the Empire, but only in geographical terms. In terms of the colonialist logic of the Empire, it is the scene of confrontation between the Empire and the other it attempts to colonize, the "barbarians." This makes it the nerve-center of the Empire. For this Empire, like all before it, rationalizes it existence through a sophisticated process of "othering" the "barbarians."

Abdul JanMohamed describes this process of "othering" the native in a way that corresponds to Coetzee's imperial allegory. Employing terms similar to those used to explain the motivation of the sadist, JanMohamed explains the desire of the colonialist to designate the native as "Other." "If every desire is at base a desire to impose oneself on another and to be recognized by the Other," he argues, "then the colonialist situation provides an ideal context for the fulfillment of that fundamental drive" ("The Economy of Manichean Allegory" 85). As in the scenario given in *Waiting for the Barbarians*, the colonialist's military superiority enables him to impose his will on the native as other, and thereby gain the recognition he desires from that "other."[8] This recognition however, constitutes a narcissistic self-recognition, since there is no recognition on the part of the colonialist that the native has a subjectivity independent of the one that the colonialist has constructed for him or her. For the colonialist recognizes the native only as a "recipient of the negative elements of the self that the European projects onto him" ("The Economy of Manichean Allegory" 86).

This projection is characterized by the colonialist's attribution of positive aspects to the self and negative aspects to the native other. *Waiting for the Barbarians* describes the operation of this duality, which JanMohamed identifies as "the economy of the Manichean allegory," in which "to say 'native' is automatically to say 'evil'" (84). However, as in the case of the sadist, the dynamics of projection dictate not fulfillment but interminable dissatisfaction for the colonialist. He has imposed on the native his construct of the other, but at one and the same time directs animosity toward the native for not being someone (as opposed to some*thing*) other than that construct. Such is the disadvantage of the colonialist's objectification:

> the gratification that this situation affords is impaired by the European's alienation from his own unconscious desire. . . . [T]he self becomes the prisoner of the projected image. Even though the native is negated by the projection of the inverted image, his presence *as an absence* can never be cancelled ("The Economy of Manichean Allegory" 86; emphasis added).

JanMohamed is writing of the operation of manichean allegory in colonialist literature; Coetzee's *Waiting for the Barbarians* examines the implementation of manichean allegory in the field of imperialist power politics. Coetzee's Empire depends upon the operation of the imperialist manichean opposition, whereby it can identify itself as just(ified) by identifying the "barbarians" as the enemy. The novel emphasizes the violence necessary for the manichean economy to be implemented in the form of imperialist relations. The narrative achieves this end by focusing on the rhetoric of inquisition and its culmination in torture. The description of the process of inquisition and its "dead-end," torture, certainly demonstrates the extent of the violence required for the imperialist project to survive. Further than this, however, the narrative bears witness to the fact that the procedures of inquisition and torture re-produce the history of colonialist-native relations that JanMohamed has outlined. Torture is the final means used by the Empire in the process of interrogation to "bring the Empire home" to those whom it considers as yet-to-be-converted renegades. The last frontier upon which the Empire undertakes to impress itself upon the manichean other is the skin of the "barbarian" captives of the tale, and at one point also that of the magistrate who sympathizes with them.

The figure of Colonel Joll demonstrates the specular relation between inquisition and colonization. He comes to the frontier, an imperial officer in search of the (for him) fundamental confrontation between the Empire and the "barbarian" other that will afford him meaning. The opening scenes of the novel indicate that he is frustrated that no such confrontation is taking place; or at least, not one of enough stature to carry the overdetermined significance he wishes to ascribe it. The magistrate explains that conflict between "barbarian" and imperial interests is virtually nonexistent, and certainly of little consequence to the Empire in terms of material loss. The two prisoners he is holding at the time of Joll's arrival, the magistrate explains to the colonel, should be regarded as an anomaly: "normally we would not have any barbarians at all to show you," the magistrate explains. "This so-called banditry does not amount to much" (4).

Joll, we soon realize, considers the information that the magistrate gives to be irrelevant, because it does not conform to his notion of the "barbarians" as the enemy. He responds to the lack of significant conflict by attempting to construct the originary imperialist/barbarian confrontation he desires—the urtext of colonization. He does this by trying to re-present the "barbarian" prisoners, the old man and the sick boy and the series of "barbarian" prisoners that follow them, as guilty. The means of doing so are, to use Colonel Joll's own description, the "set procedures" (4) of inquisition and torture.

These "set procedures" for interrogation by torture, like the colonialist enterprise described by JanMohamed, conform to the pattern of the quest. The object of the quest in both cases is very specifically defined by the quester. The colonialist seeks proof of the inferiority of the native; the inquisitor—as we have learned in theory from Foucault and in practice, from Breytenbach—seeks proof of the guilt of the prisoner. In the "economy" of the Colonel Joll figure, these two objectives become con-fused: he is both colonialist and inquisitor. The object of his quest is proof of the guilt of the "barbarian" prisoners, which for him constitutes proof of the animosity of the "barbarians." These dual agendas are married in the term Colonel Joll gives to his objective: "'the truth.'" This "truth" is, of course, "fixed." Whereas the magistrate assumes, naively, that the old man and ailing boy may prove to be innocent, or at least pays lip service to this notion, for Joll "'the [only] truth'" lies in proof of their guilt; what remains is merely for them to be proved guilty.

Colonel Joll's "truth" is determined in a specific context that mirrors that of the colonial confrontation in that it consists of a violent confrontation with the prisoner—the "barbarian" other—engineered by Colonel Joll—the person in the position of power. Proof of the guilt of the "barbarians" is the prize that awaits the inquisitor at the successful conclusion of his task. Colonel Joll explains this to the magistrate, who "bring[s] the conversation around to torture" (5). The magistrate presents a scenario, impossible from the point of view of Colonel Joll, in which the prisoner under interrogation is innocent and is telling the truth, but is nevertheless not believed. "How do you ever know when a man has told you the truth?'" the magistrate asks. "Can you pick up this tone [the tone of the truth] in everyday speech?" Colonel Joll points out that he is not concerned with truths that may pertain to "everyday" activities; he is interested only in the "truth" produced by interrogation, the "guilt" of the "barbarians." Indeed, in his response to the magistrate, he privileges the site of torture as the origin of truth:

> This is the most intimate moment we have yet had, which he [Colonel Joll] brushes off with a little wave of the hand. 'No, you misunderstand me. I am speaking only of a special situation now, I am speaking of a situation in which I am probing for the truth, in which I have to exert pressure to find it. First I get lies, you see—this is what happens—first lies, then pressure, then more lies, then the break, then more pressure, then the truth. That is how you get the truth.' (5).

The magistrate tells us that what he bears away from his conversation with Colonel Joll is that "Pain is truth; all else is subject to doubt" (5). His subsequent behavior suggests that the magistrate has taken this to heart; he retraces the footsteps of, or rather the signs of torture made by, Colonel Joll in search of truth. He is not present at the interrogations that Colonel Joll performs on his first mission to the frontier town—Joll indicates that he does not want the magistrate to be there (4)—but he does investigate the scene after Joll has finished. He tears open the shroud of the old man, to reveal a body tortured to death. Both the bloody hole of the eye-socket and the gap in the shroud that refuses to close without being resewn indicate what the magistrate already knows: having trespassed "on what has become holy or unholy ground, . . . preserve of the mysteries of the State," he cannot turn back. He regrets that he did not go on a hunting trip, "with no question about what the word *investigations* meant, what lay beneath it like a banshee beneath a stone" (9), but he has been "infected" (21): henceforth he is set on a quest of his own.

The violated body of the dead man, and the wounds that the boy suffers after Colonel Joll's second interrogation of him the following night, are only the first in a series of torture marks with which the magistrate becomes obsessed. This obsession finds expression in his relationship to the "barbarian girl." He investigates the room where the "girl's" feet were broken and her eye blinded—the same room where her father was tortured to death. He observes that it is a clean room, marked only by soot on the ceiling above the fireplace and on the wall. He asks her how they blinded her, and she describes to him the instrument they used to brand her skin. He observes in detail the wound this torture has left near her eye:

> I notice in the corner of one eye a greyish puckering as though a caterpillar lay there with its head under her eyelid, grazing. . . .
> Between thumb and forefinger I part her eyelids. The caterpillar comes to an end, decapitated, at the pink inner rim of the eyelid. There is no other mark. The eye is whole (31).

The magistrate's fascination for the "barbarian girl" stems from her body as the site of torture, rather than any desire for the "girl" herself. He worships the surface of her body, the skin, the site of interaction between torturer and tortured. Rather than having intercourse with her, he washes her body, finding in the exploration of her features an ecstasy. Often he falls asleep "as if poleaxed," oblivious, and wakes an hour or so later "dizzy, confused, thirsty." These spells are to him like "death . . . , or enchantment" (31). He massages her feet, deformed by Joll or his subordinates. When he discovers the torture mark at the corner of the "girl's" eye, he observes: "It has been growing more and more clear to me that until the marks on this girl's body are deciphered and understood I cannot let go of her" (31). He treats her body as a text that, if he pays it enough attention—if he "reads" it "properly"—will alert him to the truth behind the scene of torture.

The magistrate's need to "read" the "girl" as the subject of torture prompts us to consider the nature of his implication. From the beginning we are given information that suggests that the magistrate is not involved only in the innocent sense of "know[ing] somewhat too much" (21) and having to deal with the political difficulties that this creates for him. His demand that the boy tell the truth to Joll after Joll has tortured him, and his reprimand to the boy for having made a false confession after Joll's second torture of him, suggest a kind of lethal ignorance on the part of the magistrate as to the real effects of torture on the body. His obsession with the marks of torture on the "girl"—his incapacity to be interested in her as anything else but victim of Joll's "procedures"—also suggests that he too has invested in a quest for truth involving torture. Both Joll and the magistrate, following the Foucauldian paradigm,[9] turn the "girl" into a text from which they believe the truth will originate, Joll through implanting the marks of torture upon her and reading the result as proof of her guilt, and the magistrate by attempting to possess the truth behind torture by reading the "script" that Joll has "written" on her body.

The magistrate's "reading" of the "barbarians," and therefore also of the "barbarian girl," is not the same as that of Colonel Joll's; he has never believed the "barbarians" to be the enemy, or the "barbarian" prisoners to be guilty of plotting against the Empire. However, there is one aspect of his "reading" of the "barbarian girl" that corresponds to Joll's "writing" and "reading" of her. Both Joll and the magistrate, by making her body into a sign that will develop into the figure of the truth, turn the "girl" into an other whose person, outside of that figuring, is irrelevant to them. Both Joll and the magistrate violate the "girl" by treating her body as a means to a truth that lies beyond it, or to use the magistrate's expression, "beneath it like a banshee beneath a stone" (9). Here the tortured body, in Lucia Folena's terms,

> is an object of the violence of interpretation, a mere text to be read by the hermeneutics of inquisition. The body is thus just a means of access to its own real meaning, and simultaneously an obstacle, an opaque diaphragm interposed between the interpreter and the full disclosure of that meaning. Reading the body must needs amount to destroying it in order to substitute for an empty signifier the plenitude of inquisitorial signifiedness ("Figures of Violence" 228).

As Lucia Folena points out, even if the accused offers a confession, torture is still necessary to the inquisitor as a text whereby he can provide himself with physical proof of the prisoner's guilt, which constitutes the truth he is seeking. For if "the voice generated by torture is not, cannot be, the voice the body identified as its own before the torture" (228), the marks of torture, in the tautological rhetoric of the inquisitor, come to constitute physical proof of guilt. Torture, operating as a kind of punishment regardless of what the prisoner may be pleading, produces signs—the marks on the body—of the prisoner's guilt; for if the body bears signs of punishment, how can it be innocent? For "the body interrogated in torture," as Foucault points out in his discussion of eighteenth-century judicial procedure, "constitute[s] the point of application of the punishment *and* the locus of extortion of the truth" (42; emphasis added).

Obviously Joll is much more readily identifiable, in terms of this scheme, as an inquisitor than the magistrate is. Still the magistrate is aware of his proximity to Joll, and he is ultimately unable to disassociate himself from Joll in terms of his relationship to the "girl." Reflecting upon his concern for the tortured boy after having told him to answer every question Joll asks him truthfully, the magistrate remarks that "It has not escaped me that an interrogator can wear two masks, speak with two voices, one harsh, one seductive"

(7). With regard to the "girl" he comments that "The distance between myself and her torturers, I realize, is negligible, I shudder" (27).

Although these comments reflect the magistrate's disgust for Colonel Joll, even his conscience is ultimately unable to eradicate his fascination for the Colonel and the acts of torture he performs. It is true that he is fascinated by the "barbarian girl" too, but only because of her connection with Joll—the marks of torture she bears. He himself asks if it is not "the marks on her which drew me to her" (64). His treatment of her—the washing, the massaging, the tracing of her torture wounds—indicates that he fetishizes her, rather than loving her for herself. It is no wonder he is mesmerized in the course of his attentions to her body: he is not seducing her, but rather is himself seduced by the marks on her skin. This fetishism links him once again with Colonel Joll.

Both Joll's torturing of the "barbarian girl" and the magistrate's "love" for her conform to Suleiman's definition of fetishism: "Fetishism is that perversion," Suleiman argues, "which substitutes a fabricated object for a natural one perceived to be missing" (148). Joll, like JanMohamed's colonialist, directs aggression at the native/barbarian not only to force her to conform to the image he has of her, but also to punish her because (as a result of this very violation) she is not present as herself. Similarly, the magistrate mirrors his dissatisfaction by falling in love with not her, but her "presence as an absence" ("The Economy of Manichean Allegory" 86).[10] His fetishization of her is no less an expression of a desire to violate her, to gain access to her through her body by obliterating it, than Joll's torture of her is. The only difference between their actions toward her is that the one provides physical evidence of this desire through torture. Indeed the magistrate, once he understands to some degree the nature of his desire for the "girl," asks himself if he is not jealous of Colonel Joll for his success in expressing his desire through torture:

> Our loving leaves no mark. Whom will that other girl with the blind face remember: me with my silk robe and my dim lights and my perfumes and oils and my unhappy pleasures, or that other cold man with the mask over his eyes who gave the orders and pondered the sounds of her intimate pain? Whose face was the last face she saw plainly on this earth but the face behind the glowing iron? Though I cringe with shame, even here and now, I must ask myself whether, when I lay head to foot with her, fondling and kissing those broken ankles, I was not in my heart of hearts regretting that I could not engrave myself on her as deeply (134–35).

From this perspective, that is, the perspective of the magistrate, the object of affection and of violent attention are logically one and the same—the "barbarian girl":

> From the moment my steps paused and I stood before her at the barracks gate she must have felt a miasma of defeat closing about her: envy, pity, cruelty all masquerading as desire. And in my lovemaking not impulse but the laborious denial of impulse! (135)

The magistrate's realization of this is perhaps the only thing that prevents him from abusing her physically.

The most remarkable aspect of Coetzee's tale of inquisition and torture is that, despite the hope that the interrogators cherish that their efforts will reveal the truth, nothing is actually accomplished in the course of these "procedures." Joll's and the magistrate's desire is to find an original truth concerning the "barbarian girl," even if that truth takes on a somewhat different meaning in each case; their projects with regard to the "girl" both involve "proposing the possibility and the necessity of a restoration, presented as a reconfirmation to an origin(al)" (Folena, "Figures of Violence" 220). However, this "original" is never reconstructed. Joll's project, that of trying to designate the "barbarians" as originally evil, proves to be futile; he has to attempt to torture all the prisoners he rounds up, an undertaking that becomes meaningless as it proves to be interminable. Indeed, the torture at times appears to have become more of an amusement to Colonel Joll, one of which he could actually tire, rather than the obsessive search that was initially presented to us. The magistrate too, having left the euphoria of his "treason" behind, claims at the conclusion of the novel that he has learned nothing of what has happened: "I have lived through an eventful year," he says, "yet understand no more of it than a babe in arms" (154–55).

A metaphor for this failure is provided by the magistrate's hobby—archaeology. The magistrate's digging for the poplar slips in the hope that they will enlighten him, and his continuing attempts to decipher the writing on them, represent in material form an analogy to the kind of "reading" that supplies the logic of the hermeneutics of inquisition. It is, in Teresa Dovey's words, a "reading" that "takes us on a search for origins, and locates the mastery of truth, or meaning, in factual documentation [in *Barbarians*, the mark of otherness, the mark of torture] that anticipates the historical moment in which the act of reading, or interpretation, is located" ("Coetzee and Critics" 17). This type of "reading" and the hope that motivates it is described by Derrida explicitly in terms of the archaeological project:

> As always this archaeology is also a teleology and an eschatology; the dream of a full and immediate presence closing history, the transparence and indivision of a parousia, the suppression of contradiction and difference (*Grammatology* 115).

Dovey points out that this reading is violent in that it reduces the text to a preordained meaning, referred to as "the truth": for Joll as colonialist, the "barbarians" are the enemy; for Joll as torturer, the "barbarians" are guilty; for the magistrate as quester, the only location of truth is the scene of torture. Here lack of evidence for a single truth is followed not by recognition of the irrelevance of that truth; rather, that lack is compensated for by the production of signs that are intended to convey that truth. The marks of torture function in this capacity both for Joll and the magistrate: Joll sees them as evidence of "barbarian" guilt, whereas the magistrate sees them as proof that the "girl" must express some truth that he and Joll both wish to possess but which, the magistrate recognizes, Joll has failed to reach. Even those elements that conceivably have nothing to do with the object of the quest, such as the slips of wood, are harnessed by Joll and the magistrate as an element in their respective quests. For Joll they represent further evidence of the "barbarians" as conspirators and for the magistrate, further evidence of his (and Joll's) failure to "read" the truth that they believe lies behind the "barbarians." What Martin says about the narrator in this situation refers to the magistrate but is equally applicable to Joll, the narrator of the scenes of interrogation and torture:

> Everything, in short, is reduced to its irreducible objectivity, conceived of as a sign, as bearing some intrinsic significance, as representing some eternal order, and so is able, if understood, to reveal to the narrator the truth, to situate him definitively in an order beyond that of mere appearances. But despite his interpretive drive throughout, the narrator cannot discover the truth: his archaic "codes" no longer suffice (14).

If, as Watson points out, "the only tongue that the colonialist can speak is the circular one of tautology," then clearly the same can be said for the inquisitor. For the only answer that the inquisitor recognizes as the truth is that which he has preordained as the answer to his question. The production of signs that confirm that truth, and the transformation of potentially extrinsic material into signs that perform the same function, render meaninglessness endemic. Where everything is reduced to signs of a preexistent code, only the simulated reading of the archaeological project is possible; reading for meaning generated by subjects and the events they precipitate is inconceivable. What Watson says about the relationship between colonization and language in such a situation may be extended to apply to the relationships among colonization, inquisition, and language in the context of *Waiting for the Barbarians*: "In the same way that human relations are opaque and destructive in the colonial situation, so, Coetzee would seem to suggest, language itself fails to signify, to mean at all, under the conditions prevailing in such a situation" (373).

In this context we need to move away from seeing the narrator's fetishization of torture as a privileged site capable of producing the as yet elusive "truth" as evidence of a remarkable ability to stand up to the horrors presented by the Colonel Jolls of this world, and investigate the notion that his fascination with such sites (or rites) is rather less than laudable. For the magistrate as narrator occupies a position similar to those writers that Coetzee discusses in "Into the Dark Chamber"; as a narrator figure he is troubled by that

> problem that troubles the [South African] novelist—how to justify a concern with morally dubious people involved in a contemptible activity; how to find an appropriately minor place for the petty secrets of the security system; how to treat something that, in truth, because it is offered like the Gorgon's head to terrorize the populace and paralyze resistance, deserves to be ignored ("Dark Chamber" 35).

Now Coetzee states clearly that he is "not arguing that the world of the torturer should be ignored or minimized" (35). But he is arguing that we need to question the motives behind a preoccupation with the scene of torture by investigating the method of its portrayal. He criticizes three authors for their portrayal of scenes of torture and violence, his complaints being twofold. He criticizes Sepamla for the erotic fascination that his description of the torture of Bongi in *A Ride on the Whirlwind* displays, and then goes on to suggest that Mongane Serote and la Guma are somewhat more successful in their attempts (*To Every Birth Its Blood* and *In the Fog of the Season's End*). He nevertheless criticizes the latter two authors for their use of a dark lyricism. "If the novelist finds in squalor the occasion for his most soaring poetic eloquence," Coetzee asks, "might he not be guilty of seeking out his squalid subject matter for perversely literary reasons?" (35)

What is interesting about these criticisms in the context of *Waiting for the Barbarians* is that its narrator, the magistrate, is described as having fallen prey to both these traps. His obsession with the "girl," based as it is on her body as the object of torture, suggests that he too is guilty of erotic fascination with regard to scenes of torture. Secondly, his narrative attributes to the torturer and the torture chamber, the primary elements of the scene behind closed doors by which he is so compelled, that "evil grandeur" that Coetzee regards as "false portentousness, a questionable dark lyricism" (35). This elevation of the status of the torturer and his activities is evident in the magistrate's (dubious) curiosity concerning Joll, which results—no matter how good the magistrate's conscious intentions may be—in a kind of fruitless voyeurism. He is particularly interested in the "doorway" through which the torturer initially passes to take up his task, and which he now moves into and out of with apparent ease; the expression "first time" suggests the pornographic element of the magistrate's interest:

> Looking at him [Joll] I wonder how he felt the very first time: did he, invited as an apprentice to twist the pincers or turn the screw or whatever it is they do, shudder even a little to know that at that instant he was trespassing into the forbidden? I find myself wondering too whether he has a private ritual of purification, carved out behind closed doors, to enable him to return and break bread with other men (12).

The magistrate's concern with separating the torturer from "other men" and the torturer from the tortured is one that follows him through his tale, to the point where he identifies Joll as the enemy, pointing out to him that he is the threat, and not the "barbarians." This is the kind of blinding truth that one expects from the kind of archaeological reading the magistrate undertakes; this kind of identification of self/good other/evil is the kind of "parousia" we expect from such an enterprise. However, despite this "full and immediate dream" (to continue with the Derridean metaphor), this knowledge gets the narrator nowhere. Like the dreams he records within his narrative, this dream too "resemble[s the world] only in [its] resistance to meaning" (Zamora 8). At the close of the novel, the narrator is still trying to impose his (and Joll's) old way of reading, of judging, on a world that rejects such categorization. Confronted by a scene that "is not the scene I dreamed of," he comments that "like much else nowadays I leave it feeling stupid, like a man who lost his way long ago but presses on along a road that may lead nowhere" (155–56). The only knowledge he has gained of any potential use is not that Joll is the enemy—how could he make such knowledge useful?—but that his way of "reading," the archaeological project, has not worked; he has lost the thread of his tale, the motivation for the quest.

Through the failure of the narrator's quest, Coetzee appears to suggest the limitations of the practical benefit of fictions that deal with situations in which violence is endemic and torture common by trying to assign these ills to an evil other of magnificent significance, the eradication of which will bring back Eden; after all, Joll's interrogations "deteriorate" into games of which he finally tires, but which will no doubt occur again: it is the rise and fall of "Empires" that assures such activities, and any Joll will do. The only thing that the novelist can do under such extreme circumstances, Coetzee

suggests, is to point out the violence of the meaninglessness that such circumstances engender.

Coetzee concludes his discussion of the representation of torture with
praise for a scene from Gordimer's *Burger's Daughter* which he highlights as
"one episode in particular that, in an indirect way, addresses the same moral
problems I have been trying to put my finger on" (35). This is the episode in
which Rosa Burger is driving around on the outskirts of the black townships
of Johannesburg and comes across a family of three in a donkey cart. The man
is flogging the donkey in a drunken rage. Gordimer, through Rosa, the narrator, describes the scene as one in which she sees

> the infliction of pain broken away from the will that creates it; broken loose, a
> force existing of itself, ravishment without the ravisher, torture without the tor-
> turer, rampage, pure cruelty gone beyond the control of humans who have spent
> thousands of years devising it. The entire ingenuity from thumbscrew and rack to
> electric shock, the infinite variety and gradation of suffering, by lash, by fear, by
> hunger, by solitary confinement—the camps, concentration, labour, resettlement,
> the Siberias of snow or sun, the lives of Mandela, Sisulu, Mbeki, Kathrada, Kgos-
> ana, gull-picked on the island . . . (208).

Coetzee points out Rosa's options: to chastise a poor black for treating his
animal as he himself has been treated, or to ignore the scene and drive on, left
however with the suspicion that she did so only in order not to think of herself
as one of those whites who regards animal above human life. Once again the
situation has become one in which meaningful action is impossible. Coetzee
emphasizes this aspect of the scene:

> It is important not to read the episode in a narrowly symbolic way. The driver and
> the donkey do not respectively stand for torturer and tortured. "Torture without
> the torturer" is the key phrase. Forever and ever in Rosa's memory the blows will
> rain down and the beast shudder in pain. The scene comes from the inner reaches
> of Dante's hell, beyond the scope of morality. For morality is human, whereas the
> two figures locked to the cart belong to a damned, dehumanized world (35).

What Rosa Burger waits for, "*beyond* this dark moment of the soul" is, Coetzee
comments, what the author must suffer and wait for; a world in which the
author may once more legitimately claim meaning for her or his narrative:

> a time when humanity will be restored across the face of society, and therefore
> when all human acts, including the flogging of an animal, will be returned to the

ambit of moral judgement. In such a society it will once again be *meaningful* for the gaze of the author, the gaze of authority and authoritative judgement, to be turned upon scenes of torture. When the choice is no longer limited to *either* looking on in horrified fascination as the blows fall *or* turning one's eyes away, then the novel can once again take as its province the whole of life, and even the torture chamber can be accorded a place in the design (35).

If Coetzee's critical comment suggests that the author who writes scenes of violence should ensure that such scenes are always, in a sense, "in waiting" for, rather than representative of, meaning, his novel *Foe* suggests what form fiction "in waiting" might take with respect to its subject: the colonized figure of the indigenous other.

NOTES

1. This aspect of Coetzee's thought is emphasized in Stephen Watson's "Colonialism and the Novels of J. M. Coetzee." Watson quotes an interview with Coetzee in this regard:

> In an interview conducted in 1978, J. M. Coetzee remarked that he was inclined "to see the South African situation [today] as only one manifestation of a wider historical situation to do with colonialism, late colonialism, neo-colonialism." At the same time, as if to underline his sense that South Africa's situation was bound up with a global historical process, he added, "I'm suspicious of lines of division between a European context and a South African context, because I think our experience remains largely colonial" (370).

2. David Attwell discusses both of these elements of Coetzee's work in *J. M. Coetzee: South Africa and the Politics of Writing.* Yet while he discusses Coetzee's rather unique position in terms of the contemporary debate in South Africa over the merits of realism in his first chapter, and defends the aggressivity of the narrative of *Dusklands* as a critique of the pragmatics of liberal humanism and the literary forms it takes in the South African context (55), Attwell does not link these two projects explicitly. That is to say, he does not argue, as I do, that it is in the case, specifically, of actual depictions of violent scenes, that realist narratives are most likely to contribute to reproducing the violence of history, by structuring their readers' interest as pornographic.

3. The title of the novel alludes in a general sense to the "dusk" of the long "day" of Empire (Gardiner 174). This is indicated by the title's affinity to titles of fin de siécle works such as Nietzsche's *Twilight of the Gods* and Spengler's *Untergang das Abendlandes* (Christie 175–76). More specifically, as Teresa Dovey has pointed out, the latter allusion indicates the affinity of Coetzee's narrative to the notion of history as repetition or

Vico's *ricorso*, from which Spengler develops his notion of history as a cyclical process ("Coetzee and His Critics" 17).

4. In the context of this study I am using the male pronoun to represent the sadist, following Suleiman who, in her study of Robbe-Grillet's novels, makes a correlation between the narrator as male and the narrator as aggressor, one which is appropriate also in the context of *Dusklands*:

> Language, rhetoric, and above all the right to *invent* (narrate) belong to the aggressor. This rule is confirmed even in the instances that seem to constitute exceptions to it; I mean the narrative sequences that are first narrated by female voices . . . [in *Projet*] [T]he female narrative voice soon 'slides' into that of the chief narrator (the one who begins and ends the book), and he does not relinquish control from then on (66).

5. This is why David Attwell, in response to Teresa Dovey's application of Hegelian philosophy to Coetzee's work in *The Novels of J. M. Coetzee*, points out that it is not a master/slave dialectic that Coetzee is offering a critique of in *Dusklands*, but the implementation of a master/savage dialectic (51). This distinction is important, in that it illustrates, once again, that specific contextualizations of Hegelian philosophy demonstrate the danger of its assumed universality—a "universality" which amounts, of course, to its assumed inevitability. While Attwell re-defines the slave here as a manichean other rendered savage, rather than slave, by his racial difference, I am arguing that racial and sexual differentiation are identified in *Dusklands* as patterns of manichean othering that mimic and confuse one another in the colonial context.

6. Eugene Dawn has only disgust and contempt for his wife Marilyn, describing her as

> a masturbator who needs steady mechanical friction to generate on the inner walls of her eyes those fantasies of enslavement that eventually squeeze a groan and shudder out of her (12).

7. Coetzee is accused of both of these faults. For two of the more sophisticated arguments in this regard see Nadine Gordimer who speaks of Coetzee's "revulsion" from history ("Gardening" 3–4); and Peter Knox-Shaw who, unlike Attwell (*J. M. Coetzee* 55) and myself, claims that

> Nothing offsets the sadistic agency of the narrator [in *Dusklands*]: in so far as the suffering of Coetzee's victims is recorded it is through the gloating eyes of their killer . . . —the effect [of the narrative is] deliberately produced, but in the absence of any other resource it must be said the writing itself furthers the claims of true savagery. This is an art that can only re-enact (32–33).

8. By using the masculine pronoun to designate both colonialist and interrogator I do not mean to imply, for example, that all colonialists are male: to do so would be to deny the function of racial difference in colonialist power structures, a move that Susan Andrade identifies correctly as brutally simplistic. However, I have chosen not to in-

clude the female pronoun here, in order to avoid giving the impression that there is an equal potential for the colonialist-interrogator to be female. Although I am dealing with textual figures and not existing individuals, I nevertheless think that this would give a misleading impression of the power politics attending sexual difference.

9. Attwell remarks upon Foucault connecting torture and the construction of the accused's "identity," pointing out that "after being tortured himself, the Magistrate uses language similar to Foucault's: 'He [Mandel] deals with my soul: every day he folds the flesh aside and exposes my soul to the light' (*J. M. Coetzee* 118)" (80).

10. Lance Olsen's article entitled "The Presence of Absence: Coetzee's *Waiting for the Barbarians*" also employs this phrase in a discussion of the novel, but in a somewhat different context.

CONCLUSION

THE NARRATIVE "LOSES ITS VOICE"

In my introduction I discussed Susan Barton's dilemma as that of the postcolonizer. To suggest that she can be adequately described by that category, however, would be to simplify her position drastically, and to undermine the complexity of Coetzee's fiction. In this conclusion I intend to demonstrate two features of *Foe* which look toward a novel approach to violence. The first of these is the narrative's ability to deal with multiple violations—its rejection of any narrative that creates a hierarchy of victimization—and its capacity to discover the complex power structures that govern the relationships among those violations. The second feature of the novel which I want to stress is the way in which it proposes a narrative strategy for confronting the scene of violation without erasing it in narrative. *Foe* illustrates a way of seeing the violated figure without re-inscribing that violation, without imprisoning it, interminably, in the construct of victim.

Susan Barton is one of Coetzee's "reluctant colonizer" figures (Watson 377–79), and is herself controlled and dominated to a significant degree by discourses or narrative structures not of her own making. Her double project, that of her search and rescue operation with regard to Friday and of her writing of her story to "save" herself, are both threatened by the power of discourses that she is incapable of controlling. The history of her failure to achieve this dual goal constitutes the history of her growing awareness of her inability to create narratives that are not always already controlled—indeed, violated—by the effect of preexisting discourses on their form.

It is at this point that Susan Barton's own body, marked as both white and female, intrudes upon her own narrative. We are aware from the start that Susan Barton's gender is important to the goal of her creative desire, which is to produce the first female castaway narrative. Yet the novel potential that her gender holds for her creative future is overwritten by the predominantly male-determined attributes of her racial identity, namely her inheritance of and admiration for the masculine traditions of writing and colonization.

This aspect of Susan Barton's dilemma—her inheritance of traditions that undercut her attempts to liberate her narrative—is demonstrated by her struggles against the authority of Foe. Susan Barton resists Foe's attempt to colonize her story by making it "fit" a pattern that is largely a composite of *Robinson Crusoe*, the great English colonial narrative of the eighteenth century, and *Roxana*, the great English "fallen woman's" confessional narrative of the same period. This is Foe's description of the story he intends to write of Susan Barton, to which she responds with dismay:

> 'We therefore have five parts in all: the loss of the daughter; the quest for the daughter in Brazil; abandonment of the quest, and the adventure of the island; assumption of the quest by the daughter; and reunion of the daughter with her mother. It is thus that we make up a book: loss, then quest, then recovery; beginning, then middle, then end. . . .'
> All the joy I had felt in finding my way to Foe fled me. I sat heavy-limbed (117).

Susan Barton rejects Foe's latest narrative proposal. The wording of her refusal highlights the conjunction of colonization and patriarchy in his conception of narrative:

> 'Once you proposed to supply a middle by inventing cannibals and pirates. These I would not accept because they were not the truth. Now you propose to reduce the island to an episode in the history of a woman in search of a lost daughter. This too I reject' (121).

Much is at stake in Susan Barton's rejection of the discursive forms, those of the fallen woman and of the colonizer, with which Foe proposes to "make up" her story. Certain elements of Susan Barton's life mimic those of Roxana's—the lost daughter, for example—but only in the eyes of the male author Foe does Susan Barton become Roxana. Susan Barton rejects his construction of her as Roxana: she goes in search of her daughter, whereas the infamous Roxana rejected her daughter's (legitimate, in Defoe's eyes) maternal claim on her. Susan Barton's rejection of the second Susan Barton of the story, the false daughter that she believes Foe is forcing upon her, represents Susan

Barton's resistance to the violation that she perceives Foe to be imposing on her by demanding she recognize his creation, Susan Barton II, as hers.

If Susan Barton were to recognize Susan Barton II, whom she believes to be Foe's creation, as her own, this recognition would mask the fact that Foe would then be at liberty to "colonize" Susan Barton, to appropriate her; he would be able to claim Susan Barton's story, even Susan Barton herself, as his own. Susan Barton rejects the "daughter" that Foe proposes to her and his recuperative theory of narrative, that of loss-quest-recovery, in one and the same breath. Susan Barton tells the girl not only that she is not her mother, but that the girl has never had a mother, and therefore cannot recover one. The girl is a by-product and therefore victim of the male authorial fantasy of self-engenderment:

> "'You are father-born. You have no mother. The pain you feel is the pain of lack, not the pain of loss. What you hope to regain in my person you have in truth never had'" (91).

One of the reasons why critics have difficulty in reading Susan Barton as a feminist heroine[1] is that her own narrative begins to indicate that she is aware that she has "treated" Friday in a manner analogous to that in which Foe wishes to "treat" her. Her claim to Friday in the first two sections of the novel expresses her sense that she "owns" Friday in much the same way that Foe wants her to own Susan Barton II, so that he can own Susan Barton and her story. This is so despite Susan Barton's sense of possession being initially somewhat obscured from the reader by her notion of responsibility toward Friday. Yet ultimately these two attitudes, responsibility for and ownership of Friday, amount to one and the same thing. At the close of Part Two Susan Barton declares that she cannot rest easy knowing that she may have put Friday "back on the boat" to another plantation. Her language is that of possession, notwithstanding the fact that she has just "given" Friday his "freedom": "'. . . I do not love him [Friday], but he is mine. That is why he remains in England. That is why he is here'" (111).

It is in Part Three that Susan Barton, becoming aware of Foe's manipulation of her, describes her own violation of Friday to Foe, and warns him against performing the same violation. She rejects Foe's desire to tell the story of her life, claiming that she has a right to fulfill her own desire to be known only by the story of the island. She argues that this story includes the story of Friday. However, for the first time she suggests that the story of Friday should not be a recuperative one. She does this by pointing out that while she can at least attempt to tell her story according to her own desire, Friday cannot. Susan

Barton rebukes Foe for not taking this distinction between her silence, that is, her self-determined silence, and Friday's silence into account:

> 'You err most tellingly in failing to distinguish between my silences and the silences of a being such as Friday. Friday has no command of words and therefore no defence against being re-shaped day by day in conformity with the desires of others. I say he is a cannibal and he becomes a cannibal; I say he is a laundryman and he becomes a laundryman' (121).

Susan Barton's rebuke suggests that the writing (out) of Friday's sorrows may well result in a narrative that obscures the fact of Friday's violation, while it simultaneously masquerades as an exposé of that violation. In such a narrative, disclosure becomes simultaneously both concealment and closure. Susan Barton, speaking specifically of the scene of Friday's potential or projected castration—the fact that we remain uncertain as to the nature or extent of this violation bears out her comment—phrases the dilemma of trying to locate that scene in narrative this way: "'I do not know how these matters can be written of in a book,'" she tells Foe, "'unless they are covered up again in figures. . . .'" (120). Susan Barton registers her own project of narrativizing Friday as a violation of Friday when she points out the impossibility of Friday's self-representation to Foe with brutal clarity: "'No matter what he [Friday] is to himself (is he anything to himself?—how can he tell us?), what he is to the world is what I make of him'" she says (122).

Susan Barton begins to view the power she has over Friday, which exists in her capacity to control the representation of Friday, in a dubious light. At first Susan Barton enjoys her ability to control her story through her choice of what to write. This project involves not only the creation but also the absolute control of narrative.[2] She associates the exercise of this power with liberation; and, tellingly, views it as an expression of the masculine authorial fantasy of self-engenderment. Susan Barton claims that:

> 'It is still in my power to guide and amend. Above all, to withhold. By such means do I still endeavour to be *father* to my story' (123; emphasis added).

Yet once Susan Barton is confronted with the "daughter's" and Amy's claims to the "daughter's" authenticity, Susan Barton doubts her own renunciation of the "daughter" as legitimate, and thus begins to doubt her own, and Foe's, and any other conceivable narrator's, authenticity.[3] This radical questioning of who, if anyone, has a right to speak or write whom, pitches Susan Barton into a kind of postmodern dilemma. She suffers from a growing inability to recognize one narrative as more legitimate than another, even if that narrative is her own. This confuses the original organizational principle of Susan Barton's narrative and brings it to a kind of dead end, in which Susan Barton "loses" her voice:

> 'In the beginning I thought I would tell you the story of the island and, being done with that, return to my former life. But now all my life grows to be story and there is nothing of my own left to me. I thought I was myself and this girl a creature from another order speaking words you made up for her. But now I am full of doubt. Nothing is left to me but doubt. I am doubt itself. Who is speaking me? Am I a phantom too? To what order do I belong? And you: who are you?' (133).

The situation in which Susan Barton finds herself certainly displays the apparently democratic strategy known to postmodernism, namely that in which multiple "voices" or discourses are presented as potentially equally legitimate, or equally illegitimate.[4] As the adherents of postmodernism have pointed out, the climate of this postmodern skepticism does not encourage the kind of violation of another which Foe's projected narrative would inflict upon Susan Barton, and which Susan Barton's original recuperative strategies inflict upon the figure of Friday, in the form of appropriation. However, the expression of a radical doubt, extended as it is to all narrative propositions, brings with it its own set of violations; indeed, under scrutiny, such doubt can be seen to be far less radical than may at first have seemed the case.[5]

The attempt to present multiple narratives as equally valid, while it may appear to "give voice" to a number of conflicting claims, can function as a cover operation for the silencing of specific, or embodied, others. Susan Barton becomes a victim of this kind of silencing of the individual voice, when Foe proposes to her that a voice that contends with hers may be as valid as hers. Foe threatens Susan Barton's voice directly when he presents her with the notion that the claims of Susan Barton II, the "daughter," may be as legitimate as Susan Barton's own disclaimer of the girl. This contending voice belongs, significantly, to a character legitimated, if not created, by Foe himself. Here the violation consists of the imposition of a specifically male construction of the female character upon Susan Barton, since the daughter is both Defoe's Susan Barton, daughter of Roxana, intertextually, and, it is implied, Foe's creation, intratextually.

The ending of Foe, or more specifically, the fact that the story ends beyond the "loss" of Susan Barton's voice, suggests that the novel itself goes beyond the deconstructive project of its own postmodernism. The figure of Friday in Foe can and has been described as a postmodern figuring of the other.[6] However, the figure of Friday can also be read as a kind of critique of the postmodern strategy for representing the other. In this light the figure of Friday can be seen as suggesting an alternative to the violations that both recuperative and postmodern strategies for figuring the other inflict upon their subjects.[7]

The postmodern strategy for avoiding the recuperative fallacy for which Susan Barton initially falls is, following Lyotard, to regard the other as unrepresentable (*The Postmodern Condition* xxiv). However, without careful attention on the part of the author to the figures used to depict others as unrepresentable, this theory can result in another violation of the distinct, embodied other.[8] The location of that which is other in figures of the un-representable is a practice prone to the violation of reducing all others by representing them as a single other—the unrepresentable—within the discourse of the self. A second, and related, violation consists of the fallacy that to represent an other as unrepresentable is to avoid contamination of that other by the interests of the writing self, the authorial voice that creates the figure intended to express the unrepresentability of that other.[9] In his article entitled "Modernism's Last Post," Stephen Slemon argues that while both postmodernism and postcolonialism share deconstructive strategies, postcolonial texts are not only deconstructive, but are also at the same time "recuperative." The adjective in this context does not mean recuperative in any simplistic sense; that is to say, postcolonialism does not dictate that Coetzee should give Friday a tongue, and thus a voice. Slemon examines a text by the Jamaican writer, Neville Farki, to demonstrate his point. He describes how Farki's novel, *The Death of Tarzana Clayton*, employs deconstructive strategies that, as in *Foe*, result in a "'decolonized' sense of historic event" ("Modernism's Last Post" 11). However, he points out that this is not the only concern of Farki's novel; its deconstructive project is accompanied by "the remembering or relearning of the role of the native as historical subject and combatant, possessor of an-other knowledge and producer of alternative traditions" (Parry 34).

Slemon stresses these two interests in Farki's novel: its will to decolonize, and its (simultaneous) will to resurrect the notion of an extracolonial subjectivity from the colonized people's past and for their future. He does so in order to support his argument. He proposes that postcolonial criticism aims to maintain for postcolonial writing a mimetic or referential purpose; post-colonial writing can describe the effects of colonialism. However, such criticism also recognizes that the "'referent'" of postcolonial writing—the extracolonial subjectivity—cannot be pinned down or "totalized" (9). This may seem contradictory to our postmodern-attuned ears, but as Slemon points out, the crisis of representation confronted by postmodernism is one of the Western philosophical tradition's making. "Post-colonial cultures," he argues, "have a long history of working towards 'realism' *within* an awareness of referential slippage" (12).

The figure of Friday, noncenter of the narrative of *Foe* (as Susan Barton keeps on pointing out to Foe), can be situated at the nexus between these two "contradictory" (from our point of view) movements in postcolonialism, namely the maintenance of a mimetics that is not simplistically recuperative but is nevertheless recreative, and the simultaneous refusal of a fixed referent. For the space that Friday both does and does not occupy is not represented as unrepresentable in an absolute sense; rather it is the location of an identity that has specific attributes, but which can nevertheless not be fixed or named for all time. Friday plays a tune, throws petals on the water, dances—but the meanings of these actions are a constant puzzle to Susan Barton: she cannot "fix" them. This aspect of Friday is also figured in his speech, which is of course not speech, but an endless "stream" (157). Thus the space that Friday occupies is not one that represents the black hole of an other that subsumes all others. As Susan Barton puts it,

> 'the story of Friday . . . is properly not a story but a puzzle or hole in the narrative (*I picture it as a buttonhole, carefully cross-stitched around, but empty, waiting for the button*)' (121; emphasis added).[10]

This figuring of Friday is a solution of sorts for Coetzee's specific discursive position, that of a white South African dissident, or a "reluctant colonizer," to use Watson's term, as Attwell has pointed out (*J. M. Coetzee* 103–17). Through the figure of Friday, Coetzee avoids making the other speak (as Susan Barton and Foe try to make Friday "speak" in various ways, the last of which is by trying to teach him to write). However, the figure of Friday, as Susan Barton describes it here, does make room for a specific other, the embodied Friday who cannot "speak" to the text. The narrative does this by "losing" the voice of its named narrator, Susan Barton, and speaking in the voice of the unnamed, indeterminate narrator of its last section.

It is in this final figuring of Friday that *Foe* comes to terms with both the violence of recuperative narrative and that of the postmodern project, in which it is assumed that the representation of multiple voices as equally legitimate, and/or the representation of the other as unrepresentable, marks the postmodern discourse itself as a noncolonizing one. In the last "dive" of the fiction, the unnamed narrator and Friday come face to face with one another. It is as if the *O*'s Friday is "writing" at the end of the third part have created an opening through which the narrator may enter to inhabit, for a moment, the (nonnarrative) space where Friday dwells. The narrator relinquishes words in favor of the "slow stream" produced by Friday, untranslatable into any language at all:

> I tug his wooly hair, finger the chain about his throat. 'Friday,' I say, I try to say, kneeling over him, sinking hands and knees into the ooze, 'what is this ship?'
>
> But this is not a place of words. Each syllable, as it comes out, is caught and filled with water and diffused. This is a place where bodies are their own signs. It is the home of Friday (157).

Here the metanarrative of the text, through the unnamed narrator, recognizes the violation that the attempt to describe, to "write" Friday's body, and especially the mutilations of that body, constitutes. It is as if the authors in/of the story—Susan Barton and Foe, and behind them Daniel Defoe and J. M. Coetzee—have relinquished their attempts to dominate and thus violate their subjects, and have given themselves over to a narrative that is willing to confront the other as an other whose body it—as narrative—has always been unable to master completely. This narrative no longer wants to dominate all others, its subjects, but rather to experience, to feel, this specific subjectivity:

> He turns and turns till he lies at full length, his face to my face. The skin is tight across his bones, his lips are drawn back. I pass a fingernail across his teeth, trying to find a way in.
>
> His mouth opens. From inside him comes a slow stream, without breath, without interruption. It flows up through his body and out upon me; it passes through the cabin, through the wreck; washing the cliffs and shores of the island, it runs northward and southward to the ends of the earth. Soft and cold, dark and unending, it beats against my eyelids, against the skin of my face (157).

NOTES

1. For a critique of *Foe* as a patriarchal novel, see Kristen Holst Peterson's reading of Susan as a character "framed" by Foe and, by extension, Coetzee himself. See also Gayatri Chakravorty Spivak on Susan Barton "as agent, as the asymmetrical double of the author" for an alternative reading ("Can the Subaltern Speak"? 175).

2. Susan Barton indicates that the quest for absolute mastery is doomed never to be completed in practice, when she complains of her inability to make her narratives conform precisely to her intention:

"'Alas, my stories seem always to have more applications than I intend, so that I must go back and laboriously extract the right application and apologize for the wrong ones and efface them'" (81).

3. For detailed discussions of the question of Coetzee's authority in relation to his narrators and subjects, see David Attwell, *J. M. Coetzee: South Africa and the Politics of Writing*, and Brian Macaskill and Jeanne Colleran.

4. This is the practical consequence of that aspect of the postmodern which Jean Lyotard describes as its "incredulity toward metanarratives" (*The Postmodern Condition* xxiv).

5. The desire to have Coetzee's fiction conform to the postmodern conception of the radical questioning of all authorial voices leads to a number of readings in which the ultimate authority is given to the figure of Friday at the same time that it is claimed that "In the end, Coetzee challenges his readers to demystify the writer's art (including his own), to find the traces of other voices, and to question any attempt at authority" (Maher 40). The problem here is twofold; the claim is contradictory—Friday's voice is chosen as the authoritative one, but all authority is questionable: and second, the claim reformulates Friday as one who can speak, thus ignoring the radical instability that the deliberate obscuring of access to Friday requires from its interpreters. Friday, I suggest, is the focus of the novel: but this is not a focus whose "content" is accessible, as I hope to indicate.

6. See Dovey, *The Novels of J.M. Coetzee* and "The Intersection of Postmodern . . .": Gräbe; and Hutcheon, *The Politics of Postmodernism*.

7. Brian Macaskill and Jeanne Colleran make this point, but do so using a vocabulary that recuperates postmodernism in a manouvre that exhibits an eternally accommodating, and thus interminably assimilating, construct of postmodernism: Coetzee "resists . . . by undermining, while participating within, a postmodern critiqe of representation" (454). For an acute discussion of the problem that postcolonialism poses to this concept of postmodernism in reference to Coetzee's oeuvre and the South African literary context, see David Atwell, *J. M. Coetzee* 20–23.

8. Linda Hutcheon, in her discussion of the points of congruence among postmodernism, postcolonialism, and feminism, indicates the danger of collapsing postmodern, feminist, and postcolonial projects into one another under the rubric of postmodernity:

Postmodern representation itself contests mastery and totalization, often by unmasking both their powers and their limitations. We watch the process of what Foucault once called the interrogating of limits that is now replacing the search for totality. On the level of representation, this postmodern questioning overlaps with similarly pointed challenges by those working in, for example, postcolonial and feminist contexts. How is the 'other' represented in say, imperialist or patriarchal discourses? But a *caveat* is in order. It may be true that postmodern thought 'refuses to turn Other into Same' (During 1987: 33), but there is also a very real sense in which the postmodern notions of difference and a positively valorized marginality often reveal the same familiar totalizing strategies of domination, though usually masked by the liberating rhetoric of First World critics who appropriate Third World cultures to their own ends (Chow 1986–7: 91). Postmodern critique is always compromised. The ex-centric 'other' itself may have different (and less complicitous) modes of representation and may therefore require different methods of study (*The Politics of Postmodernism* 37–38).

9. Helen Tiffin demonstrates how what may appear to be an interest in the welfare of a so-called "other" may often operate as a secondary function in a project whose primary goal is in reality one of self-interest. Here she describes certain influential strains in contemporary Euro-American criticism (poststructuralism and postmodernism) to demonstrate her point:

> For all this theoretical investment in the question of "otherness", certain tendencies within Euro-American post-structuralism and post-modernism have in practice operated in the same way in which the Western historicizing consciousness has operated, that is, to appropriate and control the "other", while ostensibly performing some sort of major cultural redemption—specifically, for post-structuralism, the reformation or revolutionising of Western epistemological codes and cognitive biases (170).

10. David Attwell explains the implications of this position for a reading of Friday. Because it is indicated that Friday has a world of his own, Attwell argues, "this does not mean, obviously, that the novel can *represent* Friday's history: it simply means that Friday is acknowledged to have one"(*J. M. Coetzee* 115).

EPILOGUE

I am going to release you soon
from this rope of words.

—The narrator, *Age of Iron*

The writings of Brink, Breytenbach, and Coetzee which I have ex-
plored in the previous chapters span the years from 1974 to 1986. They represent the attempt of one rather specific group of dissident writers and
intellectuals to describe the operation and effects of violence engendered by
the daunting and multiple hierarchies of imperialist thought. Brink,
Breytenbach, and Coetzee have very different ways and very different priorities
in their individual approaches to the problem of such violence; but in each
case, their constructions of it have been fuelled, directly or indirectly, by their
experience of the South African context. That context has changed, dramati-
cally, since the period during which these texts were written. I can, and will,
indicate the implications of some of those changes and their impact on the
work of the three authors. What will then remain, and it is a task I can only
point toward, rather than complete at this historical juncture, is an evaluation
of the history of investigating violence through narrative—of which this study
comprises a part—in terms of its resourcefulness for the immediate task at
hand in South Africa. I mean, of course, the business of constructing liberation
in the wake of apartheid's demise.

The writings I have discussed in detail here were written in the years
that preceded 1985, that crucial and bloody year in the history of apartheid
oppression. The imposition of the State of Emergency in that year seemed to
leave even those most inured to the ability of P. W. Botha's Nationalist government to dream up yet more atrocities, in a state of shock. The novels written
by Brink and Coetzee in the aftermath of 1985 register—in very different ways,
as one would expect—the impact of the Emergency. In 1988 Brink published
States of Emergency, a novel whose narrator—a writer—is obsessed with the
inability of words and conventional narrative forms to express the horror of

148

the period. In *An Act of Terror* (1991), Brink is still wrestling with the extreme violence of the South African state. In the first-person narrative of Thomas Landman, he has a white character make the same claim that put Mandela in Robben Island in 1963: that in an extreme condition of violent oppression, such violence can only be combatted by strategic and symbolic acts of counterviolence. These novels mark a new development in Brink's fiction. The questioning of the adequacy of realist narrative to cope with the events of 1985 in *States of Emergency*, and the proposal of an ethics of terrorism in *An Act of Terror*, register a post-1985 shift in consciousness, one which is intolerant of any perceived, facile aestheticization or historicization of violence, and radically suspicious of the assumptions of liberal pacifism.

An analogous shift in consciousness is evident in Coetzee's *Age of Iron* (1990), although its manifestation is characteristic of Coetzee. Here Coetzee continues to refuse to align himself with either the progressivist beliefs of liberal humanism or those propagated in the name of an ethical terrorism by staging a fictional confrontation between the two. *Age of Iron* is set in South Africa, in a recognizable landscape (the Cape) and a recognizable time (the South Africa of the State of Emergency).[1] In this respect it differs from his earlier work: of his other works set in landscapes recognizable as South African, "The Narrative of Jacobus Coetzee" and *In the Heart of the Country* are metaphysical in a way that *Age of Iron* most emphatically is not; and *Life & Times of Michael K.* is set in apocalyptic time. The narrator of *Age of Iron* is an elderly white woman, who ostensibly writes the narrative to her only surviving relative, her daughter who lives in the United States.[2] Mrs. Curren is dying of cancer; however, the deterioration of her health is accompanied by experiences that make the violence of the society in which she lives an equal preoccupation for her.

The most formidable of these experiences is a trip to the township of Guguletu, which she makes together with her maid, Florence. The purpose of the trip is to look for Florence's son, Bheki, whom they later discover to be dead, apparently shot by the military guards who are "keeping order" in the area. For the ailing Mrs. Curren, whose classical education has left her with a vocabulary that is as persistent as it proves to be inadequate (the latter point is one that, as Derek Attridge has pointed out in his essay on the novel, Mrs. Curren herself acknowledges), the scenes of devastation in the township come straight from Hades. Wanting by her own admission only to return home, she is challenged by Mr. Thabane, Florence's cousin. I shall quote the relevant passages in full, because they perform the function of explaining by analogy the position from which these authors have worked.[3]

Mrs. Curren relates:

My back was in agony from the walking. I slowed down and stopped. 'I must get home soon,' I said. It was an appeal; I could hear the unsteadiness in my voice.

'You have seen enough?' said Mr. Thabane, sounding more distant than before. . . .

'Yes, I want to go home. I am in pain, I am exhausted.'

He turned and walked on. I hobbled behind. Then he stopped again. 'You want to go home,' he said. 'But what of the people who live here? When they want to go home, this is where they must go. What do you think of that?'

We stood in the rain, in the middle of the path, face to face. Passers-by stopped too, regarding me curiously, my business their business, everyone's business.

'I have no answer,' I said. 'It is terrible.'

'It is not just terrible,' he said, 'it is a crime. When you see a crime being committed in front of your eyes, what do you say? Do you say, "I have seen enough, I didn't come to see sights, I want to go home"?'

I shook my head in distress.

'No, you don't,' he said. 'Correct. Then what do you say? What sort of crime is it that you see? What is its name?' . . .

I glanced around the ring of spectators. Were they hostile? There was no hostility I could detect. They were merely waiting for me to say my part.

'There are many things I could say, Mr. Thabane,' I said. 'But then they must truly come from me. When one speaks under duress—you should know this—one rarely speaks the truth.'

He was going to respond, but I stopped him.

'Wait. Give me a minute. I am not evading your question. There are terrible things going on here. But what I think of them I must say in my own way.'

'Then let us hear what you have to say! We are listening! We are waiting!' He raised his hands for silence. The crowd murmured approval.

'These are terrible sights,' I repeated, faltering. 'They are to be condemned. But I cannot denounce them in other people's words. I must find my own words, from myself. Otherwise it is not the truth. That is all I can say now.'

'This woman talks shit,' said a man in the crowd. He looked around. 'Shit,' he said. No one contradicted him. Already some were drifting away.

'Yes,' I said, speaking directly to him—'you are right, what you say is true.'

He gave me a look as if I were mad.

'But what do you expect?' I went on. 'To speak of this'—I waved a hand over the bush, the smoke, the filth littering the path—'you would need the tongue of a god' (90–91).

The pain of her cancerous body Mrs. Curren can claim as her own—
she calls her tumor her child: "a child inside that I cannot give birth to" (75);
but the suffering of the township people is not her own. Her distress stems
from not being able to name their pain. Like Mrs. Curren, the writer as spectator of violence needs to come to terms with the insurmountability of this
limitation—the insufficiency of describing another's violation—without
fetishizing the distress that results from her or his recognition of it.

It would be tempting to give J. M. Coetzee's Mr. Thabane, Mrs.
Curren, and—let us not forget—the speakers from the crowd, the last words.
To do so, however, would be to risk suggesting that the apocalyptic scene from
Coetzee's novel in some way stands for all post-1985 South African fiction
and literary discourse, including its most recent developments, and that contemporary white South African literature reaches both its apotheosis and its
match during the violence of the Emergency. To "fix" the moment in this way
would be to overwrite the significant developments in South Africa since the
release of Mandela on February 11, 1990—developments more recently
marked by Mandela and de Klerk's joint winning of the Nobel Peace Prize in
October of 1993.

On April 27, 1994, in the first democratic election held in the country, South Africa elected Nelson Mandela, President of the African National
Congress, as President. Of course, unless one is an idealist of the absurd
variety, one cannot expect the official termination of the Nationalist regime
to coincide with an abrupt cessation of the widespread violence South Africa
is currently experiencing. The legacy left by apartheid to generations of blacks
in the form of faux-tribalism, poverty, and mal-education, and the consequence of the latter, no education at all—all of this will continue to have an
impact long into the postapartheid future. However, in this moment of
change South Africa is reminding the West of a factor that the latter seems to
have forgotten, an aspect of knowledge that any work against violence must
have assumed: that freedom is something that has to be worked for, consistently and continuously; it is not a state one achieves, in either the political
or personal sense, whose assumptions can be relied upon for ever after.
Coetzee speaks of this as the truncated vision of liberal democracy in a 1990
interview with the *Washington Post*:

> There is a certain controversy, isn't there, going on right at the moment in the
> United States about the "end of history"? . . . The position, expressed in a very
> crude way, is that the Western democracies have reached a stage in historical
> development in which development ceases because there is no stage beyond it. For
> better or worse liberal democracy is the form toward which all history tends. . . .

That very way of seeing the history of mankind is a symptom of the First World. . . . It's actually the Third World where history, real history, is happening. And the First World has played itself out of the game ("Author on History's Cutting Edge" C4).

David Attwell cites this very passage of the Coetzee interview in his book to demonstrate that *Age of Iron* manifests this same sense of the West, in this case specifically the United States, as moribund. Mrs. Curren's address to her expatriated daughter suggests, Attwell points out, that the very prosperity that ensures that the daughter and her children enjoy physical safety of the kind unavailable in the township, is a symptom of a kind of death of politicized, historical awareness.[4]

The death by complacency to which Coetzee refers is not, thankfully, possible within the contemporary South African context. The interregnum (to use Gordimer's famous term), in which the only task left for the white South African dissident is to die out of history, is over. The state no longer dictates such limited options. (Mrs. Curren's death, you will remember, is—to her frustration—most emphatically not caused by the state.) The ambivalence of white apocalypticism, associated with white writing during the seventies and early eighties, and expressed so radically in Gordimer's *July's People*, appears in the present circumstances to have been rejected, unequivocally, in favor of the work entailed by freedom. "It is one thing to die for liberation," Brink points out; "it is something entirely different to live with freedom" ("Reinventing the Real" 47).

Overseas reviewers and commentators will perhaps miss the attractions of white masochism because of the appeal it holds for international audiences; but those living in South Africa now have too keen a sense of the scarcity of resources not to reject such masochism for its devalued currency, its present uselessness in a context of immediate and dire need. In this respect, South African writers and cultural workers have moved postcoloniality beyond its North American impasse, which has been constructed by the academic apprehension of the subaltern as incommunicado and the careless definition of appropriation as any attempt on the part of the nonnative to envision the oppression of the indigene. This movement away from North American postcoloniality's theoretical dead-end, in which there can be no settler imagining of the indigene without appropriation, also avoids the other side of the coin, namely, the neocolonialist—or in South African terms, white liberalist—assumption that the indigene requires the imagination of the settler for the liberation of her or his community. This is a point that Brink's latest historical novel, *On the Contrary* (1993), which demonstrates its author's recent interest in the ability of nonrealist narrative to rethink history, is at pains to point out.

Instead of the parameters of the old arguments, then, current South African cultural discussions include debates over the construction of a space in which, alongside the prospect of other, new formulations, the white South African may for the first time hold a subject position whose legitimacy can be earned— without imprisonment—by its ethical apprehension of the evils of the constructions of race to which it, along with black South African subjectivity, has been subject; evils that the white liberal position has been brought to the point of recognizing in terms of the limits of, not to say flaws in, its own historical dissidence. The idea is that this consciousness of the fatal shortcomings of historical dissident acts can operate critically, in the act of reconstructing current dissidence to meet the changing face of oppression.

The construction of such a space is at the center of the debate over Albie Sachs' controversial (not to say notorious!) African National Congress "in-house" workshop paper, "Preparing Ourselves for Freedom." Sachs' paper is relevant here, not simply because, at present, it forms the focus of debates about the ANC's postapartheid cultural policy (see de Kok and Press, and Brown and van Dyk); but because in it, Sachs suggests how the legacy of anti-apartheid literature, if it continues to mean, simply, identifying an enemy, can act as an influence that continues to oppress, rather than to stimulate, creativity.

In "Preparing Ourselves for Freedom," Sachs proposed, polemically, that there be an ANC ban on saying that "culture is a weapon of struggle" for "a period of, say, five years" (de Kok and Press 19). Herein lies the basis of the controversy. If the move toward liberation has been served so well by the dictum about culture—and few would deny that it has, due to the expertise and leadership of such writers as Mongane Wally Serote, former head of the ANC's cultural wing—why would Sachs propose, so provocatively, its obsolescence?

Sachs' concern is that South African dissidents will make the same error that Brink outlines as the historical fault of Afrikaner nationalism: that we will continue to define ourselves as a community only within the framework of the manichean opposition. More specifically, he is concerned that, if the sole preoccupation of a community whose potential to inaugurate a postapartheid reality remains an exclusive focus on white oppression, that reality will be one dictated yet again by the disempowering lack of options necessitated by the apartheid age, rather than one based on self-exploration of a particular, essentially difficult, sort:

> *The oppressor stalks our vision.* We should be speaking more about ourselves and exploring *ourselves*. It's another form of domination if you like, where the whites dominate the image, even if it's the image of the enemy and the focus of our artistic endeavour is trying to dispel—to reduce to size—this overwhelming pres-

ence of the oppressor. Even if the oppressor is there, physically is there, and is
trying to penetrate our minds and to push us, and even to tell us how we should
win our freedom. . . . We should also not be afraid to enter into our own contradictions and difficulties, because we have sufficient confidence to do that. If we
can reach down to our roots—and not invented roots, *real* roots—with all the
tragedy of contradiction, the interest, the variety that's involved in that, then I
think that will do more to destroy the domination of the oppressor than simply
putting the oppressor up as a target all the time (Sachs 99).

What kind of form can this self-exploration, this reaching down to
our roots for what Sachs calls the tragedy of contradiction and the interest of
variety, take in literary terms? If the conclusion of Coetzee's *Foe* is seen to point
toward an activity beyond avoidance of the other, be it on the basis of racism
or due to the contrived, or even sincere, fear of appropriation, his portrayal of
Florence, Mr. Thabane, the dispossessed youths, and the township inhabitants
of *Age of Iron* would seem to suggest that tentative exploration of the other, the
imagining of the violence inflicted upon the oppressed, is necessary to the
project of reconstituting community on the basis of an ethical apprehension
of alterity. Derek Attridge has argued for a reading of *Age of Iron* that outlines
the value and provisionality of such an exploration in detail. Accepting his
argument, that the portrayal of alterity in the novel involves risky self-exploration, rather than neocolonial appropriation, depends, I think, not only on
Coetzee's refusal to represent his own authority in the narrative in terms of an
implied self-knowledge; it also depends upon a belief in the possibility of
change, as opposed to that fear of it expressed so well by Alan Paton;[5] a trust
(to use Attridge's word) in the validity and utility of an ethical existence for
white writing in the postapartheid era.

The claim that I make here is not—let me be quite clear on this—that
white writing in the postapartheid era will suddenly, magically, be free of its
racist heritage and the negative implications of that heritage for work against
violence. However, I do make a claim, in place of the intellectual apartheid
implicit in white masochism, for the ethical legitimacy of a multiracial community, and consequently, for the possibility that white writing can involve
itself in the act of listening to the other in its portrayals of alterity.

Indeed, Coetzee's *Age of Iron* is not the only example of such a project.
Take, for instance, Brink's fable, *The First Life of Adamastor*, first published in
English in 1993. In this fable Brink imagines Adamastor in the form of T'kama,
leader of the Khoi, who falls in love with a woman brought by a ship to the
Cape; it is a narrative that rehearses the trauma of first contact. What is telling
about this piece is that Brink, too, enacts a rehearsal in this work, which seems

to comment upon the weaknesses of his earlier fiction. Here, the myth of the giant penis of the racial other is parodied, not believed, in the Rabelaisian excesses of the novella. Also, there is no multiracial union that survives, symbolically and apocalyptically, only because it precedes political execution, as in *A Chain of Voices* and *An Act of Terror*. The woman returns to her people of her own volition, much to T'kama's impassioned regret; and his attempts to buy her back through a marriage settlement from the sailors fail, due either to cultural misunderstanding, the sailors' greed, their maltreatment of her, her recalcitrance, or a combination thereof. History, in this particular Brinkian narrative, does not relate, or, for that matter, dictate.

Mario Vargas Llosa's assessment of the significance of the relationship in his review of the novella—that intercultural relationships bear only the fruit of violence—depends upon a deterministic reading of history denied by the narrative in its overt, parodic conception of itself. Llosa, it would seem, insists on reading the separation of the couple as "prediction" (24); but what of its rehearsal, or, in its author's own words, its "reinvention of the past" ("Reinventing the Real" 54)? This is one example of the international critical appropriation of South African literature, in which the meaning of a variety of narrative forms is reduced because these forms are evaluated exclusively in terms of their ability to offer a diagnosis of apartheid, and a prognosis concerning its effects. In this example Llosa undermines the way in which Brink's fable offers an alternative history to that characterized by inevitable violence. *The First Life of Adamastor* is not simply a repetition of the fable of miscegenation, but a parody of it. Critical determinations of the sort exhibited by Llosa deny the possibility of relinquishing that obsession with the spectacular that Njabulo Ndebele, as early as 1986, identified so persuasively as reactionary in the terms of a changing South Africa. It is not only domestic writers and cultural workers who have a responsibility to rehearse their assumptions in the light of incipient freedom. Whether international cultural workers will be prepared to envision the ethics of what Ndebele calls "the rediscovery of the ordinary," in place of their traditional addiction to the spectacular in matters South African, remains to be seen.

I have tried to demonstrate that there are multiple criteria that need to be acknowledged in a consideration of violence. This point is crucial, it seems to me, in evaluating properly the various kinds of contributions made to the effort to combat apartheid. The moment has now arrived when such contributions, including, as Sachs has pointed out, their contradictions, can be assessed in view of a liberating future, the condition that has been so painfully absent in South Africa in the past decades. This opportunity for complex reevaluation can allow us, for example, to value Brink's work in terms of its popularization of the South African tragedy, and its contribution to the making of an international conscience with regard to apartheid, without denying the sexism and racial nostalgia that occasionally flaw his concept of history in, for example, *A Chain of Voices*; or to value Breytenbach's autobiography for the resistance it embodies, without ignoring the painful element of masochism involved in its genesis; or to allow Coetzee his narrative self-consciousness without regarding it as an unassailable defense on all counts, since even careful defensibility on ethical grounds is no guarantee of ethical effectiveness. Such are the implications of an emerging freedom for criticism—if criticism wishes to conceive of them.

NOTES

1. Coetzee comments on this aspect of the novel:

It was written during the years of the State of Emergency in South Africa. It reflects not only the outward manifestations of those years—the boycott of schools, the running battles in the townships, the relentless control of the media by the state— but some of their inward temper as well: bitterness and rage on the one side, despair and exhaustion on the other. In that sense one can call it an emergency novel, I suppose (Viola interview, 6).

2. The narrator, "addressing" her daughter, remarks: "To whom this writing then? The answer: to you but not to you; to me; to you in me" (5).

3. This includes Breytenbach in terms of his relationship to the victims of apartheid but not, of course, in the context of his own victimization by the apartheid regime.

4. David Attwell cites Mrs. Curren's reflections upon a photograph of her grandsons paddling a canoe at a resort, in this instance (*J. M. Coetzee* 124). The passage locates life in an awareness of the closeness of violent death, and death in the obtuseness, as Mrs. Curren perceives it, of American complacency:

Why is it that this material, foreign to me, foreign perhaps to humankind, shaped, sealed, inflated, tied to the bodies of your children, signifies for me so intensely the world you now live in, and why does it make my spirit sink? . . . Since this writing has time and again taken me from where I have no idea to where I begin to have an idea, let me say, in all tentativeness, that perhaps it dispirits me that your children will never drown. . . .

You say you will have no more children. The line runs out, then, in these two boys, seed planted in the American snows, who will never drown, whose life expectancy is seventy-five and rising. Even I, who live on shores where the waters swallow grown men, where life-expectancy declines every year, am having a death without illumination. What can these two underprivileged boys paddling about in their recreation area hope for? They will die at seventy-five or eighty-five as stupid as when they were born (178–79).

5. You will remember that Paton has his characters express the fear associated with changes, even as he himself advocated them. Kumalo recalls Msimangu's words toward the close of *Cry, the Beloved Country*, in a passage that spoke of the depth of white fear in a way that appeared to prophesy its hegemony during the decades after the year of the book's publication—and the Nationalist Party's rise to power—in 1948:

> And now for all the people of Africa, the beloved country. *Nkosi Sikelel' iAfrika*, God save Africa. But he [Kumalo] would not see that salvation. It lay afar off, because men were afraid of it. . . . And what was there evil in their desires, in their hunger? That men should walk upright in the land where they were born, and be free to use the fruits of the earth, what was there evil in it? Yet men were afraid, with a fear so deep that they hid their kindness, or brought it out with fierceness and anger, and hid it behind fierce and frowning eyes. They were afraid because they were so few. And such fear could not be cast out, but by love.
>
> It was Msimangu who had said, Msimangu who had no hate for any man, I have one great fear in my heart, that one day when they turn to loving they will find we are turned to hating (275–76).

BIBLIOGRAPHY

Alexander, Peter F. "Into the Wilderness." Review of *A Dry White Season* and *Mapmakers*, by André Brink. *Reviews Journal* 1 (1985): 110–12.

Althusser, Louis. *For Marx*. Translated by Ben Brewster. London: NLB, 1977.

———. *Lenin and Philosophy and Other Essays*. London and New York: Monthly Review, 1971.

Altinel, Sarkar. "Defence Mechanisms." Review of *The Ambassador*, by André Brink. *Times Literary Supplement* 10 January 1986: 35.

Andrade, Susan Z. "Rewriting History, Motherhood, and Rebellion: Naming an African Women's Literary Tradition." *Research in African Literatures* 21, no. 1 (1990): 91–110.

Antonissen, Rob. *Spitsberaad: Kroniek van die Afrikaanse lettere 1961–1965*. Cape Town, Bloemfontein, Johannesburg, Port Elizabeth, Pietermaritzburg: Nasou, n.d.

Armstrong, Nancy, and Leonard Tennenhouse, eds. *The Violence of Representation*. London and New York: Routledge, 1989.

Ascherson, Neal. "Children of the Cape." Review of *The Wall of the Plague*, by André Brink. *New York Review of Books* 25 April 1985: 55–56.

———. "The Fire this Time." Review of *The True Confessions of an Albino Terrorist*, by Breyten Breytenbach. *New York Review of Books* 18 July 1985: 3–4; 6–7.

———. "Living in the Night." Review of *Mouroir*, by Breyten Breytenbach. *New York Review of Books* 25 October 1984: 23–24.

Ashcroft, Bill, Gareth Griffiths, and Helen Tiffin. *The Empire Writes Back*. London and New York: Routledge, 1989.

Ashcroft, W. D. "Intersecting Marginalities: Post-colonialism and Feminism." *Kunapipi* 11, no. 2 (1989): 32–35.

Attridge, Derek. "Trusting the Other: Ethics and Politics in J. M. Coetzee's *Age of Iron*." *South Atlantic Quarterly* 93.1 (1994): 59–82.

———. "Oppressive Silence: J. M. Coetzee's *Foe* and the Politics of the Canon." In *Decolonizing the Tradition: New Views of Twentieth-Century "British" Literary Canons*, edited by Karen Lawrence. Urbana and Chicago: University of Illinois Press, 1991: 212–38.

Attwell, David. *J. M. Coetzee: South Africa and the Politics of Writing*. Berkeley, Los Angeles, and London: University of California Press and Cape Town: David Philip, 1993.

———. "The Labyrinth of My History: J. M. Coetzee's *Dusklands*." *Novel* 25, no. 7 (1991): 7–32.

———. "The Problem of History in the Fiction of J. M. Coetzee." In *Rendering Things Visible: Essays on South African Literary Culture*, edited by Martin Trump, 94–

133. Johannesburg: Ravan, 1990. Reprinted in *Poetics Today* 11, no. 3 (1990): 579–615.

Bakhtin, Mikhail. *Problems of Dostoevsky's Poetics.* Translated by R. W. Rotsel. Ann Arbor, Michigan: Ardis, 1973.

Bal, Mieke. *Narratology: Introduction to the Theory of Narrative.* Translated by Christine van Boheemen. Toronto, Buffalo, and London: University of Toronto Press, 1985.

Becker, George Joseph, ed. *Documents of Modern Literary Realism.* Princeton: Princeton University Press, 1963.

Belsey, Catherine. *Critical Practice.* London and New York: Methuen, 1980.

Benjamin, Jessica. *The Bonds of Love: Psychoanalysis, Feminism, and the Problem of Domination.* New York: Pantheon, 1988.

Benveniste, Emile. *Problems in General Linguistics.* Translated by Mary Elizabeth Meek. Coral Gables: University of Miami Press, 1971.

Berressem, Hugo. "Digging for Truth: Archaeology and the End of History." In *Crisis and Conflict: Essays on Southern African Literature,* edited by Geoffrey V.Davis, 117–32. Essen: Die Blaue Eule, 1990.

Bersani, Leo. *A Future for Astyanax: Character and Desire in Literature.* Boston and Toronto: Little, Brown and Co., 1976.

Bishop, Scott. "J. M. Coetzee's *Foe*: A Culmination and a Solution to a Problem of White Identity." *World Literature Today* 64, no. 1 (1990): 54–57.

Blishen, Edward. "Border Raids." Review of *The True Confessions of an Albino Terrorist,* by Breyten Breytenbach. *Guardian Weekly* [Manchester] 6 July 1986: 20.

Bloom, Allan David. *The Closing of the American Mind.* New York: Simon and Schuster, 1987.

Boyers, Robert. *Atrocity and Amnesia: The Political Novel Since 1945.* New York and Oxford: Oxford University Press, 1985.

Brantlinger, Patrick. *Rule of Darkness: British Literature and Imperialism.* New York: Cornell University Press, 1988.

Breytenbach, Breyten. *Boek (deel een).* Emmarentia: Taurus, 1987.

———. *Buffalo Bill.* Emmarentia: Taurus, 1984.

———. *End Papers.* London and Boston: Faber, 1986.

———. *Die Huis van die Dowe.* Cape Town: Human & Rousseau, 1967.

———. "I am Not an Afrikaner Anymore." *Index on Censorship* 12, no. 3 (1983): 3–6.

———. *Judas Eye and Self-Portrait/Deathwatch.* London and Boston: Faber, 1988.

———. *Memory of Snow and of Dust.* London and Boston: Faber, 1989.

———. *Mouroir (bespieëlende notas van 'n Roman).* Emmarentia: Taurus, 1983.

———. *Mouroir: Mirrornotes of a Novel.* London and Boston: Faber, 1984.

———. *Om te Vlieg.* Cape Town: Buren, 1971.

———. *A Season in Paradise.* Translated by Rike Vaughan. New York: Persea, 1980.

———. [B. B. Lazarus, pseud.]. *'n Seisoen in die paradys.* Johannesburg: Perskor, 1976. Censored version.

———. *The True Confessions of an Albino Terrorist.* London: Faber, 1984.

Brink, André. *An Act of Terror*. London: Secker and Warburg, 1991.

——. *Die Ambassadeur*. Cape Town and Pretoria: Human and Rousseau, 1963.

——. *The Ambassador*. London: Faber, 1985.

——. *A Chain of Voices*. London: Faber, 1982.

——. *A Dry White Season*. London: W. H. Allen, 1979.

——. *'n Droe wit seisoen*. Emmarentia: Taurus, 1979.

——. *Die Eerste lewe van Adamastor*. Cape Town: Saayman and Weber, 1988.

——. *The First Life of Adamastor*. London: Secker and Warburg, 1993.

——. *Gerugte van Reën*. Cape Town and Pretoria: Human and Rousseau, 1978.

——. *Houd-den-Bek*. Emmarentia: Taurus, 1982.

——. *An Instant in the Wind*. London: W. H. Allen, 1976.

——. Interview by Jean W. Ross. In *Contemporary Authors*, edited by Christine Nasso. Detroit: Gale Research, 1982: 55–59.

——. Interview by Jim Davidson. *Overland* 94–95 (1984): 24–30.

——. *Kennis van die aand*. Cape Town: Buren, 1973.

——. *Literatuur in die Strydperk*. Cape Town and Pretoria: Human and Rousseau, 1985.

——. *Looking on Darkness*. London: W. H. Allen, 1974.

——. *Mapmakers: Writing in a State of Siege*. London and Boston: Faber, 1983.

——. *On the Contrary*. London: Secker and Warburg, 1993.

——. *'n Oomblik in die wind*. Emmarentia: Taurus, 1975.

——. "Reinventing the Real: English South African Fiction Now." *New Contrast* 21, no. 1 (1993): 44–55.

——. *Rumours of Rain*. London: W. H. Allen, 1978.

——. *States of Emergency*. London and Boston: Faber, 1988.

——. "A Talk with André Brink." Interview by Geoffrey Wheatcroft. *New York Times Book Review* 13 June 1982: 14–15.

——. "An Uneasy Freedom: Dangers of Political 'Management of Culture' in South Africa." *Times Literary Supplement* 24 September 1993: 13.

——. *The Wall of the Plague*. London and Boston: Faber, 1984.

——. "Writing Against Big Brother: Notes on Apocalyptic Fiction in South Africa." *World Literature Today* 58, no. 2 (1984): 189–94.

Brink, André, and Christopher Hope. "Poet of Paradoxes." Review of *In Africa Even the Flies Are Happy* and *and death white as words*, by Breyten Breytenbach. *Index on Censorship* 8, no. 2 (1979): 74–77.

Brink, André, Nadine Gordimer, and Es'kia Mpahlele. "South African Writers Talking: Nadine Gordimer, Es'kia Mpahlele, André Brink." *English in Africa* 6, no. 2 (1979): 1–23.

Brontë, Charlotte. *Jane Eyre*. Harmondsworth: Penguin, 1966.

Brown, Duncan and Bruno van Dyk, eds. *Exchanges: South African Writing in Transition*. Pietermaritzburg: University of Natal Press, 1991.

Broyard, Anatole. "Hysteria, Scatology, Murder." Review of *In the Heart of the Country* by J. M. Coetzee. *New York Times Book Review* 18 September 1977: 14.

Brydon, Diana. "The Myths that Write Us: Decolonising the Mind." *Commonwealth* 10, no. 1 (1987): 1–14.

Burke, Edmund. *A Philosophical Enquiry into the Origin of Our Ideas of the Sublime and Beautiful.* Edited by J. T. Boulton. London: Routledge and Paul, 1958.

Campbell, James. "Learning to Walk by Walking." Review of *End Papers, The True Confessions of an Albino Terrorist*, and *Mouroir*, by Breyten Breytenbach. *Times Literary Supplement* 19 September 1986: 1028.

Castillo, Debra A. "Coetzee's *Dusklands*: The Mythic Punctum." *Publications of the Modern Language Association of America* 105, no. 5 (1990): 1108–22.

———. "The Composition of the Self in Coetzee's Waiting for the Barbarians." *Critique: Studies in Modern Fiction* 27, no. 2 (1986): 78–90.

Caughie, John, ed. *Theories of Authorship: A Reader.* London and Boston: Routledge, 1981.

Christie, Sarah, Geoffrey Hutchings, and Don Maclennan. *Perspectives on South African Fiction.* London and Johannesburg: Ad. Donker, 1980.

Chow, Rey. "Rereading Mandarin Ducks and Butterflies: A Response to the 'Postmodern' Condition." *Cultural Critique* 5 (1986–1987): 69–93.

Cixous, Hélène. "The Character of 'Character.'" Translated by Keith Cohen. *New Literary History* 5, no. 2 (1974): 383–402.

Coetzee, A. J. *Poësie en politiek: 'n Voorlopige verkenning van betrokkenheid in die Afrikaanse poësie.* Johannesburg: Ravan, 1976.

Coetzee, Ampie. "Taurus Publishers." *Index on Censorship* 13, no. 5 (1984): 32.

Coetzee, J. M. "Achterberg's 'Ballade van die gasfitter': The Mystery of I and You." *Publications of the Modern Language Association of America* 92, no. 2 (1977): 285–96.

———. *Age of Iron.* London: Secker and Warburg, 1990.

———. "André Brink and the Censor." *Research in African Literatures* 21, no. 3 (1990): 59–74.

———. "Author on History's Cutting Edge. South Africa's J.M. Coetzee: Visions of Doomed Heroics." Interview by Charles Truehart. *Washington Post* 27 November 1990: C1, C4.

———. "Breytenbach and the Censor." *Raritan* 10, no. 4 (1991): 58–84.

———. "Censorship in South Africa." *English in Africa* 17, no. 1 (1990): 1–20.

———. "Confession and Double Thoughts; Tolstoy, Rousseau, and Dostoevsky." *Comparative Literature* 37, no. 3 (1985): 193–232.

———. *Doubling the Point: Essays and Interviews.* Edited by David Attwell. Cambridge: Harvard University Press, 1992.

———. *Dusklands.* 1974. (Johannesburg: Ravan). London: Secker and Warburg, 1982.

———. *Foe.* London: Secker and Warburg, 1986.

———. "An Interview with J. M. Coetzee." By Richard Begam. *Contemporary Literature* 33, no. 3 (1992): 419–31.

———. "An Interview with J. M. Coetzee." By Tony Morphet. *Social Dynamics* 10, no. 1 (1984): 62–65. Reprinted in *TriQuarterly* 69 (1987): 454–61.

————. "An Interview with J.M. Coetzee." By André Viola. *Commonwealth Essays and Studies* 14, no. 2 (1992): 6–7.

————. *In the Heart of the Country.* London: Secker and Warburg, 1977.

————. *In the Heart of the Country* (bilingual edition). Johannesburg: Ravan, 1978.

————. "Into the Dark Chamber: The Novelist and South Africa." *New York Times Book Review* 12 January 1986: 13, 35.

————. *Life & Times of Michael K.* London: Secker and Warburg, 1983.

————. "A Poet in Prison." Review of *Mouroir* and *The True Confessions of an Albino Terrorist* by Breyten Breytenbach. *New Republic* 11 March 1985: 29–32.

————. "Tales of Afrikaners." *New York Times Magazine* 9 March 1986: 19; 21–22; 74–75.

————. "Two Interviews with J. M. Coetzee, 1983 and 1987." By Tony Morphet. *TriQuarterly* 69 (1987): 454–64.

————. *Waiting for the Barbarians.* London: Secker and Warburg, 1980.

————. *White Writing: On the Culture of Letters in South Africa.* New Haven and London: Yale University Press, 1988.

Contemporary Literary Criticism, 1981 ed., s.v. "André Brink."

Contemporary Literary Criticism, 1986 ed., s.v. "André Brink."

Contemporary Literary Criticism, 1983 ed., s.v. "Breyten Breytenbach."

Contemporary Literary Criticism, 1986 ed., s.v. "Breyten Breytenbach."

Contemporary Literary Criticism, 1983 ed., s.v. "John Coetzee."

Contemporary Literary Criticism, 1985 ed., s.v. "John Coetzee."

Cox, Robert. "South Africa's Prisoner of Conscience." Review of *The True Confessions of an Albino Terrorist,* by Breyten Breytenbach. *Guardian Weekly* [Manchester] 26 May 1985: 18.

Crace, Jim. "Blight of the Ages." Review of *The Wall of the Plague,* by André Brink. *Times Literary Supplement* 5 October 1984: 1140.

Davenport, T. R. H. *South Africa: A Modern History.* 1977. Updated and revised. Toronto and Buffalo: University of Toronto Press, 1987.

Davis, Geoffrey V., ed. *Crisis and Conflict: Essays on Southern African Literature.* Essen: Die Blaue Eule, 1990.

Daymond, M. J., J. U. Jacobs, and Margaret Lenta, eds. *Momentum: On Recent South African Writing.* Pietermaritzburg: Natal University Press, 1984.

Defoe, Daniel. *Robinson Crusoe: An Authoritative Text/Backgrounds/Sources/Criticism.* Edited by Michel Shinagel. New York: Norton, 1975.

————. *Roxana: The Fortunate Mistress.* Edited by Jane Jack. Oxford: Oxford University Press, 1964.

de Jong, Marianne, ed. Special issue on *Foe* of *Journal of Literary Studies/Tydskrif vir literatuurwetenskap* 5, no. 2 (1989): 105–235.

de Kock, Leon. "Literature, Politics and Universalism: A Debate between Es'kia Mpahlele and J. M. Coetzee." *Journal of Literary Studies/Tydskrif vir literatuurwetenskap* 3, no. 4 (1987): 35–48.

de Kok, I., and K. Press, eds. *Spring is Rebellious.* Cape Town: Buchu, 1990.

Delius, Anthony. "Conscience of the Afrikaner." Review of *A Season in Paradise*, by Breyten Breytenbach. *Guardian Weekly* [Manchester] November 16 1980: 22.

de Man, Paul. "Autobiography as De-facement." *Modern Language Notes* 94 (1979): 919–30.

Derrida, Jacques. "But, beyond . . . (Open Letter to Anne McClintock and Rob Nixon)." Translated by Peggy Kamuf. *Critical Inquiry* 13, no. 1 (1986): 155–70.

———. *Of Grammatology*. Translated by Gayatri Chakravorty Spivak. Baltimore: Johns Hopkins University Press, 1976.

———. "Racism's Last Word." Translated by Peggy Kamuf. *Critical Inquiry* 12, no. 1 (1985): 290–99.

Dodd, Josephine. "Naming and Framing: Naturalization and Colonization in J. M. Coetzee's *In the Heart of the Country*." *World Literature Written in English* 27, no. 2 (1987): 153–61.

Dovey, Teresa. "Allegory vs. Allegory: The Divorce of Different Modes of Allegorical Perception in J. M. Coetzee's *Waiting for the Barbarians*." *Journal of Literary Studies/Tydskrif vir literatuurwetenskap* 4, no. 2 (1988): 133–43.

———. "Coetzee and His Critics: The Case of *Dusklands*." *English in Africa* 14, no. 2 (1987): 16–30.

———. "The Intersection of Postmodern, Postcolonial and Feminist Discourse in J. M. Coetzee's *Foe*." *Journal of Literary Studies/Tydskrif vir literatuurwetenskap* 5, no. 2 (1989): 119–33.

———. Introduction to *J. M. Coetzee: A Bibliography*, compiled by Kevin Goddard and John Read. Grahamstown: National English Literary Museum, 1990.

———. *The Novels of J. M. Coetzee: Lacanian Allegories*. Ph.D. Diss., University of Melbourne, 1986. Johannesburg: Ad. Donker, 1988.

Du Plessis, Ménan. "Toward a True Materialism." Review of *Waiting for the Barbarians*, by J. M. Coetzee. *Contrast* 13, no. 4 (1981): 77–87.

du Plessis, Michael. "Bodies and Signs: Inscriptions of Femininity in John Coetzee and Wilma Stockenström." *Journal of Literary Studies/Tydskrif vir literatuurwetenskap* 4, no. 1 (1988): 118–28.

During, Simon. "Postmodernism or Post-colonialism Today." *Textual Practice* 1, no. 1 (1987): 32–47.

Durix, Jean Pierre, ed. Special issue on J. M. Coetzee and V. S. Naipaul of *Commonwealth: Essays and Studies* 9, no. 1 (1986): 1–58.

Eckstein, Barbara J. *The Language of Fiction in a World of Pain*. Philadelphia: University of Philadelphia Press, 1990.

Egan, Susanna. "Breytenbach's *Mouroir*: The Novel as Autobiography." *Journal of Narrative Technique* 18, no. 2 (1988): 89–104.

Fanon, Franz. *Black Skin, White Masks*. Translated by Charles Lam Markmann. Foreword by Homi Bhabha. London and Sydney: Pluto, 1986.

———. *The Wretched of the Earth*. Translated by Constance Farrington. Preface by Jean-Paul Sartre. Harmondsworth, New York, Victoria, Markham, Auckland: Penguin, 1967.

Farki, Neville. *The Death of Tarzana Clayton.* London: Karnak House, 1985.

February, Vernon. *Mind Your Colour: The "Coloured" Stereotype in South African Literature.* Revised. London and New York: Kegan Paul, 1991.

Folena, Lucia. "Figures of Violence: Philologists, Witches and Stalinistas." In *The Violence of Representation,* edited by Nancy Armstrong and Leonard Tennenhouse, 219–38. London and New York: Routledge, 1989.

Foucault, Michel. *Discipline and Punish: The Birth of the Prison.* Translated by Alan Sheridan. New York: Vintage, 1979.

Fraser, John. *Violence in the Arts.* London and New York: Cambridge University Press, 1974.

Freud, Sigmund. *Civilization, Society and Religion: Group Psychology, Civilization and its Discontents and Other Works.* Vol. 12. The Penguin Freud Library, translated by James Strachey and edited by Albert Dickson. London: Penguin, 1985.

Gallagher, Susan Van Zanten. *A Story of South Africa: J. M. Coetzee's Fiction in Context.* Cambridge: Harvard University Press, 1991.

———. "Torture and the Novel: J. M. Coetzee's *Waiting for the Barbarians.*" *Contemporary Literature* 29, no. 2 (1988): 277–85.

Gardiner, Allan. "J. M. Coetzee's *Dusklands*: Colonial Encounters of the Robinsonian Kind." *World Literature Written in English* 27, no. 2 (1987): 174–84.

Gates, Henry Louis Jr., ed. *Race, Writing and Difference.* Chicago and London: University of Chicago Press, 1986.

Gerwel, G. J. *Literatuur en apartheid: Konsepsies van 'gekleurdes' in die Afrikaanse roman tot 1948.* Kasselvlei: Kampen, 1983.

Girard, René. *Deceit, Desire and the Novel: Self and Other in Literary Structure.* Translated by Yvonne Freccero. Baltimore: Johns Hopkins University Press, 1965.

———. *Violence and the Sacred.* Translated by Patrick Gregory. Baltimore: Johns Hopkins University Press, 1977.

Goddard, Kevin, and John Read, comps. *J. M. Coetzee: A Bibliography.* Introduction by Teresa Dovey. Grahamstown: National English Literary Museum, 1990.

Gordimer, Nadine. *Burger's Daughter.* London: Jonathan Cape, 1979.

———. *The Essential Gesture: Writing, Politics and Places.* Edited by Stephen Clingman. London: Penguin, 1989.

———. "The Idea of Gardening." Review of *Life & Times of Michael K.,* by J. M. Coetzee. *New York Times Book Review* 18 April 1984: 3–4.

———. *July's People.* New York: Viking, 1981.

———. "Living in the Interregnum." In *The Essential Gesture: Writing, Politics and Places,* edited by Stephen Clingman. London: Penguin, 1989. 261–284.

———. "New Notes from Underground." Review of *Mouroir,* by Breyten Breytenbach. *Atlantic Monthly* July 1984: 114–16.

Gorman, G. E. "From History's Enclave." Review of *Wall of the Plague,* by André Brink. *Reviews Journal* September 1985: 87–90.

Gosset, Louise Y. *Violence in Recent Southern Fiction.* Durham: Duke University Press, 1965.

Gräbe, Ina. "Postmodern Narrative Strategies in *Foe*." *Journal of Literary Studies/Tydskrif vir literatuurwetenskap* 5, no. 2 (1989): 145–82.

Grant, Damian. *Realism*. London: Methuen, 1970.

Haluska, Jan Charles. "Master and Slave in the First Four Novels of J.M. Coetzee." Ph.D. Diss., University of Tennessee, Knoxville, 1987.

Harlow, Barbara. *Resistance Literature*. New York: Methuen, 1986.

Harris, Wilson. *Explorations*. Edited by Hena Maes-Jelinek. Aarhus: Dangaroo, 1981.

———. "The Frontier on which *Heart of Darkness* Stands." In *Explorations*, edited by Hena Maes-Jelinek, 134–41. Aarhus: Dangaroo, 1981.

———. "Interview with Wilson Harris." By Michel Fabre. *World Literature Written in English* 22, no. 1 (1983): 2–17.

Harvey, C. J. D. "*Waiting for the Barbarians*." *Standpunte* 34, no. 154[4] (1981): 3–8.

Hassal, A. J. "The Making of a Colonial Myth: The Mrs. Fraser Story in Patrick White's 'A Fringe of Leaves' and André Brink's 'An Instant in the Wind'." *Ariel* 18, no. 3 (1978): 3–27.

Hebdige, Dick. *Subculture: The Meaning of Style*. London, New York: Methuen, 1979.

Hegel, Georg Wilhelm Friedrich. *Phenomenology of Spirit*. Translated by A. V. Miller. Foreword and Analysis by J. N. Findlay. Oxford: Oxford University Press, 1977.

Heller, Terry. *The Delights of Terror*. Urbana and Chicago: University of Illinois Press, 1987.

Heywood, Christopher. *Aspects of South African Literature*. London, Ibadan, Nairobi, Lusaka: Heinemann; New York: Africana, 1976.

Hofmeyr, Isabel. "'Setting Free the Books': The David Philip Africasouth Paperback Series." *Research in African Literatures* 12, no. 1 (1985): 83–95.

Hope, Christopher. "The Political Novelist in South Africa." *English in Africa* 12, no. 1 (1985): 41–46.

Horne, Philip. "Tunnel Vision." Review of *States of Emergency*, by André Brink. *London Review of Books* 4 August 1988: 26–27.

Howarth, William L. "Some Principles of Autobiography." *New Literary History* 5, no. 2 (1974): 363–81.

Howe, Irving. *The Critical Point: On Literature and Culture*. New York: Horizon, 1973.

———. *Politics and the Novel*. New York: Horizon, 1957.

———. "A Stark Political Fable." Review of *Waiting for the Barbarians*, by J. M. Coetzee. *New York Times Book Review* 18 April 1982: 1, 36.

Hume, Kathryn. *Fantasy and Mimesis: Responses to Reality in Western Literature*. New York and London: Methuen, 1984.

Hutcheon, Linda. *A Poetics of Postmodernism*. London and New York: Routledge, 1988.

———. *The Politics of Postmodernism*. London and New York: Routledge, 1989.

———. *A Theory of Parody*. New York and London: Methuen, 1985.

Irwin, John T. *Doubling and Incest, Repetition and Revenge: A Speculative Reading of Faulkner*. Baltimore: Johns Hopkins University Press, 1975.

Iser, Wolfgang. *The Act of Reading: A Theory of Aesthetic Response*. Baltimore and London: Johns Hopkins University Press, 1978.

Jackson, Rosemary. *Fantasy: The Literature of Subversion.* London and New York: Methuen, 1981.

Jameson, Frederic. *The Political Unconscious: Narrative as Socially Symbolic Act.* Ithaca: Cornell University Press, 1981.

———. "Magical Narratives: Romance as Genre." *New Literary History* 7, no. 1 (1975): 135–63.

JanMohamed, Abdul R. "The Economy of Manichean Allegory: The Function of Racial Difference in Colonialist Literature." In *Race, Writing and Difference*, edited by Henry Louis Gates, Jr., 78–106. Chicago and London: University of Chicago Press, 1986.

———. *Manichean Aesthetics: The Politics of Literature in Colonial Allegory.* Amherst: University of Massachusetts Press, 1983.

Jolly, Rosemary Jane. "Aborted Voyages: Narrative Conquests in J. M. Coetzee's *Foe.*" *Matatu*, Special issue on South African literature. Ed. G. W. Davis. Amsterdam: Rodopi, 1993. 61–70.

———. "The Gun as Copula: Colonization, Rape and the Question of Pornographic Violence in J. M. Coetzee's *Dusklands.*" *World Literature Written in English* 32.2 & 33.1 (1992–3): 44–55.

———. "Territorial Metaphor in J. M. Coetzee's *Waiting for the Barbarians.*" *Ariel* 20, no. 2 (1989): 69–79.

Juillard, Alphonse, ed. *To Honour René Girard.* Saratoga: ANMA Libri, 1986.

Kafka, Franz. *The Penal Colony: Stories and Short Pieces.* Translated by Willa and Edwin Muir. New York: Schocken, 1948.

Kakutani, Michiko. Review of *Writing in a State of Siege*, by André Brink. *New York Times* 6 March 1984: C17.

Kant, Immanuel. *The Critique of Judgement.* Translated by J. C. Meredith. Analytical Indexes by J. C. Meredith. Oxford: Clarendon, 1952.

Keith, John. "Simple Love Story Can't Avoid Involvement in Apartheid Issue." Review of *States of Emergency*, by André Brink. *Vancouver Sun* 23 July 1988: D4.

Kelly, Hewson. "Making the 'Revolutionary Gesture': Nadine Gordimer, J. M. Coetzee and Some Variations on the Writer's Responsibility." *Ariel* 19, no. 4 (1988): 55–72.

Kendrick, Walter. "Adrift in Ouagadougou." Review of *Memory of Snow and of Dust*, by Breyten Breytenbach. *New York Times Book Review* 22 October 1989: 9–10.

King, Francis. "Rather a Boer." Review of *A Chain of Voices*, by André Brink. *Spectator* 8 May 1982: 23.

Knox-Shaw, Peter. "*Dusklands*: A Metaphysics of Violence." *Contrast 53* 14, no. 1 (1982): 26–38.

Kramer, Jane. "In the Garrison." Review of *A Chain of Voices*, by André Brink. *New York Review of Books* 2 December 1982: 8–12.

Kristeva, J. *Powers of Horror: An Essay on Abjection.* Translated by Jean Roudiez. New York: Columbia University Press, 1982.

Kristeva, J. *Revolution in Poetic Language.* Translated by Margaret Waller. New York: Columbia University Press, 1984.

Lacan, Jacques. *Ecrits.* Translated by Alan Sheridan. London: Tavistock, 1977.

la Guma, Alex. *In the Fog of the Season's End.* London: Heinemann, 1972.

Lane, Richard. "Embroiling Narratives: Appropriating the Signifier in J. M. Coetzee's *Foe.*" *Commonwealth Essays and Studies* 13, no. 1 (1990): 106–11.

Lazarus, Neil. "Longing, Radicalism, Sentimentality: Reflections on Breyten Breytenbach's *A Season in Paradise.*" *Journal of Southern African Studies* 12, no. 2 (1986): 158–82.

———. "Modernism and Modernity: T. W. Adorno and Contemporary White South African Literature." *Cultural Critique* 5 (1986/1987): 131–55.

Lejeune, Philippe. *On Autobiography.* Translated by Katherine Leary. Minneapolis: University of Minnesota Press, 1989.

Lindfors, Bernth. "Coming to Terms with the Apocalypse: Recent South African Fiction." In *A Sense of Place: Essays in Post-Colonial Literatures,* edited by Britta Olinder, 196–203. Göteborg: Gothenburg University Press, 1984.

Llosa, Mario Vargas. "Love Finds a Way." Review of *The First Life of Adamastor,* by André Brink. *New York Times Book Review* 5 July 1993: 1; 23–24.

Lowndes, C. D. "Beauty and Its Place in Political Statements." *Globe and Mail* [Toronto] 8 October 1988: C25.

Lukács, Georg. *The Meaning of Contemporary Realism.* Translated by John and Necke Mander. London: Merlin, 1962.

Lyotard, Jean François. *The Postmodern Condition: A Report on Knowledge.* Translated by Geoff Bennington and Brian Massumi. Minneapolis: University of Minnesota Press, 1984.

Macaskill, Brian, and Jeanne Colleran. "Reading History, Writing Heresy: The Resistance of Representation and the Representation of Resistance in J.M. Coetzee's *Foe.*" *Contemporary Literature* 33, no. 3 (1992): 432–57.

Macherey, Pierre. *A Theory of Literary Production.* Translated by Geoffrey Wall. London, Boston: Routledge, 1978.

Maclennan, Don, and Malvern Van Wyk Smith, eds. *Olive Schreiner and After: Essays on Southern African Literature.* Cape Town, Johannesburg and London: David Philip, 1983.

Maes-Jelinek, Hena. "The Muse's Progress: 'Infinite Rehearsal' in J. M. Coetzee." In *A Shaping of Connections: Commonwealth Literature Studies—Then and Now,* edited by Hena Maes-Jelinek, Kirsten Holst Petersen, and Anna Rutherford. Sydney, N.S.W: Dangaroo: 232–42.

Maher, Susan Naramore. "Confronting Authority: J. M. Coetzee's *Foe* and the Remaking of *Robinson Crusoe. International Fiction Review* 18, no. 1 (1991): 36–40.

Mannoni, O. *Prospero and Caliban: The Psychology of Colonization.* Translated by Pamela Powesland. New York and Washington: Frederick A. Praeger, 1964.

Marais, Michael. "The Deployment of Metafiction in an Aesthetic of Engagement." *Journal of Literary Studies/Tydskrif vir literatuurwetenskap* 5, no. 2 (1989): 183–93.

———. "Interpretive Authoritarianism: Reading/Colonizing Coetzee's *Foe.*" *English in Africa* 16, no. 1 (1989): 9–16.

Martin, Richard G. "Narrative, History, Ideology: A Study of *Waiting for the Barbarians* and *Burger's Daughter.*" *Ariel* 17, no. 3 (1986): 3–21.

McClintock, Anne, and Rob Nixon. "No Names Apart: The Separation of Word and History in Derrida's *Le Dernier Mot du Racisme.*" *Critical Inquiry* 13, no. 1 (1986): 140–54.

Memmi, Albert. *The Colonizer and the Colonized.* Boston: Beacon, 1965.

Mennecke, Arnim. *Koloniales Bewusstsein in den Romanen J. M. Coetzees.* Heidelberg: Winter, 1991.

Merivale, Patricia. "Ambiguous Frontiers: *Waiting for the Barbarians* as Topographical Parable." In *Proceedings of the XIIth Congress of the International Comparative Literature Association, 1988 Munich II: Space and Boundaries in Literature,* vol 2., edited by Fokkema et al, 272–76. Munich: Iudicum, 1990.

Mietkiewicz, Henry. "South African Author Shuns Ivory Tower." *Toronto Star* 25 May 1982: D1—D4.

Morrison, Blake. "Portents of Apartheid." Review of *A Chain of Voices,* by André Brink. *Observer* [London] 9 May 1982: 31.

Moses, Michael Valdez. "Caliban and His Precursors: The Politics of Literary History in the Third World." In *Theoretical Issues in Literary History,* edited by David Perkins, 206–26. Cambridge: Harvard University Press, 1991.

Moss, John. *Sex and Violence in the Canadian Novel.* Toronto: McClelland and Stewart, 1977.

Moynahan, Julian. "Slaves Who Said No." Review of *A Chain of Voices,* by André Brink. *New York Times Book Review* 13 June 1982: 1, 15.

Ndebele, Njabulo. "The Rediscovery of the Ordinary: Some New Writings in South Africa." *Journal of Southern African Studies* 12, no. 2 (1986): 143–57.

Neill, Michael. "'Groping Behind a Mirror': Some Images of the Other in South African Writing." In *Crisis and Conflict: Essays on Southern African Literature,* edited by Geoffrey V.Davis, 157–82. Essen: Die Blaue Eule, 1990.

Neumann, Anne Waldron. "Escaping the 'Time of History'? Present Tense and the Occasion of Narration in J. M. Coetzee's *Waiting for the Barbarians.*" *Journal of Narrative Technique* 20, no. 1 (1990): 65–86.

Nkosi, Lewis. "Afrikaner Arithmetic." Review of *Rumours of Rain,* by André Brink. *Times Literary Supplement* 20 October 1978: 1196.

Olcott, Anthony. "The Long Reach of Apartheid." Review of *The Wall of the Plague,* by André Brink. *Washington Post* "Book World" 17 February 1985: 1–2.

Olsen, Lance. "The Presence of Absence: Coetzee's *Waiting for the Barbarians.*" *Ariel* 16, no. 2 (1985): 47–56.

Omotoso, Kole. "André Brink: Dissident Afrikaaner [*sic*] Writer." *West Africa* 6 December 1982: 3148–50.

Parriner, Patrick. "What His father Gets Up To." Review of *My Son's Story,* by Nadine Gordimer, and *Age of Iron,* by J. M. Coetzee. *London Review of Books* 13 September 1990: 17–18.

Parry, Benita. "Problems in Current Theories of Colonial Discourse." *Oxford Literary Review* 9, no. 1–2 (1987): 27–58.

Pasley, J. M. S. Introduction to *Der Heizer; In der Strafkolonie; Der Bau,* by Franz Kafka. Cambridge: Cambridge University Press, 1966.

Paton, Alan. *Cry, the Beloved Country.* 1948. Note and foreword by Alan Paton added. New York: Macmillan, 1987.

Penner, Dick. *Countries of the Mind: The Fiction of J. M. Coetzee.* New York, London and Westport: Greenwood, 1989.

———. "J. M. Coetzee's *Foe*: The Muse, the Absurd, and the Colonial Dilemma." *World Literature Written in English* 27, no. 2 (1987): 207–15.

———. "Sight, Blindness and Double-Thought in J. M. Coetzee's *Waiting for the Barbarians*." *World Literature Written in English* 26, no. 1 (1986): 34–45.

Petersen, Kirsten Holst. "An Elaborate Dead End? A Feminist Reading of Coetzee's *Foe*." *A Shaping of Connections: Commonwealth Literature Studies—Then and Now,* edited by Hena Maes-Jelinek, Kirsten Holst Petersen, and Anna Rutherford. Sydney, N.S.W.: Dangaroo, 1989: 232–42.

Polley, J,. ed. *Die Sestigers: Verslag van die symposium oor die Sestigers gehou deur die Departement Buitemuurse Studies van die Universiteit van Kaapstad, 12–16 Februarie 1973.* Cape Town and Pretoria: Human and Rousseau, 1973.

Post, Robert M. "The Noise of Freedom: J. M. Coetzee's *Foe*." *Critique: Studies in Modern Fiction* 10, no. 3 (1989): 143–54.

———. "Oppression in the Novels of J. M. Coetzee." *Critique: Studies in Modern Fiction* 27, no. 2 (1986): 67–77.

Reading, Peter. "Monstrous Growths." Review of *Age of Iron,* by J. M. Coetzee. *Times Literary Supplement* 28 September to 4 October 1990: 1037.

Réage, Pauline. *Story of O.* Translated by Sabine D'Estrée. New York: Ballantine, 1973.

Reckwitz, Erhard. "The Broken Mirror: Die Problematik der Selbstbespielung in den autobiographischen Romanen von Breyten Breytenbach." In *Current Themes in Contemporary South African Literature,* edited by Elmar Lehmann and Erhard Reckwitz, 26–83. Essen: Die Blaue Eule, 1989.

———. "'To Break a Structure'—Literature and Liberation in Breyten Breytenbach's *The True Confessions of an Albino Terrorist*." In *Crisis and Conflict: Essays on Southern African Literature,* edited by Geoffrey V.Davis, 205–14. Essen: Die Blaue Eule, 1990.

Redman, Eric. "An Afrikaner Novelist Confronts South Africa." Review of *A Dry White Season,* by André Brink. *Washington Post* "Book World" 20 January 1980: 5, 14.

Rich, Paul. "Apartheid and the Decline of the Civilization Idea: An Essay on Nadine Gordimer's *July's People* and J. M. Coetzee's *Waiting for the Barbarians*." *Research in African Literatures* 15, no. 3 (1984): 365–93.

———. "Tradition and Revolt in South African Fiction: The Novels of André Brink, Nadine Gordimer and J. M. Coetzee." *Journal of Southern African Studies* 9, no. 1 (1982): 54–73.

Roberts, Sheila. "Breyten Breytenbach's Prison Literature." *Centennial Review* 30, no. 2 (1986): 304–13.

Rushton, Alfred. Review of *A Chain of Voices*, by André Brink. *Globe and Mail* [Toronto] 17 July 1982: E12.

Sachs, Albie. "An Interview with Albie Sachs." By Eve Bertelsen. World Literature Written in English 30 (1990): 96–104.

———. "Preparing Ourselves for Freedom." *Spring is Rebellious.* Eds. Ingrid de Kok and Karen Press. Cape Town: Buchu, 1990.

Said, Edward. *Orientalism.* Harmondsworth: Penguin, 1978.

Scarry, Elaine. *The Body in Pain: The Making and Unmaking of the World.* New York: Oxford University Press, 1985.

Schiller, Bill. "Author Wages War on Apartheid." *Sunday Star* [Toronto] 26 March 1989: H2.

Sepamla, Sydney Sipho. *A Ride on the Whirlwind.* Johannesburg: Ad Donker, 1981

Serote, Mongane Wally. *To Every Birth its Blood.* Johannesburg: Ravan, 1981.

Shrimpton, Nicholas. "Cold Feet in Moscow." Review of *Waiting for the Barbarians*, by J. M. Coetzee. *New Statesman* 7 November 1980: 30.

Silver, Louise. *A Guide to Political Censorship in South Africa.* University of Witwatersrand: Centre for Applied Legal Studies, 1984.

Silverman, Kaja. *The Subject of Semiotics.* New York and Oxford: Oxford University Press, 1983.

Simpson, John. "Angry Parable." Review of *A Chain of Voices*, by André Brink. *Listener* [London] 13 May 1982: 26–27.

Slemon, Stephen. "Modernism's Last Post." *Ariel* 20, no. 4 (1989): 3–17.

———. "Post-Colonial Allegory and the Transformation of History." *Journal of Commonwealth Literature* 23, no. 1 (1988): 157–67.

Spann, Meno. *Franz Kafka.* Boston: Twayne, 1976.

Spivak, Gayatri Chakravorty. "Can the Subaltern Speak?" In *Marxism and the Interpretation of Culture*, edited by Cary Nelson. Urbana: University of Illinois Press, 1988: 271–313.

———. *The Post-colonial Critic: Interviews, Strategies, Dialogues.* New York: Routledge, 1989.

———. "Theory in the Margin: Coetzee's *Foe* Reading Defoe's Crusoe/Roxana." *English in Africa* 17, no. 2 (1990): 1–23. Reprinted in *Consequences of Theory: Selected Papers from the English Institute, 1987–1988*, edited by Jonathan Arac and Barbara Johnson. Baltimore: Johns Hopkins University Press, 1990: 154–180.

Splendore, Paola. "J.M. Coetzee's *Foe*: Intertextual and Metafictional Resonances." *Commonwealth Essays and Studies* 11, no. 1 (1988): 55–60.

Sprinker, Michael. "Fictions of the Self: The End of Autobiography." In *Autobiography: Essays Theoretical and Critical*, edited by James Olney, 321–42. Princeton: Princeton University Press, 1980.

Suleiman, Susan. *Subversive Intent: Gender, Politics and the Avant-Garde.* Cambridge, Massachusetts and London: Harvard University Press, 1990.

Theroux, Paul. "Afrikaners." Review of *A Season in Paradise*, by Breyten Breytenbach. *New York Times Book Review* 30 March 1980: 8–9.

Thompson, Leonard, and Monica Wilson, eds. *The Oxford History of South Africa*. 2 vols. Oxford: Clarendon, 1971.

Thornton, Lawrence. "Apartheid's Last Vicious Gasps." Review of *Age of Iron*, by J. M. Coetzee. *New York Times Book Review* 28 September 1990: 7.

Tiffin, Helen. "Post-Colonialism, Post-Modernism and the Rehabilitation of Post-Colonial History." *Journal of Commonwealth Literature* 23, no. 1 (1988): 169–81.

Tucker, Martin. Review of *Looking on Darkness*, by André Brink. *Commonweal* 12 September 1975: 410.

Turrell, Rob. Review of *States of Emergency*, by André Brink. *Times Literary Supplement* 10–16 June 1988: 654.

van der Vat, Dan. "Killing Time." Review of *The True Confessions of an Albino Terrorist*, by Breyten Breytenbach. *Guardian Weekly* [Manchester] 11 November 1984: 21.

Van Wyk Louw, N. P. *Derskouende verband*. Cape Town and Pretoria: Human and Rousseau, 1977.

Vaughan, Michael. "Literature and Politics: Currents in South African Writing in the Seventies." *Journal of Southern African Studies* 9, no. 1 (1982): 118–38.

Viola, André. "André Brink and the Writer 'in a State of Siege.'" *Commonwealth* 7, no. 2 (1985): 64–71.

Wade, Jean-Philippe. "The Allegorical Text and History: J. M. Coetzee's *Waiting for the Barbarians*." *Journal of Literary Studies/Tydskrif vir letterkunde* 6, no. 4 (1990): 275–88.

Wagner, Kathrin M. "'Dichter' and 'Dichtung': Susan Barton and the 'Truth' of Autobiography." *English Studies in Africa* 32, no. 1 (1989): 1–11.

Watson, Stephen. "Colonialism and the Novels of J. M. Coetzee." *Research in African Literatures* 17, no. 3 (1986): 370–92.

White, Hayden. *The Content of Form: Narrative Discourse and Historical Representation*. Baltimore and London: Johns Hopkins University Press, 1987.

White, Hayden. "The Politics of Historical Interpretation: Discipline and De-sublimation." *Critical Inquiry* 9, no. 1 (1982): 113–37.

———. *Tropics of Discourse*. Baltimore and London: Johns Hopkins University Press, 1978.

———. "The Value of Narrativity in the Representation of Reality." *Critical Inquiry* 7, no. 1 (1980): 5–27.

White, Landeg, and Tim Couzens. *Literature and Society in South Africa*. Harlow: Longman, 1984.

White, Patrick. *A Fringe of Leaves*. London: Cape, 1976.

Whiteson, Leon. "Bad Dreams, Murky Motives." Review of *Waiting for the Barbarians*, by J. M. Coetzee. *Canadian Forum* 62, no. 722 (1982): 26–27.

Wideman, John. "In the Penal Colony." Review of *Mouroir*, by Breyten Breytenbach. *Washington Post* "Book World" 24 June 1984: 4.

Williams, Paul. "*Foe*: The Story of Silence." *English Studies in Africa* 31, no. 1 (1988): 33–39.

Wilson, Jonathan. "Counterlives: On Autobiographical Fiction in the 1980's." *Literary Review* 13, no. 4 (1988): 389–402.

Yeats, W. B. Introduction to *The Oxford Book of Modern Verse: 1892–1935*. Oxford: Clarendon, 1936.

Zamora, Lois Parkinson. "Allegories of Power in the Fiction of J. M. Coetzee." *Journal of Literary Studies/Tydskrif vir literatuurwetenskap* 2, no. 1 (1986): 1–14.

INDEX

Adamastor myth, 18
Aeschylus, 114
Africa, 58n20
African National Congress, 61, 104n26, 151, 153
Afrikaans language, 54n3, 70, 104n23
Afrikaner government: Breytenbach and, 61–62; confession to, 71; Cruso representative of, 14n7; dissident authors and, 17; individual conformity to, 69–70; lawyer integration with, 61, 101n6; literary diagnosis of, 20; novelistic fantasy and, 122–23; personification of, 105nn28, 33; postapartheid, 152; security of, 65, 66, 69; in State of Emergency, 148, 149, 151, 156n1; totalitarianism and, 104n21. *See also* Censorship Board (Publications Control Board); Security Police
Afrikaner liberalism: *Age of Iron* and, 149; *Burger's Daughter* and, 12; in *A Dry White Season*, 26–27; in *Dusklands*, 135n2; historical dissidence of, 153; neocolonialism and, 152; racial-sexual nexus and, 30
Afrikaner nationalism: Afrikaans language and, 104n23; Breytenbach and, xviin8, 70, 71, 80, 105n28; Brink on, 67–68, 153; detainee-interrogator relations and, 62, 66–71; interracial sexuality and, 30; liberal "sell job" of, 69; theological aspects of, 103n18; unified subject and, 89
Afrikanerdom: Breytenbach and, 29, 70, 101n5; British domination of, 36–37; Coetzee and, xvi–xviin8; postapartheid, 153; rebellion against, 31–32, 33–34, 35, 37; "unity" of, 68
Allied Powers, xiii
Althusser, Louis, 69, 73, 89–90, 105n30
Andrade, Susan, 136n8
Anglo-Boer War, 68
Antiapartheid movement, 16–17, 18, 61
Anti-Semitism, xviin1, 66
Apartheid: authorial response to, 11; Brink on, 19–20, 156; Derrida on, xviin2, 104n21; determinism and, 84; disassociation from, 100; fiction of, xii; institutionalization of, 68; international criticism and, 155; legacy of, 151; poetic representation of, 105n34; prison horrors and, 93; private/public do-

mains and, 65; Sachs on, 153–54; sexual aspects of, 29, 30; treasonable resistance to, 70; white liberalism and, 69
Archaeology: reading as, 130, 131, 133
Armstrong, Nancy, 1, 3
Arnold, Matthew, xviin3
Ascherson, Neal, 75
Athene (Greek deity), 113, 114
Attridge, Derek, 13n5, 149, 154
Attwell, David: on *Age of Iron*, 152, 156n4; Coetzee and, xvi–xviin8; on *Dusklands*, 119, 122, 135n2, 136n5, 137n9; on Friday character, 15n14, 144, 147n10; oversight of, 14n11; on philosophical allegories, 13n1; on "postcolonizers," 3
Augustine, St., 77
Autobiography: of Breytenbach, 75, 77–78, 86; Egan on, 92, 106n37; expressed subjectivity and, 99; fantasy-reality relationship and, 87; first-person pronoun and, 73, 74; repetition in, 108n51; self-other dyad in, 87, 94–95, 96–97; violated subjectivity in, 93

Bakhtin, Mikhail, 105n34, 108n52
Ballantyne, Robert, xvin6
Barthes, Roland, 121
Beckett, Samuel, 99
Belsey, Catherine, 68–69
Benjamin, Jessica: Breytenbach and, 65; on "false differentiation," 47, 53; on independence, 49; on sadomasochism, 44, 45, 50, 113–14, 116, 117; on self-assertion/socialization tension, 43; on *Story of O*, 51, 52
Benveniste, Emile, 73, 74, 94, 105nn30, 31, 34
Bible, 48. *See also* Exodus (O.T. book)
Biko, Steve, 22–23, 24, 55n10
Bloom, Allan, xii
Bodies: as signs, 8, 128, 145
Boer Republics, 68
Borges, Jorge Luis, 108n50
Botha, P. W., 18, 148
Bourgeois ideology, xviin5
Brantlinger, Patrick, xvin6
Breytenbach, Breyten, xii, xiv–xv, 12, 60–109, 125; apartheid victims and, 156n3; authority of, 27–28; Coetzee and, xvi–xviin8, 60, 110; miscegenation and, 29; narrators of,

A Note about the Author

Rosemary Jolly, Assistant Professor at Queen's University in Kingston, Canada, lived in Southern Africa for twenty years, both in South Africa and Lesotho. Her field of study is racial and sexual violence in postcolonial writing.